Also by Willette Kotan

Reading is 'human awakening'; John Sheldon Publishing Co.; ©1966

CISE © 1977

"Critical Thinking," in Arithmetic Teacher, Oct. 1965

Willette Kotan:
A Backward Glance

JOHN SHELDON

iUniverse, Inc.
Bloomington

Willette Kotan: A Backward Glance

iUniverse books may be ordered through booksellers or by contacting:

iUniverse
1663 Liberty Drive
Bloomington, IN 47403
www.iuniverse.com
1-800-Authors (1-800-288-4677)

ISBN: 978-1-4502-5523-3 (sc)
ISBN: 978-1-4502-5525-7 (hc)
ISBN: 978-1-4502-5524-0 (ebk)

Library of Congress Control Number: 2010912974

Printed in the United States of America

iUniverse rev. date: 01/31/2011

Dedication

An Academy Award winner more often than not recites a conglomeration of names of people who contributed toward his winning this goal. It's, more or less, the idea of a John Donne (1572-1631) sermon that no man is an island,[1] and Walt Whitman's (1819-1892) *Leaves of Grass that* reflect the idea that all events and personalities in time have an effect upon one and all, regardless whether they are aware of it or not. An individual and moral personality, a stance for beliefs and an attitude emerge because of some noteworthy individuals in one's life. There are a few who are outstanding in Willette's life. Ida Crapo, our mother's sister, is one who formed her character during the early stages of childhood. Besides her husband Emil Kotan, whom she stated as the kindest and most gentle of men she ever knew, there were Scottie, Jinne, Lois, Elda, and Daggie, who were dear friends in threading the born again faith at various times of her life. In a Hindu greeting[2] of pressing the palms of the hands together and with a slight bow of the head, I greet the Spirit of God who resides within these individuals in loving friendship, and I dedicate this book in their names.

---

1   John Dunne, "from Meditation XVII.
2   *The performer of this greeting says the word "Namaste."*

People come into our lives
And walk with us a mile,
And then because of circumstances
They only stay awhile.
They fill a need within the days
That move so quickly by,
And then are gone beyond our reach
We often wonder why.
God only knows the reasons
That we meet and share a smile
Why people come into our lives
And walk with us a mile.

Elgar Beaderstat,[3] *Bonneville Power Administrator*

---

3   Mr. Beaderstat was one of her supervisors while working in the tombs of the Bonneville Power Administration. He was not just the boss, but a gentleman who drew a friendliness and admiration from his employees.

PREFACE

There were copious notes on Willette's travels throughout the world. For her social and economical status, she probably surpassed many of her peers. By using her journals, I have written her story, connecting locations with some historical references as well as abbreviated her personal thoughts that align themselves to some philosophical descriptions.

This book, then, has become basically more than just a biography and travel log, for it portrays Willette Kotan's ordinary life. Ordinary? If it were just ordinary, then this book would not exist. To trace an individual's cause and effect world evolves thoughts of conclusions that may not always be the best. Be what they may, living life creates a pattern where one happening chooses its successor. Relating the life of Willette Kotan has been difficult in that anyone who tries to do so for another realizes that the description of that life deals with more than the sum of the total of one's experiences. Anyway, in my attempt to take this backward glance springs from... **Time**...

    is a measurement of man's life...

        it begins at birth...

            and ends at death...

                It is incorporated in units...

Second...minute...hour...day
   week...month...year...century...
are manifested by the clock...
   when to eat...quit work...
      when one will get paid ...go to bed...
         special events are marked in time..

Christmas...Easter...a birthday.
   It is a precious commodity
     for it can not be sold
       nor be replaced...

Time...like money...should be something that every man should have
  enough to spend foolishly without
    worrying about it later...
      Man can relive today
      in his memories of yesterdays.[4]

John Sheldon

---

4   Willette Sheldon Kotan, Reading is 'human awakening,' John Sheldon Publishing Co., Portland, Oregon, 1966.

Table of Contents

INTRODUCTION

L ife continually ebbs away and my sister, as probably every other senior, asked herself, "WHERE did all those years go?" They are really gone if one cannot remember the past. She was born in the same year as Lauren Bacall. Calvin Coolidge was president and on June 15th of 1924, all Indians were made citizens. What she did or didn't do will not overshadow what GOOD she could have done through all those intervening years. The biggest part of her physical life has been already lived with the conclusion of this story. Her notes reflect that she was grateful for the memories and spirit to recognize the God-given gifts which have enhanced her first 82 years: college education, opportunities for extensive travel, a marriage, and once-in-a-lifetime experiences, such as a tandem jump at age 67.

She firmly believed that God wants us to enjoy life. Her DNA gave her essence of individuality, and with the five senses God endowed her, she began her walk through life. This book validates that enjoyment.

Chapter One:

The Beginning

I am at the closing stages of my life, and thus I am motivated to somehow thread a plot of my memories into a biography relating that mine was just ordinary...or was it? My life began in the last century in 1924 in a little town named Waukegan, which is located on the west shores of Lake Michigan, just about halfway between Milwaukee, Wisconsin and Chicago, Illinois. As my great-aunt Mary Crapo stated to her grandson Richard Dyas, it's a town that was once was home to the families as the Kubelskys[5] and Ray Bradbury, whom she knew. Mildred Dyas, Richard's mother, reported that after her father Leonard O. Wainwright died, crooked lawyer shenanigans resulted in Mary losing basically all her property[6] and moved into an apartment above a grocery store and a beauty parlor while she was growing up. The smells and sounds were well remembered and conveyed to Richard in her tales of her past, and before Richard Dyas closed/sold this apartment building, he witnessed graffiti written on the walls in the basement: "The Kaiser is a dog."

---

5   Jack Benny's family name; Waukegan was also home for Otto Graham, Jr., All American college football player for Northwestern U. and NFL football player for Cleveland.

6   All was not really lost, Mary's daughter Mildred grew up, became a lawyer and returned to Waukegan and sued her mother's lawyer for his shifty actions and won.

In school, we all had to take a course in Illinois history. I learned that the French explorer Marquette as well as LaSalle and Hennepin camped here before 1700, and that a French trading post had been established during the French and Indian neocolonial wars. At that time the site was named "Old Fort River" or "Little Fort." The name lasted until 1849 when the village was incorporated and the new name Waukegan was adopted. Waukegan is a Pottawatomie word that means little fort. Earlier it had been the name of the stream that emptied into the lake below the fort.[7] It was also a town that thrived—if you could call any city "thriving"— during those depression days. There was Great Lakes Naval Station that kept an economy going in Waukegan. A series of about 16 factories operated below the bluff on which the city itself sat.

Ida Crapo

My Aunt Ida, knowing shorthand worked herself from a general clerk to head secretary at the Downey Veterans Hospital; she also worked an evening shift at Dr.Yeager Laboratories or Physician's Service located in the First National Bank Building on Genesee Street. This extra income provided her the means to recoup the house and land my grandfather lost after the crash of 1929. If there were any relative, any woman, who instilled in me my moral character, it was she. Then there was my Great Aunt Martha, who worked at American Steel & Wire Company. It was her endeavors/salary that saved the few Crapo farm acres from the clutches of greedy bank directors during those awful years of depression. My brother-in-law quit high school for the opportunity to work at Johnson Motors, one of the world's largest manufacturers of outboard motors. One benefit for Waukegan was the creation of the Johnson Motor's public beach park in front of its factory. There was Abbott's Laboratories where my Aunt Blanche worked on the assembly line for more years than I could count during my childhood.

---

7   Encyclopedias and the Waukegan New Sun, 31 January 1951.

My sister Dorothy worked for the National Envelope factory before she married the man of her life. Upon graduating, my sister Ruth went to live with the Drinkwines. Lil was one of my mother's peers who helped in the operation of a catering service. Ruth trained to become a beauty operator with Lil Drinkwine, but when business slumped, she found security working as a clerk/typist for the U.S Naval Hospital. My brother Bill eventually returned after the Korean War and worked for Nash Motor Industry in Kenosha, Wisconsin, but later became a U.S. postal employee and worked nights/weekends as a bartender to support his growing family.

An asbestos roofing manufacturer, Johns-Manville Corporation, was located on the north side of my town. You drove down on an extended Greenwood Avenue once Sheridan Road crossed this intersection. I remember it well because I was a very young girl when my mother was killed by a drunken driver who had refused to obey the traffic signs one evening on December 20th in 1936.

Waukegan had a terrific harbor where products and raw materials came and went to service its industrial needs, but there were a goodly number of fishing boats that fished fresh water salmon, which we were too poor to purchase, and an abundance of perch. I loved to buy small smoked perch for a penny or two each. There was also bedded in my memory the mile long pier. There was an elevated walk above the main pier to save the light house keeper from getting wet during storms, and it was such fun to walk up there while waves crashed into the pier sending heavenly sprays high into the air; nature at its best and fierce dramatic role. It was also the scene where my mother walked and considered suicide when she learned my father was having an affair. This is enough about Waukegan.

In those early childhood years we lived at 318 McKinley Avenue in a two story house with one bathroom. Can you imagine the groans today given by a seven member family with only one bathroom? We hauled heated water from a copper tub up to the second floor for the Saturday bath. There were four rather large bedrooms on the second floor and a sink in the bedroom where my two brothers slept. Methinks the house was designed for a two family dwelling and somebody fluked because there was only one bathroom. We had a coal furnace which sat on a barely covering cement slab and where clinkers had to be abstracted with clutching prongs from a not too often blazing fire. Not too often blazing because too often we trotted down to the railroad tracks and picked up coal fallen from laden cars along the track. There were other gleaners so the pickings were slim. My brother Bill and I dared to climb stationary cars and throw down chunks so that my other brother Jack picked them up and placed them in a somewhat dilapidated, red wagon. More than once we were chased from this dire task of deviltry. One mean railroad guard kicked/dented our wagon so badly that it had to be taken to our grandfather for repair under the guise of another reason for its fragileness. We didn't think this petty theft a sin, but one of basic survival even though we all were faithful at attending Bible school classes every Sunday at the Chapel Street Christian Church. There were enough kids in the neighborhood that we five had multiple friendships with others. Bubba Evans lived next door to the east. He had an older sister who was a friend to Ruth. We used to roast potatoes among the lilac bushes separating our houses. The lot to our west was empty and much to my constant dismay, we kids had to maintain the garden that somehow my father got permission from the owner to plant a whole mess of various vegetables. There were strict rules to follow when hoeing, weeding and picking off the potato bugs while the plants were maturing. On one very hot July day, I had not done my share of the hoeing and I enlisted one of the Mulvaney kids to hold an umbrella over me while I did my chore for a whole nickel. My elders, particularly Uncle Bondo, thought I was ingenious to hire cheap labor. Almost directly across the street lived the Gordons. They had a barn and a horse and he daily made rounds collecting what we now call recycling stuff. Old newspapers were worth money, and Ruth and my brother Bill and at times I helped collect rags, bundle them in a gunny sack with a brick in the bottom. We were paid by the pound and a little hanky-panky trickery was to our minds permitted if we wanted to buy "smoothies" at the down-the-street market and certainly nothing like the supermarkets of today. There was a clerk who waited on you and besides there might be "smoothies" marked "free" on the stick after consumption. To us it was like winning the lottery. But back to Mr. Gordon; I am sure as grass is green that he knew all too often of our deceit and said nothing. Not always, but enough to win our admiration for his kindnesses in tolerating our devilry. McKinley Street rose from McAlister Street and it adjoined Roosevelt Park. In winter it was our ice skating rink and sledding joys and in summer we searched it for "critters" in its slime.[8]

My brothers and sisters had common names like Ruth, Dorothy, William and Jack. I was named Willette, a name my mother coined by using the French suffix with Will, nickname for my father as well as Bill; thus, me, "little Willie." I've always wondered why I wasn't given an easily recognizable name. In any case I used *Willie* now for 82 years.

My grandfather was a most unusual grandfather. He was the kind grandfather in *Heidi* without the beard. He was gifted in many abilities and could fix anything. There were a goodly number of times we came running to him to fix broken stuff to escape severe penalties from our father; such an incident was romping around the dining room table and knocking a chair over so violently that it broke the higher part of the supporting back. The fixed chair was not detected as previously broken, and I escaped a whipping for misconduct; my father never knew it had been broken. Another devilment of my brother and me was taking his model A and driving it backwards into the neighboring Mr. & Mrs. Hall's house, smashing the siding severely. Good fenders in those days because I

My Grandfather

---

8   Actually these "critter" were small crabs and we used them as fish bait for perch in Lake Michigan.

can't remember much damage to the car. Anyway, grandfather made the repairs. By profession, he was a master painter and decorating contractor with a specialty skill in hanging wallpaper. He was active in politics, and espoused the views of the Greenback party.[9] His mother was Mary Esther Lakin, who was born in Maine. Mary's father brought his family to Illinois and for a time was in a business in Chicago. During the gold rush fever that permeated into every class society he went off to California and was never heard of again. His father, Walter Crapo (B. 1829), was a carpenter contractor. Walter's father was John Crapo (B. 1800), and John was the son of Samuel Crapo (B.1773) whose father was Seth Crapo (B.1724). Seth was the son of Penelope White and Peter Crapo. Penelope White is the daughter of Samuel White and he was the son of Josiah, and Josiah was the son of Resolved White, who was the son of William White, one of the Leyden Puritan congregations that fled from England during the reign of James I of England. Actually, he and his family fled first to Holland, which permitted religious refugees to enter this country. Later, he, Susanna, and son Resolved then set sail on board the first trip of the *Mayflower* to the New World in 1620. Their second son, Peregrine was born here in the New World. William died during the first winter (February 1621), and then Susannah White married Edward Winslow, who was governor of Plymouth Colony intermittently for five years (1633, 1634, 1636, 1638, and 1644). In my later years when I visited Plymouth with my sister Ruth, she bought a book entitled The Mayflower Families, published by the General Society of Mayflower Descendants. Contents therein verified my grandfather's notes tying the relationship of my family to William White. There isn't any particular central point in this hoop-de-la recitation of ancestry, except that New England pride predominates my claiming Mayflower ancestry and that pride still exists. Grandfather

---

9   The Greenbacks were formulated and somewhat effective for a number of reasons during the latter part of the 19th and early part of the 20th century: agrarians wanted government control of transportation and communications; sponsored the railroad strike of 1877; espoused shorter working hours (& effective for the coal miners of Alabama), a ban on prison labor; advocated a graduated federal income tax; and lifting of all restrictions on suffrage are just some of its principal avocations.

Crapo was born on September 18, 1869, so he was well aware of the suffering effects of the Civil War with so many relatives who participated in that conflict. He was an avid reader of Civil War history. My brother Jack has bound into two volumes his original collection of *Harper's Pictorial History of the Civil War.*
They contain so many marvelous etchings of notable people and dreaded battle scenes. Grandfather collected the National Geographic Magazine. We kids titillated through discovery of naked Africans and New Guinean photographs. I'm sure he was a devout believer and reader

General Hooker's column storming Lookout Mountain

in Darwinism. He was a lover of nature and all its creations. His ability to complete taxidermy work was reflected in preserving, upon its death, his daughter Ida's prize speckled black and white chicken. She had won more than once first prize with its exhibition at fairs. He led boy scouts out into fields to find Indian arrow heads. He had a number of Indian stone tools for grinding maze. There was a box with a glass cover that constantly, whenever I saw it, sent my imagination wondering. The box contained the arrow that had been shot and killed a friend who had joined a caravan to settle the West. I am sure that it would have made my day if I could have borrowed it for a show-n-tell school assignment. I am proud of the fact that editors found him qualified to publish a one-page tribute biography in *The Book of Illinois on page 402.*

Inheriting his father's knack in carpentry, he developed the ability in taking a piece of wood and creating unique hand carved picture frames and letter openers that were amazing.

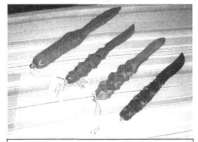

Photo: top CA sugar pine from 1892 World's Fair; 2nd, cherry from branch "sissy" broke; 3rd, Pin Cherry from Toll Gate Tavern House; 4th, black walnut from bedpost of John Q. Adams

With his jackknife, he made an infinite number of letter openers from different woods from around the world: Africa, Europe, Canada, but mostly from his neighborhood. The list of contributors who sent him pieces of wood to change from "chunks" into intricately designed letter openers to treasure always is behemoth. Regrettably, and not for the lack of trying, none of his descendents picked up his exceptional ability regardless of prolonged efforts. Included were descriptions of each wood and where it came from. I have one that he carved from the black walnut bedpost formerly belonging to John Q Adams.

I remember as a child I fell from a cherry tree in the yard and Grandpa made a letter opener from the broken branch. He also made letter openers from trees on the grounds of the Veterans Hospital where my Aunt Ida worked: one was a Black Locust and second was from a maple tree. I possess a letter opener from their 1928 Christmas Balsam Tree—he did this with all Christmas tree remnants. Years ago there was a toll gate on the road to Waukegan; the toll gate was made from a cherry tree; Grandpa made a letter opener from a piece of the Pin Cherry toll gate.

Charles & Ida Crapo June 27, 1900 Wedding photo

My Grandmother, whom we called Sanny,[10] used to get a little upset with Grandpa as he left many wood shavings on the rug or places where they should not be. She said if she had married a banker maybe there would be dollar bills on the floor instead of wood shavings.

My grandmother, Ida Lulu Brown Crapo had her own unique background; she and her family lived in the Lake County Court House which provided living quarters for the Sheriff of Lake County; Sanny's grandfather also was Sheriff of Lake County. In recalling/retelling stories about her, particulars in some cases fade as so many years have passed. Friends of my brother Jack have commented all

---

10   My sister Ruth was first born. Her ability to sound out voiced "gr" consonant blend changed to voiceless "s." She also changed "sister to "sissy," a title she still calls me.

too often, "Are you sure you both lived in the same house?" There were days I can recall my grandmother clearing pits from cherries. You may not know that cherries must be picked when fully ripe. The fruit does not ripen later as apples, pears, and some other fruits. But one thing that has stayed with me all these years is the make-believe language my grandmother and I used when watching the traffic on busy Belvidere Street in

late afternoons; the task became mundane while we pitted cherries and on another occasion peeled apples. She humored me and we'd communicate with strange sounding words spoken in a different pitch and enunciations. Sense didn't matter. The experience taught me **that the ideal density of life is relevant to the quality communications of their (those concerned) relationships.** As I was to write later in life in Reading is 'human awakening'…

The Crapo House on Belvidere Street

Oftentimes man has become extremely frustrated…
    lost…bewildered…confused
        when he can not discover…tap…
            elicit…unearth the right word
                to express his self-identity.
wordless world is
    like unfolding
        a dry heart…
        a dry soul.
Words become vital…immeasurable tools…
    instruments…having limitless…
        vast…endless unquestionable fertility
           for human awakening.

With gibberish talk my grandmother and I bonded beyond sensible thoughts and communicating a love of a grandmother for her grandchild. This love was expressed in a silly grandchild's fantasy. I still make up

Ida Crapo, Sr.

words today. I remember on a visit in Hong Kong I was riding in a taxi with another couple and spoke my make-believe language; the taxi driver could not understand me; he said he was familiar with many languages but not the one I was speaking and would like to know where I was from. My friends and I laughed as I told him, it was my own make believe language, and thus a remembrance of grandmother who cottoned to my imagination.

My mother was named Grace when she was born on April 3, 1902. There was a bonding between my grandmother and her first born that exceeds the usual, at least in my view. If there were ever two women who had united in spirit and abilities, it was these two. Great love for cooking and both attended The Waukegan Roller Rink Cooking Shows. It was not beyond her conscience even to deal in bootlegging if it benefited her family income. She even dared to ask a policeman for directions while the car being driven had "hot" booze stored within it. Our mother did all kinds of things to augment survival, including ironing clothes, especially shirts for the do-betters. More than once we got gypped out of payment. She also thought her father's influence in the Republican Party, transformed our garage into a place for voting booths during elections.

Grandmother – Mother

She was such an effective campaigner for politicians that they sought her out to work for them. She also cleaned houses for people; one such family was the Blaylocks. The man of the house was a policeman and he later became the Waukegan Chief of Police. She also headed a small group of her peers in a free-lancing catering service. It was returning home on one of these occasions that she lost her life through the error of a drunken driver. My grandmother would have joined MADD with an exuberance previously unsown had it existed. That story made headlines in our local paper The Waukegan New Sun–Mother of Five Killed!

My grandparents, aunts and uncles were now even more an influence on my life, as it was on my two sisters and two brothers. I just turned twelve years old and in the 6th grade at Andrew Cooke School when my mother died on December 20, 1936. Sanny walked a mile each school day for weeks on end to make a lunch for the five of us. At ending my childhood, I realized that I took my mother for granted. In a sense I didn't know my mother. A classic oxymoron, knowing her and not knowing her; yet I was very close to her in that small dark close place for the nine months she carried me, providing nourishment and allowing me to develop into a healthy baby girl. However, healthy though I be, I learned later I was born without wisdom teeth or tonsils, both of which I easily live without. Likewise I easily lived with two epiglottises, the little "dingy thing" that hangs down in your throat to keep food going down the wrong passageway.

From Sanny's tales and from my own experience, I know my mother's favorite song was "Pennies from Heaven,"[11] which she played on the piano so often that it was planted indelibly into our memories. Among her peers were people like Myrtle Hansen and Dorothy Zoeller. They were girls who livened up many church socials. Grace, my mother, could play trills into hymns that even made our male choir members get lost in the musical phrasing. Sanny related many an incident that involved flukes of behavior like one special incident while they were shopping at Tony's Market. Tony had made a display of food items, and my Mother took one item from the bottom, not deliberately, and the

---

11   This song came out in 1935 and became a "hit" almost immediately. Music was by
      Arthur Johnston and lyrics by John Burke.

whole display fell to the floor. My mother and Sanny were very close since my mother was her first-born child.

With insurance money in his pocket, my father remarried, and we moved to a different part of Waukegan, a block from Belvidere Street and only a block from where my Mother's family lived. This family consisted of four uncles and two very different aunts and of course my grandmother and grandfather. Since we now lived so close, we saw them almost daily, more often than not, usually on our way to school. I used to go with Sanny when she tried to collect the rent from homes she owned; it was during the depression years and most of the time the renters were unable to make payments. Eventually the homes were lost to bankers for back taxes.

Later in life I gave away books in memory of my mother; I gave books by Grace Livingston Hill, and much later books entitled *The Purpose Driven Life* by Rick Warren. The rationale in giving these kinds of books in her memory was allowing her shadow to fall where she would never be.[12] I am still doing this even 60 years later.

---

12 McElroy in *Quiet Thoughts*

Chapter Two:

❦

WWII—1942-1946

In Tom Brokaw's book *The Greatest Generation*, he related so many memorial events that everyone agreed with him that during those terrible times with so many sacrifices and resolution efforts for defeating fascism in all respects and with the loss of life counting upwards of 35 million, with 10 million alone lost in Nazi concentration camps, that he named thusly this generation cannot be anything else but *The Greatest*. The patriotism that all children/students carried in their hearts is reflected in patriotic acts as by buying "saving stamps,"[13] turning in our household grease jars for ration stamps, and giving up the begging for Mom to do baking because of sugar rations. Victory gardens were high on the list for home folks to aid the war efforts; no problem with this family as a garden was considered necessary to keep his kids out of mischief. And I know that I put more than one aluminum pan into the pile of metals for recycling. In the early days of the war with continual stream of disheartening war news, it's no wonder we had films often starring John Wayne to buck up our depressions. Life went on.

---

13   Saving stamps were as low as 10¢ and issued by the U.S. Post Office; we purchased ours in the classroom.

I ended my childhood with graduating from West Elementary School. I attended Waukegan Township High School and graduated in 1942, completing the academic in 3 1/2 years. I was anxious to be on my own and packed my bags and moved to California to find a job. The war facilitated the hiring of women in all phases of manufacturing. My interest and opportunity lay with the airplane industry. For awhile I worked in San Diego, California, after which I went to Tucson where I worked on B-24s that were being modified. My desire to join the Ferry Command grew and as a result I went to Tucson because I learned that the climate was best there to take flying lessons. As time permitted, I rode my bike to the airport and took flying lessons. You bought flying instruction at the rate of eleven lessons for $100. I made my first solo after eleven hours of instruction in a Taylor craft plane. All my flight training was for naught. My entry into Ferry Command did not materialize as many women volunteers fulfilled the need and this section of U.S. Armed Forces was closed to women. An opportunity came and I took another job in New York, working on the modification of B-24s. All these work experiences in the aircraft industry did not satisfy my desire to serve my country. You had to be 21 to join one or the other women's armed services: a WAAC or a WAVE. What to do was a dilemma. After my 20th birthday passed on August 2, 1944, I signed my father's name on enlistment forms and entered in the US Navy as a WAVE. But before being called to active service in September 1944, I wanted to make another solo flight, so drove out to Waukegan Airport and rented a Piper Cub plane and had an easy take-off. It was awe inspiring to be flying and looking down at the farmland knowing you were alone in the plane. When it was time to return to the landing field I encountered a crosswind while trying to land. When you are landing a plane like a Piper Cub, you reduce the gas and try to "mush" the plane to ground zero, but a crosswind picked the plane up higher and too high to mush and land. The first two times I bounced with crosswinds, but on the third fly "by the seat of your pants." I never flew solo again. With so little experience in flying and now quitting, I felt that I was cheating the possibilities of crashing and ending a life I wanted to continue.

By President Roosevelt's executive order, the War Manpower Commission was established (4/18/42). Paul McNutt was named chairman and along with his chairmanship, he obtained the selective service powers. All males between the ages of 18 through 38 became subject to selective service, the draft. Women were enlisted for non-combat duties in the Women's Auxiliary Army Corps (WAACs, by act of 5/15/42), and incorporated Women Appointed for Voluntary Emergency Services (WAVES), Women's Auxiliary Ferrying Squadron (WAFS), *Semper Paratus* Always Ready Service (SPARS), and Women's Reserve of the Marine Corps.[14]

My orders from the WAVES commander arrived and I traveled to New York City plus the distance to Hunter College in The Bronx, where

U.S. Naval Training School, Bronx, N.Y.

I was to receive my boot camp training. Training meant early revelry with marching here and there wherever my platoon went including meals three times a day. The strict daily classes included physical training periods, naval history and lectures on social diseases. The one thing that dominated boot camp was marching in unison. We learned this very well. Many feet pounded the pavement, and it was considered the "deck," of a ship and a part of our living quarters. "No spitting, there, sailor!" was a repeated warning. My goodness, no, we girls did not chew tobacco, but quite a few smoked and as a result spittle discharge was at times necessary. There was another gas station epithet that forbids

---

14   American History, ed., Richard B. Morris, Harper & Brothers, 1953.

my quoting verbally. Grandmother would not approve. Consequence of defiance was scrubbing the "deck" with your toothbrush. And I mean this literally. "Scrub-a-dub, sailor." The six weeks passed quickly and graduation was a "grand" parade and a display of our camaraderie. "Hip-hip Hooray," we're out of boot camp. I think the purpose of boot camp is to reflect upon the Thoreau principle that however "mean" your life is, meet it and live it; don't go calling Heaven. C'est la vie.

Shortly after boot camp graduation, new orders were given, and I was assigned to Pensacola, Florida, where I drew duty at Bronson Field and then Ellyson Field. I was a person who could be talked into doing for someone else, so it was easy for other Waves to talk me into carrying their cigarettes in my bra during muster or inspection. Rather stupid since I did not smoke. One of my duties was to "warm-up" SNJ planes for preflight. I assisted the instructor or a cadet in getting into position in the plane, have him sign the sheet, pull chocks and direct him to the take-off area. I also had to be there when the pilot returned, directed him to a specific parking place, and put chocks in place before signaling him to cut the engine. There were four flights a day. Routine, in some respects, means that there are some days you're the pigeon, and some days you're the statue.

All the WAVES on the flight line could also apply for "flight skins," which meant we would not only fly as a passenger with an instructor, but also we would be eligible for extra pay for this special duty. This was war time and I felt I was doing my part and found it exciting and interesting to be assigned to the flight lines. All of us WAVES also took turns on "flag duty," which meant directing flight traffic on the tarmac. One day I got caught communicating with a sailor with my flags as he was asking me for  a date using the flags. I was called to the Captain's Mast, a preliminary step in naval justice, and I was given a stern warning that my duty was to be directing plane traffic and not using the flags for social conversation.

After a few months I was reassigned to work in the parachute loft. In an incident of delivering parachutes to a hangar, I kept a sailor from falling off the truck. Later he called me several times at the women's barracks for a date. I was a rather naive person as I thought if you kissed a guy you would have to marry him, and I was not at the stage of my life to become involved to that degree. I refused him initially, but he persisted. He called and asked me to go to church with him one Sunday. In such a situation, I felt he would be an O.K. guy to be around. He had a Ford coupe, and later on, he took me to USO dances. He did not believe in dancing, yet he took me to these dances and waited to take me back to the barracks. Often he would park his car, not to "neck," but read the Bible to me. After he was honorably discharged from the service and returned to Pennsylvania, I was surprised to hear from him. He was now married and sent me this poem, which I treasure his thoughts put into verse.

Willie

Have you ever seen a morning dawn –
    One that was fresh and new and clean?
Have you ever seen a perfect night –
    A million stars – a dreamer's dream?
Have you reveled in a mountain brook
    That threads its way through shaded vale,
Or glimpsed the mystery of a gypsy caravan,
    Moon lit - on a mountain trail?
These things I've surely seen,
    Though just a boy from Philly,
Cause down through the winding road of life,
    I met a girl named "Willie."

Dick Hurst

My point here is to remind my reader that you never know when any of your acts, whether they are kind gestures, pleasantries, amiabilities, may be forever etched on someone's heart, something like Pippa in Browning's poem "Pippa Passes."[15]

I think every service person during the war days remembers kindnesses given to them. On the train trips I took from Pensacola to my grandparents' home in Waukegan, the train made various stops along the way where ladies provided coffee and donuts to the military personnel riding the train either on leave or returning to their military bases. Waukegan is near Chicago, and I was thoroughly impressed how the military service people were treated in Chicago. I think Chicago gained a reputation as the best place to be on liberty or leave because free tickets to shows and events were always available; this kind of hospitality was awesome.

Oh, the joy when the war was over. I thought we would be sent home right away but that was not the case. The service person received a number of points for each month served in the U.S. Navy. When you accumulated a certain number of points, you would be eligible for the honorable discharge. In April 1946, I had enough points to be released from the navy. During this process we were examined before our discharge. During the examination I was told that a tooth had to come out first. I disagreed with the officer and indicated that I had enough points to be discharged, and they could not take out my tooth. Yes, I was discharged with the tooth in my mouth; that same tooth is still there today.

In typing up my separation papers, the typist goofed on my birth date. When I challenged him to change it, rather than admit his error he just said now I have two birthdays to celebrate. When we

---

15   In this poem about Pippa, Browning illustrates the power of positive thinking; Pippa's song related a goodness that changes the lives of various nefarious characters.

witness faux pas, it's just like the government to have multiple choice consequences. In my case I got to choose.

It was many years coming to memorials for WW11 service personnel. The U.S. Postal Service put out a 32¢ stamp commerating women who served in the various five branches of the armed services. Chuck Sumerlin created a stationery depicting women who served with a background of the memorial, which in 1997, the Women's Memorial was dedicated in Washington, D.C. to recognize the women who served in the U.S. Military; my friend Reba Scott submitted her name and mine as Charter Members. The photograph of the National WW11 Memorial was designed by Friedrich St. Florian and approved in 1997; however, there are alterations to the original and wasn't completed/open to the public until April 29, 2004, with President George W. Bush making the dedication. There are now 56 pillars, one for each of the forty-eight states of 1945 and one for District of Columbia, Alaska Territory, Territory of Hawaii, and Commonwealth of the Philippines, Puerto Rica, Guam, American Samoa and U.S. Virgin Islands. The wall contains 4,048 gold stars, each representing 100 Americans who died in the war. The commentary for the memorial: "Here in the presence of Washington and Lincoln, one of the eighteenth century Father and the other the nineteenth century preserver of our nation. We honor those twentieth century Americans who took up the struggle during the Second World War and made the sacrifices to perpetuate the gift our forefathers entrusted to us: a nation conceived in liberty and justice."

The Roosevelt Memorial with his dog Falla is inscribed: "They (who) seek to establish systems of government based on the regimentation of all human beings by a handful of individual rulers…Call this a new order. It is not new and it is not order." The number of women who died in WWII is minor compared to the men who died on the battle fields of the world, and yet we service women added our strengths, our time, and our devotions to the cause that Tom Brokaw called *The Greatest Generation.*

WWII Memorial Plaza

Roosevelt's Memorial

Chapter Three:

West to Oregon—1946-1949

After being released from the navy I went back to my grandparent's home. With what money I saved being in the service, first thing I did was buy a car. The owner had it up on blocks. I was very impressed with the condition as the interior of the green sedan was very elegant. It had shades, wide space between the front and back seats and it had flower vase attached to the back sides of the back windows. I'd love to have that car today. The owner represented it as an Essex, and little did I know otherwise; we pushed it more than we drove it. I was hired, probably through my Aunt Ida's influence, to work at the Veterans Hospital. I disliked my job mainly because mentally disturbed men displayed uncouth behavior. My mind raced for alternatives. I knew my brother Jack still lived with our father and step-mother. Our father was the kind who carried the traits of his father's mother's (Mary Ann Hazen) rigid rules. Our father's mother, our grandmother Anna Hegelston, was a Swedish immigrant and saw advantage in marrying Fred Sheldon, who lived on a rather large farm with his mother. Anna gave Fred two sons before she had had enough of his mother's iron rule by whipping farm hands when they drank a little too much or disobeyed her directions. She was characterized in a book called *A Yankee from the*

West by Opie Read. The book deals with the eccentricities of a widowed woman, Mrs. Struvic, who lives in Millford, Illinois, and supplemented her income running a boarding house, a means to meet a variety of characters while the plot, in some respects, deals with huge land owners and, at times, their oppressive work conditions. Anyway, Anna ran off to Chicago to do domestic work rather than live in such a household of her mother-in-law. She took Louis, her baby, and told William he had been boarded to a neighboring farm in exchange for his labor. Times when our father's ire got out of control resulted in being whipped not spanked but whipped. Thus, I wanted my brother Jack to venture forth with me and live in Oregon out of the severe disciplinary reaches of an abusive father. And so it came to be.

I had purchased by now my second car, a 1939 Chevrolet sedan. A plan had been formulated. I saved every penny from my work and Jack worked nights at the House Of Steele out on highway #41 as dish washer and at rush times assisting the cook and making all of $36 a week; a big increase from working at the hamburger joint across the street from an entrance to the U.S. Naval Training station for 25¢ an hour. At summer's end, we packed our

1939 Chevy

meager belongings into this 1939 Chevy, said good-bye to our father, who made no objections and started west.

Our trip was uneventful except we experienced car trouble in Wyoming. There were some road grades that are much steeper than they are today. I suspect that the car over heated and stalled the engine. It was a two lane road and we had pushed the car near the road edge while seemingly a flood of cars with people irritated by the delay caused by an inoperative car. Jack stayed with the car and I hitch-hiked a ride back to the town to find a tow truck, which returned with me to tow the car. The tow truck driver hitched the car and we proceeded back to town. However, on the way back, the driver miscalculated his driving and one side of the car hit a stone wall damaging the front fender, which made me very upset. When we got back to a service station, he would not unhook the car till I paid for towing charges. This event made me more agitated, so I went to see an attorney in the town. The lawyer gave me some empathy but he would not pursue the tow driver to make amends indicating he (the attorney) lived in the town and did not want to rock the boat in his law office. So I went back to the service station, paid for the tow charge and left with a bad memory of a Texaco service station which never lived up to its later advertised "star" by realizing how the tow truck driver and attorney took advantage of two very young people in distress.

The immediate plan was to drive to Roseburg, where there was a state mental institution. Once looking over the city and the facilities, I decided that we really didn't want to live in this section of Oregon. I thought our chances of attaining a place to live and different job than what I had at Downey, Illinois, would be far greater in Portland.

We arrived in Portland the next day in the middle of August 1946. It was difficult to find a place to live as living accommodations were scarce. We did find a place in an old two story house in the Lloyd Center area. Of course the Lloyd Center was not built until much later. Three other families shared this home. We all had separate rooms but shared one upstairs bathroom. One refrigerator located in the hallway was shared among the four apartments. Since we had the larger rooms, we received possession of the larger section of this 4-door, wooden refrigerator. Actually it was the area to place ice at one time and now converted to a more modern operation. I almost begged on bended knee for the state representative to rent to us with the promise to take the best care of his property. And we promised we would not use the fireplace, as we had been warned it smoked terribly. Now that I am older and experienced, a chimney that smokes can be remedied by raising or adding on to the chimney so that its is higher than the peak of the roof. At this stage of my life we couldn't use the thing anyway as we were too poor to find or purchase wood to burn in it. We were just thankful to find an apartment and not having to resort to a rented room in some house among other strangers.

Since I was a veteran, hiring by the government worked on points. The longer you were in service the greater number of points you had over someone else being hired for the clerk-typist position with Bonneville Power Administration. Their offices were in a set of barracks on N. E. Grand Street. As that year passed, I can honestly say my peers at BPA were among those who were a great influence on my life because they urged me to use the G.I. Bill and attend college.

But, for the present, the first thing I had to do was get Jack enrolled in high school, which was a difficult process as the principal would not enroll him as a senior, telling us that he should be with his parents. I told the principal that our Mother was deceased and Jack was with me and he has to be in school. Portland Public School system was insistent that they did not enroll children who did not live with their parents. Through testimony of relating to his circumstances from relatives back home and the fact that I was his nearest kin and also paying taxes just as other Portlanders did, the administration finally relented and allowed Jack to enroll as a senior in Jefferson High School, and he did graduate a year later in June 1947.

There are always people who enter your life with grace and kindness and in Jack's case three sisters ran the lunch counter at the Holiday Drug Store there on 7th and Broadway. He worked the lunch hour rush from 12 to 1:30 and then returned at 6 for the evening shift until 10 o'clock, six days a week. Since he had gathered most of his high school credits, he had only to attend school in the mornings. On Sundays the store closed and offered

us the opportunity for young people activities, like skiing. With two incomes there was money to spend on the superfluous events of life, meaning we took up skiing, purchasing at G.I. Joes those slip over winter parkas and G.I. boots as well as skis and poles. G.I. Joes was at that time strictly government surplus and you could purchase equipment such as skis and poles cheaply. We learned to put on chains and travel off to Mt. Hood for adventure on the slopes. In those days tickets were not as dear as they are today. At times we'd park at Government Camp, take the bus to the Mt. Hood Hotel area, take the ski toll to the top slopes above the hotel and ski down all the way back to Government Camp. If I remember correctly, doing this once was just about an all day effort. And we loved it. When I compare prices then with what prices are now, you have inflation personified.

Jack took the street car to school and with the school pass; he could ride the bus, street car for 5¢ as long as he stayed away from public transportation between 4 and 6 P.M.

In the Spring Jack joined the Mazamas with his high school friend Oliver Johnson. Oliver's parents, Jessie and Oliver Sr. (Red) were great friends. They invited us into their home for many special celebrations. Oliver had his parents' permission to use the family Ford for all kinds of occasions and even over-night trips with the Mazama hikers who made annual jaunts to the top of both Mt. Hood and Mt. St. Helens. Jack said his trip to Mt. St. Helens was more difficult to climb than Mt. Hood because the continued steepness of the climb on St. Helen's. According to Mazama rules, you began the climb below the timberline forest. On St. Helens, this line was far below that of Mt. Hood. Jack said that reaching the top of St. Helen's was awesome because the rim was massive with steam coming out. To fall sliding down inside probably couldn't be stopped with ice picks and clamp-ons on your boots. Since St. Helen's eruption in May 1980, jaunts to St. Helens Park is always enjoyable by taking visiting relatives and our friends there because St. Helens certainly displays what can and did happen when Mother Nature unleashes its maternal force. And if you haven't visited St.

Helens, then you need the opportunity to hear rangers discuss and to show you original film footage of the eruption with other exhibits. You are in for a treat. Do go for a visit.

While working at BPA barracks, I was often invited to go to lunch with a group of gals. I was still shy and naive and I would order my lunch yet was too hesitant to eat it. I was afraid to say that I was shy and just kept indicating that I wasn't hungry and someone in the group would eat what I ordered. Of course that does not bother me anymore as I grew out of that personality quirk with time.

The year slipped by quickly and upon Jack's graduation we both decided we would go to college, so we took an entrance exam. We passed but the college testing program was not all the determining factor. Space was limited and if you were not at the very top of academic standing, then you were passed over because of the overwhelming number of applications from veterans; the vets had priority. Since I was in the navy during World War II, I was accepted as a student.

Having lived in one of the older Portland homes converted into a multiple dwelling by one of Oregon's state congressman, we became determined to get out of having to share one bathroom with three other families. The apartment that we had rented consisted of a living room with a parlor when you entered into the front premises. I had the parlor for my bedroom while

Going Street house

Jack slept on a divan couch in the living room area. A hallway separated this living space from a small but adequate kitchen. An ice box sat in the hallway with four compartments of which our box was on top and the largest. We paid $50 a month for this "luxury" accommodation and we were anxious to relinquish this for a small home. Our house mortgage which included payment, interest as well as insurance was $50 monthly. We jumped at the opportunity to become house owners. We sold the 1939 Chevrolet for $500 to make the down payment, which was very fortunate that cars that looked good were still in demand. The Johnsons still had their 1939 two-door Ford with gears on the floor. Mine, at least, had the gears under the steering wheel. Anyway, the total cost of the house was $3,000. The Pullman kitchen meant that you could stand at the kitchen counter and reach the stove, refrigerator and cupboards basically without taking a step. One of the best things about the house was the marvelous laundry room and not having to share a bath with nine other residents. Oh, how fortunate we are today with most homes having two heavenly bathrooms. The Johnsons were invited over for coffee and cake, for they were dear friends, and they always took an interest in our welfare: how we were doing. I could tell that they thought this venture in buying property was a mistake, but they said nothing negative about this investment.

Jack was now working for Balfore and Gutherie, an English flour/grain industry, I guess. He was making less money than he earned working in the drugstore, but there were possibilities of advancement. The draft was still on, and he received notice to report to the draft board. In a humorous note, he decided that he didn't want to wear khaki under drawers — G.I. Joes has such wear available. Besides, our brother Bill visited us when he was stationed in Fort Lewis, Washington, and Jack just knew khaki drawers were not to his liking. He decided he would rather enlist in the navy. I enrolled as a freshman at Lewis and Clark College. While he was in the navy, he sent me an allotment of $50 a month and every three months a savings bond which helped defray my living costs of attending college.

While attending Lewis and Clark classes, I had to give up my clerk-typist position with Bonneville Dam Administration. I found part-time work in an office for a credit company. I was one busy student, I did not have time to go to the games or attend any of the many social events associated with college life. I suppose this was true of most veterans returning to school to advance themselves in life. The G.I. Bill was one of the most influential acts Congress could have passed to better its citizens. I, for one, am forever grateful. I worked and studied hard. No one ever saw my grades as I was alone. It took me three years to graduate with a double major in Business Administration and Psychology. In June 1950, I received my Bachelor of Science Degree from Lewis and Clark College. Elated I had been, for I, upon graduation, was offered a teaching position in southeastern Oregon even though I did not take any courses in education. I accepted the position knowing that I would have to take summer school classes in education to change a temporary teaching certificate to a permanent one. So, I sold the house for the same price we had paid for it. It had served its purpose and it was far better living than paying rent for an apartment of equal footage space.

There is a passage from Thoreau's thought that pertains to living each season as it passes, and be resigned to the fact there will be influences of each—in my case it's been four and half years that I have had great influences on me. Read on for more telling.

Chapter Four:

Andrews & Lacomb, Oregon—1950-1953

My first year of teaching in this remote area of Andrews, Oregon, was quite a challenge and experience. Andrews isn't even on the more recently published maps of Oregon, but it exists east of the Steens Mountain range and north of Fields. The heights may vary from 6,300 to 9,600 ft in elevation. Andrews is at an elevation of approximately 2,900 ft. I had five students; one youngster rode to school on his horse. My living accommodations were inside the school building itself behind the classroom. The accommodations were very meager. I had to use a pump every day to retrieve water for cooking and washing. There was a hot springs in the area and I took advantage of it to take a bath when weather was normal enough to use; you could not use it in the winter months.

Andrews school house

During this school year I got acquainted with an elderly gentleman, Billy Bruckwilder, a semi-retired rancher who lived in the building next to the school He was from Germany and very intelligent; we had many discussions, and I was invited to eat with him after school. He made the most delicious Buckaroo Stew. It became an evening ritual to have dinner with him. We discussed many current events, some of which we did disagree on at times. Once the discus-

Steens Muntains

sion was re-ally intense, and Billy became ag-itated with

Billy Bruckwilder

me and asked me to leave. I said "not until I eat," which sounded so ridiculous and we both laughed. From then on our daily discussion never got to that degree of disagreement.

Reflecting back into time and my experience here at Andrews, I learned much that formulated thoughts and I later expressed in *Reading is 'human awakening'* and in *CISE* publications. Pumping water and not quite loving to endure an Andrews environment, I decided, at the end of the school year, and I would accept a new teaching position near Lebanon, Oregon. I kept in touch with Billy until the end of his life. He had been very good to me and made my first year of teaching a remarkable experience. I don't know who first said it, but

John, Ray, John, Maria & Rose

friendship is a word that the very sight of it in print makes the heart warm. I shall always remember my first teaching experience here at Andrews with gratitude. I learned much and the experience was indeed an asset for my later accomplishments.

Lacomb, Oregon -1951

My second teaching position was to be in a little farm community east of Lebanon. When I was hired for the principal-teaching position, I was also asked if I would like to pick up a school bus in Lima, Ohio. I was given $300 to fly to Lima and to drive the bus back to Oregon. This was a serious challenge for me. My trip to Lima was in the latter part of August. When I arrived at the Superior Bus Company, there were minor details to be done before taking possession of the bus. It became a rush situation as it was almost the end of the work day, close to 5 p.m. They gave me some instructions indicating that I would be breaking in the engine and I was not to drive over 50 MPH. Later I learned the bus was rigged so I couldn't drive over 50 miles per hour no matter how leaden my foot rested on the accelerator in any case.

My grandparents' home at Waukegan wasn't too far afield from my designated route to the West. It would be a good place to make a rest stop. Driving this bus approximately 2,500 miles across the country was a challenge for me. I was apprehensive and too naive to consider what a chore I was assuming. The drive was quite easy if I considered positioning the bus in such a way that I could drive out stopping areas without any difficulty, especially on occasions when stopping for gas or stopping at motels parking areas. This didn't always work in my favor as someone parked in front of me at times. When this happened the first time, I was unsure on how to drive the bus in reverse. Better to ask a humiliating question than suffer undue consequences. I strode over to the gas attendant—these were still the days when gas attendants checked the motor oil, checked air in tires and washed windshields at no additional cost other than purchasing a gallon of gas—and quickly learned a reverse driving lesson. Thereafter, when I stopped for gas or other reasons, I was continually diligent in positioning the bus in such a way that I had clear passageway to continue my journey without having to drive in reverse for any distance.

I arrived in Waukegan either extremely late in the evening or maybe it was in the following morning of my first day of driving. I was so tired

I went to bed and slept and slept. My grandfather called to me by late morning to say people were checking out the bus since one does not see a bus in a family driveway, especially with Lacomb, Oregon, stenciled on each side. I spent the rest of the day preparing myself to leave the following morning. Before I did, I took Grandpa and Sanny for a ride on the bus. I drove down Genesee Street which is the main street in Waukegan. The bus caught the attention of people who wondered why a bus from Oregon was on the main street,

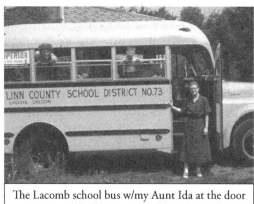

The Lacomb school bus w/my Aunt Ida at the door

and why there were two older citizens riding as passengers. I don't think my grandparents forgot that experience. It was their first ride on a school bus, for they belonged to an era of walking knee deep in snow for miles to attend school. Lord Byron wrote, "All who joy would win… Must share it…Happiness was born a twin." What joy there is in encountering the unexpected.

One encounter that would not have fazed an experience driver was the challenge of reading a sign before crossing a river indicating the bridge would only hold so many tons. I checked instructions in the jockey box to see if I passed the weight limits. At that stage of the game I didn't know how to relate or compute weight of my bus against the tonnage allowed crossing the bridge. Finally I became brazen enough to decide that surely whoever builds bridges wouldn't build one so fragile that it couldn't carry the weight of school bus. Firmly convinced of my logic, I just drove across the bridge, hoping it would not fail and thus resulting in finding me and the bus in the river below. It took me five long days to reach Portland. I was amazed how much other drivers gave me the right-of-way. Some shook their head when they noticed a young girl as the driver of a bus so far from Oregon. I was 28 years old at the time and consider myself young gal. This experience just proves that good judgment comes from experience and a lot of that comes from bad judgment. *C'est la vie.*[16]

School had already started by the time I arrived back at Lacomb, Oregon, and I entered my second year of the teaching profession. These two years at Lacomb slipped by quickly. I didn't keep much of a journal/notes and there was nothing of particular interest in running this school. But I did meet Josephine Kotan Riddle, sister of my future husband, Emil. I took board and room with the Riddle family as this was convenient to be in the vicinity of the Lacomb school and also because it was economical. Farm communities everywhere have this one common connection. Real people with never an inkling of pretense about anything are always hospitable and ready to invite you into their homes for dinner. Say your prayer, pass the dinner on platters or bowls with enough for second helpings and obviously much to refrigerate afterward. Always considerate about displaying their folk crafts and shown only if you ask. I purchased many quilts and potholders freely given along with respect as so-and-so's teacher. Emil and his

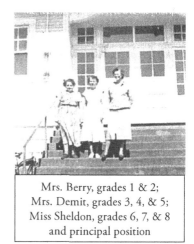

Mrs. Berry, grades 1 & 2;
Mrs. Demit, grades 3, 4, & 5;
Miss Sheldon, grades 6, 7, & 8
and principal position

Lacomb students in the 6th, 7th, & 8th grades and me

16   That's life.

brother Joe were a part of the Kotan family who owned 440 acres of land with two barns and all this comprised a cattle and a feed operation. The farm/ranch bordered Fish Hatchery Road and included acreage bordering the Crabtree Creek. My first impression of Emil was that he was a shy farming man who had great experience with animals. He was devoted to his land and walked with trepidation, which means he was always the gentleman in my presence. Never heard any gas-station English leave his lips regardless of frustrating events that appeared in his kind of work. But more information will come forth about Emil Kotan in my narration of my later years of life.

Chapter Five:

Verdun, France - 1953/54

During the ending of my second year teaching at Lacomb, I had applied to teach in military schools overseas. It was for my teaching experience that I had been elected for this appointment as noted in a letter from Charles Furman, Chief, and Recruitment Branch Overseas Affairs Division. My letter of acceptance was to teach in Verdun, France. Transportation abroad for us teachers was on board the U.S.N.S. General Hodges. From the menu on the following page, my reader should be able to tell that it just wasn't teachers who rode this vessel across the Atlantic, but mothers with their children/babies that were to join loved ones abroad. The captain's effort to make this a pleasant sailing was a concerted effort by the officers and crew members. I was amused by "attention announcement" shot over the loud speaker system for cabin class passengers that the dance with live music would be the finest between New York and Bremerhaven. And during intermission there would be a beauty contest and crowning of Miss USNS Hodges. Anyway, this would be my first trip overseas and I was "up-tight" with excitement.

The famous battle of Verdun in WWI took place here in February 1916[17] and lasted for almost a year before the Germans withdrew their forces. The Germans thought that they could basically crush the French army here and in doing so would damage the morale of the other armies elsewhere along with the French citizens. France hailed General Henri Pe'tan as a hero of this

Monument a' la Victotre

battle, but later critics firmly believed that the slaughter of both French and German soldiers was due to the inept generalship.

Makes you cry to see so many graves as a result of this French/German conflict.

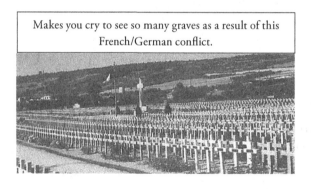

While visiting this WWI memorial, the idea was in the back of my mind and the idea became stronger as I realized by looking at all these graves how fragile a life can be and end so soon for all those beautiful people lost so suddenly on a battlefield and had not a chance to say goodbye to their loved ones. Their lives cut so dramatically short. What were their lives like and what would the rest of their lives have been like had they lived through this horrific battle. Makes you cry.

---

17   Verdun, besides the great battle site of WW1, it was the site where three Frankish kings (all grandsons of Charlemagne) agreed upon the embryonic kingdoms of France & Germany in 843 C.E.

PLEASE INDICATE EITHER LARGE OR SMALL
PORTIONS WHEN ORDERING
MILITARY SEA
TRANSPORTATION SERVICE

USNS GEN H F HODGES

SATURDAY   **MENU**   22 AUGUST 1953

B R E A K F A S T

CHILLED SLICED FRESH PEACHES W/CREAM

CHILLED GRAPEFRUIT JUICE

BOILED HOMINY GRITS WITH MILK

ASSORTED DRY CEREALS

EGGS TO ORDER

FRIED, BOILED OR SCRAMBLED

BAKED CORNED BEEF HASH

POACHED EGG ON TOAST

EGG MUFFINS   DRY OR BUTTERED TOAST
ASSORTED FRUIT PRESERVES   FRESH MILK
COFFEE   TEA   COCOA

STRAINED BABY FOOD

3ND-P&PO-2137

Upon arrival in Verdun, we were told that we would have to live on the French economy and to find our own living accommodations. They put us up at the hospital that first night. I was fortunate and located a room in a beautiful new home where the owner was looking for renters. It was just a room and I had to share the bathroom with two civilian secretaries who rented the second bedroom in this new home.

My residence while in Verdun

Maxine, one of the secretaries, owned a Triumph and invited me to take outings with them. I really got to see much of France with these two gals. One of the trips was touring Mont-Saint-Michel off the coast of Normandy near St. Malo. From a distance it appears to be a cathedral. The only way to get to this historic site was by driving on a narrow cause-way

If you walked along the causeway during high tide, you would be in trouble as the water comes in faster than you could outrun it. Once at St. Michel you will have to do the walking. Yes, there are small trucks that can scoot about the narrow streets, but basically cars are banned on St. Michel and the place is not for the handicapped, for streets are steep and climbing steep steps can bring about heavy breathing even for the younger crowd.

Mont St. Michel 1954

The historic monastery on this small island has marvelous arched passageways and you'll find a humongous kitchen no longer in use. If hunger strikes you, unlimited kinds of omelets are featured in most cafes. Besides numerous small shops and restaurants, there is even a hotel. Many tourists and French people visit this unique site.

Twice I went with Maxine to see Paris. The first time was on Washington's Birthday when we had a three day holiday. Scottie flew from London to meet us at the St. Francis Hotel. Scottie was stationed with me at the Pensacola Naval Base in Florida. After the war she opted to stay in the Navy until her retirement.

It was a thrill for me to be in Paris as I had heard so much about the city, and now I finally arrived to see it for myself. In front of the hotel I threw open my arms and yelled, "So this is Gay Paree." Some Parisians happened to be walking by and gave me a questionable look. In any case, here were three Americans right in the middle of this fabulous metropolis, unbelievable, but true! We three gals were ready and willing to scoop up all its splendor, gaiety, ancestral history, and architectural ambience of Paris. We were young and gay and not in the sense of what "gay" means in sitcoms or in the vernacular English today.[18]

On the way to Paris, our conversation centered on seeing the Folies-Bergère. The more they discussed the show, the more I decided not to attend. Being naïve, I thought the program would be too risqué for my taste; they went and I stayed

Arc de Triomphe at Champs Élysées 1954

in my hotel room that evening. Included in these trips was shopping at the Galleries Lafayette, eating at a small restaurant on the Champs Élysées, and walking to the Arc de Triomphe, where one had a fantastic view of Paris including the Eiffel Tower in the distance; you could see how the seven avenues run to the Arch and to a circle; all roads leading in and out join this circle. This arch was built in 1808 and a monument

---

18   Do read *Our Hearts Were Young and Gay* by Cornelia Otis Skinner. It's a marvelous read.

for French Soldiers. Under this magnificent structure lie the ashes of the French Unknown Soldier.

We took a tour to see some of the famous Paris sights close up. It also included a trip to the Louvre where we saw the *Mona Lisa* by de Vinci. I had heard and read much about this famous painting and here it was now in front of me. I thought it was quite small compared to other famous art work. I tested the theory that the eyes follow you from whence you stand to gaze upon her contented face. The painting is more than just a painting of a woman, for it reflects dignity of its era. It has splendor, and imagine it was painted back in the 1400's. We viewed the *Angelus* painted by Millet. A farmer and his wife praying over a basket of potatoes and my thoughts went back to those depression days when potatoes were the only nourishment on our plates. Methinks I would not be praying; I'd be cursing. We were expecting to see the *Gleaners* but it was borrowed for another art show.

We had some wonderful food on our visit in Paris. I remember one of the first economy meals was in a little French restaurant near our hotel. I ordered a Swiss sandwich and some *pommes de terre frites*. Gee, did it look good and tasty; however, I did not get to eat much as the gals were hungry and ate most of mine. From then on I cleverly made it clear that from now on they should order enough so I could eat my own.

We stopped long at the Eiffel Tower, which was built in 1887, and for 50 years was the tallest building in the world. I took time to walk part way up to the second landing as the elevator was not working to go higher. I came to realize the contention of Mr. Gordon's horse straining to pull that wagon up the McKinley Street hill. Never again for me, and yet what I saw from the second level was fantastic scenery; I feasted my eyes on this fabulous city and exploded with thoughts of French history.

We also had the opportunity to see the *Carmen* at the Opéra Comique. The building itself was rebuilt in 1889. It wasn't a large building and appeared like a regular movie house; the four balconies were portioned off into loges, each lined with red velvet. The Opera singers were wonderful and the voices singing the libretto made the plot come endowed with life right in front of my eyes. In a later visit I saw the production of *LaTraviata* here at the Grand Opera House on the busy Place de l'Opéra; the Grand Foyer and Grand Staircase are dramas themselves to visit.

Several times we took a taxi to wherever we needed to go, and riding in a taxi is an experience I shall not forget. The French drivers believe that Americans have taken the sport out of driving by obeying all rules and signals. Maybe so, but it is easier on one's nerves and patience. Returning one evening to my hotel, one cab driver would shoot off his lights and zoom through a traffic light or stop sign. Yes, I traveled across Paris quickly, but! Driving in Paris means you need a horn and plenty of guts.

My students helped me write a poem about the first visit to Paris. Fun exercises in counting syllables, making rhymes, creating stanzas, checking spelling, looking up places compiled multiple lessons in English, some history and some geography. It was a time when this teacher became an ally with her students, emphasizing that writing can be fun and doesn't have to be perfect.

Maxine and Willie in Paris

It wasn't April but Washington's Birthday in Paris
For an Oregonian and a Missourian from USA fairest.
In Maxine's little "Mayflower" which was black as ink
The girls went to gay Paree feeling in the pink.

They checked into the St. Francis, the finest hotel,
Their service was deluxe, with bidet and vitals.
To a little French restaurant, they went for something to eat
Where Willie was as hungry for all she could be
Ordering a cheese sandwich and ignoring St. Joseph's feet
Sampling pomme dauphines and some French brewed tea.

Alas, her friends really so hun—gar..rey!
So ordered enough to feed three little fleas.
But when Willie came back, she holl'ered out__ Hey!
You jerks have eaten all my Swiss cheese.

They went shopping at the Galleria, buying a hat

Which was green, perfume, kerchief, all cheap at that?
Maxine bought a cloud blue sweater; oh how she did hate
As she could not wear it now with all her excess weight.

But Willie laughed and looked at the skinny figure
She luckily had by fate, and danced a fancy jigger
Whistling for a taxi and taking the comers in a hurry
With Willie and Maxine, two mourners full of worry.

A ride by the Sorbonne, Sacré Coeur and Bastille,
Then back to the Pam-Pam for an American meal.
Sunday night to the opera Comique, Carmen for to see,
She got squashed in the last act; Don Jose was as fat as could be.

Monday morning to see paintings at the Louvre off were they,
Great art by DeVinci and Angelus by Millet
Maxine with her tripod and Willie with her AR—gus!
Taking pictures of masters with guards making a fuss.

Yes, Willie and Maxine left this wonderful town of renown,
Dreading hoping and wishing that Verdun was never found
By a lot of Yanks—not one alone!

At Christmas vacation I took it upon myself to see Garmisch, a little
town in the Bavarian section of Germany. Garmisch is a very colorful
town with many decorated shops and restaurants. The exterior of many
buildings are uniquely decorated with scenes portraying the occupation
of the owner. I'll have more to say about the Bavarian area of Germany

Garmish area

later as I returned to this area
again and again. Another time
Maxine and I drove to the
Vogelsberg area in the Hessen
Province of W. Germany, where
the countryside was flooded in a

growth of jonquils/daffodils.[19] It was a custom to pick the jonquils and decorate your car with them. There is a wonderful admiration to see so many who are so enthusiastic for the coming spring. In my first visit into Switzerland, I visited a little village of Wildhaus. I was so impressed with the countryside scenery and Wildhaus that I repeatedly made every effort to visit this area every time I visited Europe.

During my spring break I took the US military train to Berlin. The fare was not expensive at the time; I was assigned a private compartment. One thing that stuck in my mind as each time we would stop or slow up at a railroad station, I saw the word, Bahnoff. This made me curious as I could not figure why Bahnoff would be on a sign at each station. I learned later that Bahnoff meant railroad station. At the time of this visit, the Berlin Wall had not been erected.

Oh, I enjoyed Berlin, and since I am a shopper I had a great time browsing merchandise in the stores. As I walked down Kurfurestamdam Street I saw this shop that displayed the most beautiful red accordion. I can neither play nor read music, yet I bought a red accordion. Obviously I was thinking of Joe, Emil's brother, and he played the accordion, but after I bought it, I wondered how in the world I would get it back to Oregon.

While teaching in Verdun I purchased an Italian Fiat car. We received our pay monthly and many of us would go to the Brussels' central railroad station in Belgium to exchange our money, for French Francs at the exchange office there was so much better than in France. I drove the Fiat once and had to push it more than drive it. The Fiat turned out to be a "lemon" and it was fortunate I was able to sell it to someone else on the military base who needed a car and knew how to maintain it to keep it running. I think I sold it for a hundred dollars.

---

19   To this day I still have difficulty distinguishing between the two. Both belong to the Narcissus, a family having perhaps 9 main classes or divisions. Jonquils are fragrant and flower cup is longer or shorter than petals. Two to six fragrant flowers are borne per stem. The trumpet flower of daffodils is as long or longer than petals and one flower borne per stem. And who cares what the difference is; I love 'em

Maxine and I would rent bikes in Verdun and ride around the countryside. Verdun is a famous place for the memorial and cemetery for those soldiers who fought in the First World War. Once we biked to an area that had an underground tunnel which was used during The Great War or World War I. I was curious, so I walked into the tunnel, and I learned later that this was not a good idea as there still could be live ammunition in some of these tunnels.

The right side photo is one that shows where Verdunites do their washing. The little shed on the right close to the water in the photo is where they do this. It's a block from my rooming house.

Each school day I would ride the military bus to the dependents' school on the base. One day while standing at the bus stop, I felt something on my leg, and before I realized, a dog was taking advantage

Washing facility & Meuse R.

of my leg to urinate. There were four or five people waiting for the same bus, and I noticed that they had a hard time to keep from laughing at the incident. When I got to the base I immediately took off the hose to wash it and my leg. I never realized that my legs took on the appearance of a tree trunk.

While in France I had my first look at a French aspect of plumbing, the bidet. I wondered what the bidet was used for. I was as naive as Cornelia Skinner.[20] While in France I did not learn much French except combien (price) and the word toilette. When school ended I accepted a four-week position as a Girl Scout counselor near Mittenwald, Germany. After that job I planned to go to England.

---

20   Again, this is a reference to *Our Hearts Were Young and Gay* about Cornelia's travels in France and England.

With the closing of my first year abroad teaching, I learned so much from my travels, especially of my teaching in Verdun. The year infused me with the desire to travel everywhere. I like Agatha Christie's attitude about living,

> I have sometimes been wildly, despairingly, acutely miserable, racked with sorrow, but through it all I still know quite certainly that just to be alive is a grand thing.

Chapter Six:

England 1954 - 1955

I was supposed to teach in an American Base school near the town of Kings Lynn, which is about 100 miles North of London on the East Coast of the North Sea.[21] This teaching assignment became one with a number of clashes with the head administrator. The classroom furnishing was sparse. There were orange crate boxes for book cases. We teachers did not even have desks. My peers were united in vesting our complaints, which landed on deaf ears. Since I was probably more incensed than others, I was elected to voice strong objections to our physical classroom facility. The administrator and I had strong words and I was pushed—perhaps not quite true—but at least left with the only alterative of either shutting up or resigning. There were also other little straws that beat down on my shoulders. Students complained that they were taught otherwise for the use of the apostrophe. I taught students they should avoid using the possessive case for inanimate objects. The room's ceiling; the room cannot own the ceiling. Everyone agrees that adding apostrophes after a noun to show possession and just an apostrophe should the noun ends in s, but not in all cases regardless of what US Government Style Manual states. We should follow what

---

21   Actually the bay there is called "The Wash."

is said in the reading of the word in question; i.e. Gladys...Gladys's coat; Dickens...Dickens' novels; the boss...the boss's daughter, bosses' daughters, etc. If the possessive s is pronounced then the s should be written. And why in the world we use an apostrophe to cite numbers is ridiculous; it's perfectly clear to the 1s (ones) will stand to the right; and the 5s (fives) to the left. And for pity sakes, why are we writing "Dear" in the salutation of a letter firing off criticism for some service or product. We're mad as hell. Forget it. Just begin the letter and state your complaint. Maybe "attention" is applicable: "Attention Customer Service" or "Sir." Applying "Dear" in your salutation is no big deal. Do as you wish.

This seems to be a place to cite my philosophy of education, which I cited to the Director of American On-Base Schools and included some of my ideas of why I was resigning from my post: "Our country is a democracy which is predicated on the concept that all members of our society should participate. The quality of participation will hinge upon the quality of literacy each individual member has attained. The school, to my way of thinking, will need to take more initiative in doing a more effective job in helping the individual to achieve the highest form of literacy he/she is able to achieve. Our society values education. Encompassing this value will be two basic tenets to which I whole-heartedly subscribe: a) individual worth, and (b) the dignity of the individual. As an educator, I am committed to this, and I must make every effort to appeal to the learner's power of understanding and to prepare the individual to think for himself/herself. Each learner's development will be unique; the purpose will not make him/her a wise individual, but equip this unique being's progress toward wisdom in his own unique way. Physical climate of the classroom must be one that at least supports learning." I left much out of my letter of why I felt this English classroom did not support an environment for learning. Since I did not receive a response, I made a personal appearance at the director's office in London. He had not heard of my complaint, and he had not received my letter of resignation that was to have gone through the channels: principal of my school first. This is all water under the bridge. And I'm sure I'm boring my readers. But reader, know this: all teachers have encountered their *Up the Down Staircase*[22] at one time or another.

But I am getting ahead of myself. I rented a room with an English family consisting of a mother, father and their young son. The rent included room and board for the total sum of $5 a week. They did not have central heating or air conditioning. My room was on the second floor. Often after dinner we would sit by the fireplace to listen to the wireless. On Saturdays the father would usually go to the nearby English pub, and the wife and I would listen to plays on PBS, which were excellent entertainment.

Mr. & Mrs. Oliver

My friend Reba Scott (Scottie) lived in London and worked at the American Embassy. Scottie, a born-again Christian, and, as I previously stated, she and I were stationed together in Pensacola during World War ll. Scottie shared her apartment with two other Waves. After working hours, it was she who took the time to show me London. London, alone has so many places of interest and historical value. On a weekend she took me to see a play at the Old Vic Theater. What amazed me was being served tea or coffee in our seats during intermission, which orders were placed in advance. The popcorn crowd of theatres today will never know the services of yesteryears.

One day I shopped at Selfridges there on Oxford Street which has items from Gucci bags and Hermes scarves to household gadgets and a food section in the basement where I purchased some beautiful green grapes; I was shocked to learn that I had paid over $3.00 for this small bundle of grapes. I quickly realized that I would have to pay closer attention to the currency exchange so I would understand how much I

---

22   Bel Kaufman's book is a hilarious account of her secondary teaching experiences.

would be spending. The English decimal currency of today is far simpler than it was in the 1950s. English coins, for instance, numbered in pence (d) and 1/2 pence, called a half pence, pronounced haypence. You could have a two pence and three pence.[23]

Pence were copper, nickel, and zinc coins and 12 pence (12d) equaled a shilling (1s) and 20s equaled a pd (£1).[24] So the cost of the grapes had to be more than 20s. According to Fielding's exchange guide the £ in exchange in U.S. dollars would be $2.80 and then there was the guinea, which had a value of $2.94. Confusing, yes, and yet I learned to be more careful is appraising an object for purchase.

In 1999, I returned to shop again at Harrods—now owned by a very rich Arab. I could not help but be intrigued by its food court where various food specialties were cleverly and provocatively presented. All most tempting, but realizing the prices, I thought again to look elsewhere such as Selfridges or Mark and Spencer's to satisfy hunger pangs for such-n-such.

I did not have a car and it seemed to everyone rode a bike; I purchased a beautiful red Raleigh, which became my mode of transportation while in Kings Lynn. One Sunday my landlady suggested that we could bike to Sandringham since the Royal family attends the small church in the village when in residence. She also told me that they do allow people besides the royal family to

Oliver and I are on our bikes.

attend the service; however, the church was small and only 20 visitors/residents were permitted to attend on these occasions. We got in line and

23   Pronounced təpence and thrəpence
24   My brother ordered from the British Museum a copy of Jacque Callot's explanations of the numbers printed on his steel engraving titled La Siege of La Rochelle and he paid 51£ sterling, which equaled to slightly over $100.

I was #20; my landlady insisted that I attend the service, and she would wait for me. I took a photo of Queen Elizabeth and her husband and later learned that it was forbidden to take photos of the Royal Family. Yes, ignorance is bliss, for I have my own photo of this royal couple.

Elizabeth & Phillip

Since I did not have a job and my funds were running low, I opted to return to the States. I was fortunate and bought a third-class ticket on the *Queen Mary* to sail out of Portsmouth, England. When the *Queen Mary* was preparing to embark, passengers began throwing rolls of party paper at the people on the pier. I was caught up in the emotion and began throwing the paper and even began waving to people on the pier as if I knew them personally. I even had tears in my eyes while waving. The trip was great and time passed all too fast crossing the Atlantic. On board the *Queen Mary* I remember entering a contest for the lady passengers; the contest was to make a hat and model it one evening. I took the commode--yes, third class passengers had them-- that was in my cabin; I got two cups from ships personnel and hung them on the handles of the commode. When it was time to show my hat, I asked the band to play "Tea for Two," and I walked

My commode hat

slowly before the audience. It was a little dramatic, and the people clapped and laughed; however, I did not win a prize. I thought the experience making this kind of hat would be something to remember. Happiness comes not from exterior situations but from the joie de vivre[25] within you. Joy is never in things, it is in us. I have included copies of the luncheon and dinner *Queen Mary* menus on the next page; they changed daily.

When we docked in New York I had a little difficulty hiring a taxi to take me to Pennsylvania Station to catch a train to Chicago. I had my Raleigh bicycle, and the taxi driver did not know how he would transport it; finally he placed it on the roof of the car. Can you imagine a cab driver in New York City today

Dining on R.M.S. Queen Mary

taking on a young lady with this entire luggage and a bicycle? His kindness is ten volumes of indulgence. I had covered the Raleigh bicycle with paper Mache for protection, which was holding up nicely.

When I finally arrived at my grandparents' home, I still needed to find a way to get back to Oregon with so much baggage and very little funds left. I solved the problem by checking the *Chicago Tribune* newspaper and discovered that a company in Chicago hires people to drive cars to other places in the states. They needed to get a station wagon to Portland, and I inquired to take the job and got it probably because I was the only one in the office heading for Portland that day. It was a lot easier than driving a bus I tell you. The tires were not good, and had to replace one; the company reimbursed me when I arrived in Portland. I stayed with friends until I received an appointment for teaching the 7th and 8th grades on an Alaska on-Base School for the 1953-54 term. Evidently my resigning from such in England was not held against me. My recent past confrontation with a school administrator would not be my last—and evidently swept under the rug, hidden from observers. Stranger things happen are my experience.

---

25   Joy of Life.

49

England

Juices: Tomato   Vegetable   Grape Fruit

HORS D'OEUVRE

Sardines   Œufs, Rémoulade   Antipasto, Italienne
Pickled Lambs' Tongues   Salade Parmentiére   Bismarck Herrings
Tunnyfish in Oil   Salade, Italienne   Chou-Fleur, Portugaise
Marinated Cod Roes
Saucisson: Liver and Lyon
Olives—Green and Ripe   Iced Table Celery

SOUPS

Consommé Cheveux d'Anges   Old Fashioned Bean Soup
Cold: Beef Bouillon

FISH

Fillets of Weakfish sauté with Almonds
COLD: Norwegian Prawn Salad, Mayonnaise Sauce

FARINACEOUS

Macaroni, Calabraise

VEGETARIAN

Vegetable Cutlets, Cream Sauce

EGGS

Shirred, Miroir
Omelettes (to order): Friar and Joinville

ENTRIES
Creamed Chicken à la King   Frankfurters with Sauerkraut

CONTINENTAL SPECIALITY
Sauerbraten
Fresh Round of Beef, previously marinated with Salt, Vinegar, Sliced Onions,
Lemon, Sugar and Spice. Braised and cooked with addition of chopped Raisins
and Ginger. Served with Potato Latkes

GRILL (to order):

Loin Lamb Chop, Maître d'Hôtel
Fresh Calf's Liver and Bacon

JOINT

New England Boiled Dinner

LUNCHEON

R.M.S. QUEEN MARY

SUGGESTED MENU

Hors d'Œuvre, Variés

Consommé Cheveux d'Anges

Froid: Salade de Crevettes, Norvégienne

Poulet à la Crème
Brocolis, Mornay   Pommes en Purée

Compote de Fruits, Chantilly

Fromage   Café

Passengers on Special Diet are especially
invited to make known their requirements
to the Chief Cabin Steward
Specialty Foods for Infants are available on request

Red and White Wines are available per bottle or
en carafe 7/6, per glass 1/3

VEGETABLES

Brocolis, Mornay   Mashed Swedes
Macédoine of Vegetables

POTATOES

Baked Jacket   Purée   French Fried

COLD BUFFET

Roast Ribs and Sirloin of Beef, Horseradish Cream
Roast Turkey, Cranberry Sauce   Fresh Home-made Brawn
Rolled Ox Tongue   London Pressed Beef   Boiled Ham
Roast Leg of Lamb, Mint Sauce   Galantine of Chicken

SALADS

Hearts of Lettuce   Fresh Fruit   Sliced Tomato
Tourangelle   Miami

DRESSINGS

Cream   Thousand Islands   Roquefort   French

SWEETS

Peach Custard Pudding   Pineapple Crush Pie
Gâteaux: Devil's Food   Banbury
Compote of Cherries and Apricots—Whipped Cream

ICE CREAM

Vanilla   Chocolate   Rum Raisin

CHEESES

Camembert   Wensleydale   Gorgonzola   Cheshire
Cheddar   Edam   Cream   Roquefort
Danish Blue   Port Salut

Fresh Rolls

Tea (Hot or Iced)   Coffee (Hot or Iced)

Luncheon menu – H.M.S. Queen Mary

50

England

QUEEN MARY   Thursday, June 16, 1960

Juices: Orange   Grape Fruit   Clam
Chilled Cantaloup Melon
Sea Food Cocktail
Smoked Salmon with Capers

HORS D'OEUVRE

Sardines in Oil   Anchovy Fillets   Antipasto, Italienne
Œufs, Diable   Salade Orientale   Green Pepper Salad
Thon à l'Huile   Oignons à la Grecque   Gendarme Marinés
Tomatoes, Génoise
Olives—Queen, Ripe and Stuffed
Salted Mixed Nuts   Iced Table Celery

SOUPS

Consommé Royale   Crème Juanita
Cold: Jellied Herb Consommé

FISH

Suprême of Brill, Palace
Fillets of Sole, Amandine

FARINACEOUS

Macaroni au Gratin

VEGETARIAN

Cheese and Tomato Pie

ENTRIES

Poussin en Cocotte, Forestière
Vol-au-Vent, Mogador

CONTINENTAL SPECIALITY
Tête de Veau en Tortue
Calf's Head, boned and cut in pieces, cooked in a Blanc. Served in a Tomato-
half glaze with an infusion of Turtle Herbes, Madeira Wine and quartered
Mushrooms and Sliced Olives

JOINT

Roast Ribs and Sirloin of Beef, Horseradish Cream
(Yorkshire Pudding)

SORBET

Raspberry

GRILL (to order):

London Mixed
Boiled Ham Slice with Glazed Banana

DINNER

R.M.S. QUEEN MARY

SUGGESTED MENU

Melon Cantaloup frappé

Consommé Royale

Suprême de Barbue, Palace

Poussin en Cocotte, Forestière
Haricots Verts sautés   Pommes Macaire

Pouding Black Cap

Dessert   Café

Passengers on Special Diet are especially
invited to make known their requirements
to the Chief Cabin Steward
Specialty Foods for Infants are available on request

Red and White Wines are available per bottle or
en carafe 7/6, per glass 1/3

RELEVE

Roast Long Island Duckling farcie, Apple Sauce
(Green Peas)

VEGETABLES

Fresh French Beans sautés   Cauliflower, Mornay
Fried Salsify

POTATOES

Boiled New   Roast   Macaire

COLD BUFFET

Roast Lamb, Mint Sauce   Rolled Ox Tongue
Roast Chicken   Boiled York Ham, Vegetable Salad
Roast Sirloin of Beef, Railfort   Home-made Brawn

SALADS

Hearts of Lettuce   Sliced Tomato   Fresh Fruit   Waldorf

DRESSINGS

Mayonnaise   French   Vinaigrette

SWEETS

Black Cap Pudding   Sherry Fruit Trifle
Pear Melba

ICE CREAM

Vanilla   Peach   Strawberry   Coffee

SAVOURY

Quiches Lorraine

FRESH FRUIT

Apples   Pears   Bananas   Oranges

Coffee (Hot or Iced)

Dinner menu – H.M.S. Queen Mary

Some London photos and commentary follow on the next page.

Upper left, London Bridge; upper right, St. Paul's; Middle left Westminster and middle right, Westminster as seen from across the Themes near the Westminster Bridge; Lower left, Piccadilly Square; lower right, spot where Anne Boleyn was beheaded. I included these photos of some historical buildings to note how dingy the buildings were after the war and praise the government's effort to clean their public buildings; thankfully, Piccadilly prominent & garish signs have disappeared.

Chapter Seven

Alaska—1955-1959

Teaching in American-on-base schools may have the advantage of traveling to far away places, but there is a disadvantage in that the physical facilities are often cut short, meaning there is no activity room or gym or counselors to contend with children with problems.[26] Nor are there specialist in art or music or special education classes that are often remiss in the system; not always, but more often than not. What military on-base schools do is deal with problems as best they can. Little did I think that I would spend roughly three years teaching in Alaska, and yet I benefited from the experience.

In the 50s, there were approximately 570,000 square miles in Alaska, which was home for approximately 128,643[27] residents. You could say that there were 39 people who live in every 100 miles. Elementary history books relate the story that it was the Russians who were the first settlers mainly in Sitka, Kodiak and the Aleutian Islands. Natives were primarily the Eskimos to the north and Bering Sea, Aleuts in the Aleutians and the Athapaska Indians in the interior; there were other tribes I'm sure. I think my brochure stated that 14 out of every 100

---

26   Note, she didn't say problem children; there is a difference.
27   U.S. Bureau of the Census 1950

residents in Alaska belonged to one of these tribes. There are only two valleys that are suitable for farming in Alaska, and they are the Tanana (near Fairbanks area) and the Matanuska (Anchorage area) Valleys.

All that this means is most foods have to be imported at great costs, especially fresh produce. Salary had to be higher here to cope with this kind of additional expenses.

Adak

My government appointment provided the means to be flown to Anchorage, and then the navy transport booked me a flight to Adak, which is a small island in the western end of the Aleutian Islands that extend roughly 900 miles westward from the tip of the Alaskan peninsula. Adak was

Adak Harbor

primarily populated by navy personnel and civilians who worked for the government in some capacities. Adak is not particularly attractive. The only foliage outside the perimeter of the navy base was a heavy, thick coarse grass.

During the winter you could check out ski equipment to ski on the high ground. There wasn't much to do with free time. There was the base

Adak hikers

cinema that one attended. What I did enjoy was organizing a group of my students, the Adak Hikers,[28] to take part in hiking; I even designed a patch with a totem pole and awarded it to students who had fulfilled a certain requirement.

---

28   On 2/11 I had 5 students complete 4.4 mile hike and then on 2/18 hike to Finger Bay the group expanded to 19.

Out of 23 students who hiked periodically, 6 earned the badge. On 2/18 we hiked from the Adak Commissary to Finger Bay a total distance of seven miles and at other times we would hike from the Quonset school house just around the base for 4.4 miles. There were only 4 girls and 2 boys who had to be disciplined and eventually dropped from the hiker club because their continued skylarking was dangerous or just foul play. And then there was bullying, if you like. Too often in the world today, teachers have an over-loaded schedule in dealing with these kinds of situations, and yet we all must be more attentive to those who later may become the central cause of school violent disruptions. In these formative years of students in my class, I must agree with Emerson who cited good manners are made up of petty sacrifices. The school days here on Adak are much like school days elsewhere, especially when compared with my first teaching days at Andrews, Oregon, with the exception that here I had running water.

I suppose I should say something about the Alaskan malamute, a dog bred and used as a sled dog. We all are endeared to Jack London's short story *To Build a Fire* in which man faces a powerful protagonist, the elements of nature. Man succumbs while the dog survives. My experience here

Alaskan Malamute dog

brings vivid details of clarity with nature. *White Fang* and *Call of the Wild* have been popular readings for junior high people and incite interest in this northern expanse which is no longer a wasteland. The year passed quickly.

Kodiak

In the next 1955-56 school year, I was assigned to teach 7th and 8th Grades at the Kodiak Naval Base on Kodiak Island. Kodiak is a much larger island than Adak, and it is much closer to the mainland. On Kodiak there were many trees, streams, lakes and foliage which provided

Kodiak fishermen

the most beautiful scenery. There were a goodly number of navy personnel who lived on the base; I lived in the women's barracks where I had a room. There was a kitchen and refrigerator which I shared with others. I rode the navy bus regularly into the town center of Kodiak. Kodiak was populated by civilians who made Kodiak their home; some were engaged in the fishing industry as Kodiak was noted for catching salmon. When you visited the pier area, you could see many fishing boats; some selling fresh salmon to anyone who wanted to buy them. The city of Kodiak had some stores and a bakery where I became a regular customer.

There was a unique looking church in the town center; it was a Russian Orthodox with a blue "bubble" on the roof of the Church. There were some unusual practices as in all faiths I am unfamiliar with. Here, the separation of the males and females were segregated in the sanctuary, and neither was women permitted if they were menstruating.

I didn't sponsor a hiking club here, but there were times I'd go bike riding with students and riding past the local golf course and down to some off-beaten road by a stream where we carefully built a small fire and roasted (mostly burned I might say) marshmallows. The word "cool" was coming into existence. Skiing season wasn't what

Russian Orthodox church

it should have been at all that year—more rain than snow. Dreary days abound at times. Longfellow made the comparison that a feeling of sadness or melancholy is akin to pain just as some thoughts of a mist may resemble rain. I think he made a valid judgment, and my point is that dreary days abound at times if one doesn't keep active. Enjoyment declined, especially for two students who had mishaps serious enough for them to wear braces/cast for a lengthy time. I urged my students to take a Junior First Aid course here at the school. I attended also and received my First Aid Certificate along with some of them.

My cost of the living accommodations was low, which provided me the opportunity to save money. When I took this assignment I promised myself that I would save so I could take the next school year off and attend the University of Oregon to obtain a Masters Degree. Before I flew back to the states to attend the University of Oregon at Eugene, I flew to Anchorage where I caught the train that would take me into Mt. McKinley National Park to visit my brother Jack and his wife. Jack had taken a temporary position as a park ranger for the summer. I took the scenic trip by train to the park; actually it was the only way to enter the park at this time since there was no road to drive there. Trains ran north one day and then south the next. The ride north was spectacular during its run through the foothills of the Alaskan Range. The McKinley train station was close to the entrance to McKinley Park and the hotel itself lacked the majesty of other hotels in other national parks. Jack and his

Mt. McKinley/Mt. Denali

wife drove me to some areas not available to the public. Winter is the best time to view the whole mountain and it is unusual to have a clear picture of Mt. McKinley/Denali in the summer.

This photo here was taken when my brother

got me up as I remember about 2 A.M., and drove about 30 miles for this captivating view of this humongous mountain. It was an awesome view; a thrill to stand in its presence even at this distance and view such a mountain where it has been climbed successfully only six times.[29] There is also a wonder of wild flowers. I met Tillie, the Alaskan Red Fox who apparently trots out from her den to amuse park travelers on a bus from the hotel. The parka squirrels are another common feature to amuse visitors. But it is hard to appease the lust of seeing/meeting at a distance, of course, the Alaskan brown bear. There was a taxidermic one standing on his hind legs more than 9 feet high in the lobby of one of the banks.

Dr. Murray's nailed cabin door deters bears from breaking in.

Jack stopped at one place where there was a noticeable number of dwarf fireweed. Fireweed is so named because clusters can sprout first on the scene of a past fire. Multiple Ptarmigan abounded in this wilderness. They do not fly south for the winter and they do change from a summer brown, speckled plumage for a wintry white. It was Marcus Aurelius who commented that the natures are the things that have a union with all from the beginning. So, while looking at this 20,230 ft peak with just a flutter of a cloud at its peak, I can see below the treacherous trail leading to tundra, a reflecting lake where caribou, doll sheep, marmoset, etc. live; all as in primeval circumstances. In a platonic thought I am looking at the secondary substance and capturing its primary existence. Nature is a name for an effect whose cause is God. I stand on hallow ground. If you fail to catch my feeling then perhaps you should definitely add this park to your list of places to visit, for an ideal density of life is dependent upon the quality of their (you and nature) communication.

---

29   My brother stated that this number applies through the year 1951.

At the close of the school year I departed Alaska for Eugene, the second largest city in Oregon in 1957. Eugene is situated on the Willamette and McKenzie rivers and the southern end of the Willamette Valley. The university itself is bounded by Franklin Blvd, 11th and 18th Avenues, and Alder and Moss Streets. Like all universities I have visited or attended, it has a pleasant campus pictured so often in the movies. The Willamette River worms itself through the city and strangers or non-habitants may find themselves not exactly where they want to be and seek guidance to traverse the road to the coast or a specific area of this city.

My studies leaned more to school administration and supervision, for I know that there are grants and other monetary gifts for operating a school system and learning the procedures would benefit any school system that I become associated. My earlier experiences taught me that there are special government funds for the maladjusted child, and classes here at the university were offered on how to tap into those kinds of resources. I also had an intense interest in mathematics. It was here at the university that I was finding the basis for my article in the *Arithmetic Teacher*. In the course of everyday living, one should know and understand the business terms of discount, regular price, net price, interest, writing a check, and installment buying, etc. And thus I was learning methods to stimulate my inclinations of tinkering with intriguing numbers. Most of my students generally followed where I led them into numbers and probabilities. If you have watched the sitcom *Numb3rs*—regrettably I never reached the level of the stars— you will understand my interest in mathematics probabilities. Life doesn't offer coincidences; the cause and effect reigns.

The year passed quickly. I did a variety of jobs including grading papers for professors with enrollment of undergraduate students. There were many I had to call in to the office and guide them through the processes of elementary English usage and the proper way of presenting their term papers. Thankfully, I had saved sufficiently for my tuition and for the most part basic living costs. Basically, my tuition here was cheaper than the tuition paid for my undergraduate work at Lewis &

Clark College. Need I remind my reader I'm talking about a time when a cup of coffee could be purchased for 5¢ and you could get a hamburger for 10¢. On June 14th, 1958, I was awarded my Master's degree. The worries of yesterday were now cancelled by this achievement; regret here never had a chance to exist. And oh, I was thankful, proud, and one happy girl.

It was late in the year for searching/applying for a teacher's job. In September 1958, as luck would have it, I returned to Kodiak for my second teaching assignment for the school year 1958-1959 Again, I lived in the women's barracks. Other civilians rented room spaces as well. On our floor we had a kitchen which we shared. We bought food items from the commissary as well as from stores in town. When a ship came in with supplies, the commissary was quite busy; often we were able to buy fresh fruit like bananas. The milk was frozen when we bought it and we allowed it to thaw in our living quarters.

During the school year I had the opportunity to originate the Teenage Roundtable with students in my class. It was a program presented on Saturdays at 9:30 a.m. over the radio station the Navy operated. Bob Mallek, US Navy, worked earnestly with all of us on our first program to get us into a routine and to get us at ease with using the microphones. We were good enough after our first taped productions so that the panel made live appearances on the Navy Radio Station. The Kodiak Naval Station was generous in making this half-hour available for us. I think the programs were good; I may be ex-

Teenage Roundtable

aggerating, but it was a fabulous opportunity for the students. The panel usually consisted of six members who discussed such topics as study habits, discipline, good manners, good grooming, conversation, allowances, first aid, dating, plan a party, and how to get the most out of high school. Our 14th and last program dealt with how to plan a vacation.

Mrs. King, mother of one of my students, was a great help in this project; she was knowledgeable and faithfully appeared on every program. Her input and direction were highly valued, and I convinced her to become the moderator of the program. The youngsters really enjoyed working with Mrs. King. I felt that it was her direction and guidance that made the program such a huge success.

While doing this program I had the opportunity to meet other personnel who operated the radio station. One day I was assisting the engineer in his program dedicated to music. It went so well I was asked to substitute for him on other Sunday mornings. It was only a half hour show of easy-listening music. I played David Rose's rendition of "Tenderly,"[30] which is one of my favorite songs; I played it every time I was asked to substitute for the regular sailor agent who had the program. When I took over the show, I told my audience to just call me "Lynne,[31] when a listener wished to make a musical request.

During the school year I made an appointment with local airways to fly with the pilot on his mail route. During the winter months, scenery appears dull and wintery, but when the weather changed, it was a delight to be on Kodiak Island for the school year. I use the analogy that my Alaskan experience is like a bridge; you cross over a bridge but you don't establish yourself upon it. I think the government of on-base schools frowns upon civilians making a life story with them. And besides, I was ready to return to the states where products of civilization are a necessity for one like me. I eagerly wait with exciting

---

30   Lyrics by Jack Lawrence and music by Walter Gross; copyright in 1946.
31   The name stems from my experience from Kings Lynn, England, a place which held special memories for me.

anticipation for an ephemeral existence in a contemporary civilization. It's when all my impulsive reaction can be released...to be refreshed with tantalizing everyday occurrences that exist only around your wonderful friends in the delightful Portland atmosphere. Of course, there will be frustrations, just as there are here in Alaska, but I can cope with those. I find/ anticipate an exhilaration of devouring fresh fruits and vegetables again; even a banana split or hamburgers from the Carnival in southwest Portland. Yes, I would enjoy even the simple ride on an elevator or escalator appeal to me. My extrovert tendencies can once again recover control as I may find myself yelling "fore" on the golf courses of Portland. Mark Twain created humor for me when he phrased my present attitude as one that becomes "a limitless multiplication of unnecessary necessaries."

Chapter Eight:

Teaching in Oregon—1959-1969

I n the 1959-60 school years, I accepted a teaching position with the Reynolds School District in Troutdale, Oregon. Troutdale is at the western entrance to the Columbia Gorge itself. Those who have traveled the old route US 30 know it well by finding relief from the most curvaceous road that competes with the Amalfi drive in Italy. With a hop-skip-n-jump from Troutdale on US30 is Crown Point with its panoramic view of the Columbia Gorge; thus at the western end and driving east for the following 12 miles, a visitor encounters numerous, spectacular water falls culminating at the Multnomah Falls, second highest fall in the country with its 620 foot drop. Scenic grandeur and panoramic view-points abound.

I kept my position here for three years: first year I taught 7th grade in a self-contained room. In my 2nd year, my subjects were English and Math for two 7th grade

Troutdale students presenting their prized efforts

sections, and in my 3rd year I taught math for two 7th grades and two 8th grade sections.

For the next succeeding years I taught these grades with the Siskiyou County School system and then Hood River, and finally Rainier, Washington. Thus, this chapter will deal with my experiences teaching this range of students. I make some guesses about my charges, which I think every teacher does likewise. Whatever challenges I met, I always enjoy my position and learned much from these teaching posts.

Upon returning to the US, I decided it was time to buy a home. In August 1959, I was fortunate to know the owner of the house I wanted to purchase as she inherited another house, which she decided to keep and live in. She agreed to sell her house ($8,500) with a mortgage and interest rate of 4 percent, which was the same rate I could apply under the G I Bill for a mortgage loan. Not so today. And when I think of all those people who are losing their homes because they cannot make their mortgage payments that jumped in some cases as much as $500 to a $1,000 a month, I think of all those people who lost homes in the depression when I was just a child. Where is the integrity of men who have a responsibility for our monetary system? Honesty seems to be the most abused word in our courts of law and with the dealings of our present U.S. Administration (2000-08).

One of my 6th grade students, Diane Hoyt showed exceptional artistic ability. I asked her if she would paint a copy of a postcard that I bought in London. The painting reflected the thought in praying to God to help her to be good—a life long process. Forty years later I decided to see if I could locate her so I could return the painting to her. I located her in northern California and was very impressed to learn that she had written 37 books for children published by

My sixth grade class

Holiday House Publishers in New York City. She sent me one entitled Apache Rodeo, which had exceptional content with marvelous illustrations. It's always a reward to learn that one of your former students did so well in life. Diane's sister still lives in the Troutdale area, and she came to lunch one afternoon. During our lively conversation of meeting after so many years, she conveyed to me that although I was liked by most of my students, I was also feared as the "holy terror" teacher by some of the boys.

Fairview School grade 7, 1960-61 school years

All children's photos should be taken as individuals and never by a class group as noted in too many yearbooks, and such group pictures are probably completed for expedience sake. There are skin tones that should be taken into consideration. I am submitting photos of my 7th grade class here to ask my reader to look and guess who has a genuine smile that reflects great joy in their lives.

On the succeeding page 72, I am showing tasks completed as school decorations. No matter how insignificant the project may be, there should always be pride and praise for accomplishments.

As any elementary school teacher will recite that she is fortunate to have a gifted student who takes the lead, and will find that this student's peers will likewise attempt exercises/lessons that is a stretch for them. With encouragement, everyone wins. The two years that I spent here involved students who as a whole were the children of parents who loved them, interested in their progresses and anxious for them to excel. They sent them off to school in clean clothes and fed them a breakfast to start their school day. What keeps a teacher pinned to her charges advancement is the infinite recognition of effort and achievement regardless of the goal. Just cutting out letters for a window sign "Happy New Year" is an enjoyment and achievement with scissors for some in the class. Enveloping ourselves in tissue to illustrate a science project produced a question of why and who can relate a reasoning answer.

There are rewards in teaching and one is praise from a student who has infinite admiration. George C. is one such student, who wrote a note to me: "to the best teacher I have ever had."

There are also times when headache circumstances come into being. For instance, when teaching high school English students, and during my third hour exam period, I presented the class with a huge pan cake delivered at the school, frosted "The results of 'you know'" in

George

gaudy colors. This class agreed to pay 1¢ every time anyone said "you know'" and collected $3.25. Cost of the cake was $6.57. I was careful never to request payment. It was the class who demanded payment. It was a game and I believe I could see everyone made a conscious effort to eliminate this useless over-used expression. Use of my eyes, my stance, reminded the class of one who had offended the class rule. I think everyone enjoyed this usage game. During their taking of the exam, I cut and passed out huge pieces of this heavily sweetened treat (if you consider the condition of this method "you know" taught, it may have been an artifice). I expected some Marie Antoinette to arise and say, "See, you can have your cake and eat it too." It's such a corny line. I only mention it here in this biography because I was called on the carpet that I had made a conscious effort for students to pay illegal sums of money. I was caught only because the exercise got published in the local newspaper as a humorous article. My answer to the charge to the administration was that I never asked students to make any payment, and that it was the class who whole-heartedly endorses the game usage and forced offenders to fork over recompense.

And this wasn't the only instance of being called into the superintendent's office. I'm enclosing a candid snapshot of me to illustrate that we teachers were concerned about our appearance. We dressed neatly and spent hours in the evenings with fixing our hair and with grading papers. And yet the superintendent had the gall to call me into his office and reprimand me for not wearing make-up. Can you imagine such a thing happening today?

Superintendent's criticism

I have never been keen on make-up. I thought cosmetic expenses were not a high priority with me. Thus, as the fourth year closed, I decided to seek employment elsewhere, and this I did.

Fortunately, I had a goodly number of artistic students in my class.

It seems as other teachers know that we are always taking more classes to become more efficient in dealing with our teaching careers. My classes at Monmouth, Albany, Lebanon and Portland were all in the Oregon system of higher education of which some I found helpful and expedient to my philosophy of education, which included workshops in Montessori as well as motor perceptual methods. All dealt with elementary education.

When it was time to leave Reynolds School District I had accumulated sufficient credits to earn an elementary principal certificate in July 1963 and enough sick leave which I wanted to use legally. I knew I could not use it unless I was sick; I washed my hair and sat on the front porch hoping I would catch a cold so I could use my sick leave; in fact I did not catch a cold so my sick leave was never used.

My salary at that time was almost at the high end of the pay scale of $10,000. My beginning salary with Reynolds was $7,600. If I kept myself on a strict budget, I would be able to pay off the mortgage in less than 10 years. My salary was paid for only the nine months. I was expected to go out and get a summer job to eke out my living expenses. And yet my salary with a Master's also allowed me to make a trip to Europe, especially to re-visit Switzerland and to see the 1960 production of the Passion play.

This Passion play is performed every 10 years; the cast is usually comprised from the people who live in Oberammergau, which is a Bavarian village not too far from Munich. The townspeople put on this portrayal of the suffering and death of Jesus every ten years to honor their ancestors who made the commitment to God since they survived those crucial times during the era when the plague ravaged so many other cities. One must reserve tickets for this play a long time in advance, for the peoples' production is renowned for its excellence as is the Passion Play held during the summer months by the townspeople in Zion, Illinois, a community united together in tithing 10% of their wages from Zion Industries: the curtain, the cookie, etc. factories. The Oberammergau Passion Play is scheduled for an all day affair. In the morning you see part of the production in a theater that has superb acoustics.

All leave at noon for lunch and then return to see the remaining part of the play. If you have seen The Passion, produced and directed by that Australian

Oberammergau Theater

fellow, Mel Gibson,[32] you can sense the suffering endured by our Lord and the revelation of the purpose of His life. At least the Pope thought so.

While on this extended trip to Europe, I could not tell you why I drove to the Austrian and Czechoslovakia border to take photos. Whether it was my curiosity or with intent to show photos to the Kotans back in Scio or a dare to myself to enter into the strange and well publicized fact about the Iron Curtain. It was a mistake on my part to cross into No-Man's Land to get a closer picture of the sign that said Bratislava. The Kotan parents emigrated from Czechoslovakia, actually from the outskirts of Prague in 1890s. My purpose was to return to the States with souvenir shots. Before I knew what was happening, two guards on duty from the gate area arrested me. What else can I say? They approached me and took me to the small building near the entry gate. As a youngster I was taught never to lie, and that behavior was practiced all my life. When the Russian or Czech soldiers caught me, they communicated via shown-n-tell pantomime that they wanted to know what I took photos of and such were forbidden. I did not want to lie and not sure what to say, so I kept saying the word "focus." Obviously I did not communicate anything sensible to the two guards. I spoke repetitively the phrase "focus" and thought I held the countenance of an angelic child, which probably looked more like the countenance of a half-witted adult. I thought such created puzzling thoughts on the part of the soldiers and produced a "humph," and they walked away from me. Without Messrs. Sourpuss guards scrutinizing me, I immediately clutched my belongings to me and walked out of the guard shed and hurried to the gate into Austria. Oh, my, so long ago. Maybe that's why I appear to have my characteristic gait of always being in a hurry. Get back to Austria.

I had many more adventures in my travels in Europe and I relate to them later within this autobiography.

Upon leaving the Reynolds School District, I spent 30 semester hours at U. of California, Berkeley, California, during the years 9/1964 through 6/1966. My doctoral program specialized in Elementary

---

32   Actually Mel was born in the U.S. and emigrated to Australia at the age of 12.

Education and Curriculum. Tuition and living costs had to be subsidized with various employments. One job that I held was at an adult day school in Oakland, which was a basic education for adults; actually, it was a functional literacy program. Another job from 9/1965 to 1/1966 was teaching basic education for adults; basically high school English for adults and taught as a separate course in Reading Development for adults at the US Naval Supply Center. During this same time period, I worked as an intermediate typing course at Laney Junior College, Oakland. And then in 1/1966 to 6/1966, I worked part-time as the remedial reading teacher at the Catholic Diocese of Oakland.

My studies at Berkeley undoubtedly resulted in my article about "Critical Thinking," which was published in *Arithmetic Teacher, Volume 12, October 1965, page 501*.[33] "Critical Thinking" is an article dealing with the influence by the personality of the individual and well reflects the backlog of his/her experiences. My point in this article is that we need a generation of something beyond surface thinkers. Having knowledge does not guarantee a good thinker, but a good thinker does need good knowledge.

Running out of money and technical difficulties with choosing a thesis, I took employment with the Siskiyou County Schools and with Mt. Shasta School District as the reading technician elementary schools. My program as the reading technician gave the slow learner a second chance for learning basic skills which he was unable to grasp the first time around. This program of basic education is in tune with a concept which is becoming more in focus of continuous learning.

During the 1967-68 school years, I took the position as developmental reading—special, if you please—and English with the Hood River School District. Methinks the school district was impressed with my publication of *Reading is 'human awakening.'* And I think one way of expressing my theory is that the reading teacher show three films at the same time, silently run of course, two slides show—it can be any subject. In my case, the slides pertained to the modern classroom and slides of primitive classrooms where my brother taught Micronesian teachers English. At

33   See appendix A.

the same time I'm reading my blank verse contents of my book along with the playing of the well-known musical arrangement of Beethoven's Fifth Symphony. Ninety percent of audience identified the contents of all three films, the comparison and contrast of schools, identified, at least, knew that it was a well-known symphony, and concluding that the mind can truly have more than one thought at the same time. There was an "awakening," meaning is a reflection of one experiences and that experiences are brought to the word and not the reverse.

While we here in Oregon were not harassed by inner city racial problems, there were many teachers elsewhere who took the brunt of inner city and school riots. So, a comment is applicable to remind us that 1968 was also a time that "tries men souls." My brother wrote:

> I can still hear the Vice-principal's voice reverberating over the PA system like the voice of God commanding his frantic angels to attack Satan: 'Teachers, step out of your rooms and clear the hallways.' I happened to be in the tiny corridor on the second floor near the study hall and immediately went to protect the Tattler room with its $1,000 worth of senior pictures and one hundred and ten hours of labor it took to identify, classify and alphabetize the some thousand individual photos of underclassmen when they came stomping though like a wild herd of elephants that they were those few minutes. One kid picked up a five foot plastic type fern plant, vase and all, and threw it at me. It crashed against the Tattler door, smashing into a million bits. And the voice of God commanded out of the squawk box, 'Teachers, we must clear the hallways!' And literally 1,000 kids pushed teachers aside, casting aspersions that only gas-station illiterates resort to in anger. 'Teachers, clear the halls!' shrieked our commander-in-chief, and I felt like yelling, 'Go to hell!' The students threw rocks, toppled file cabinets, smashed windows, jerked shades from their spinners, tore up bulletin boards, started two bon fires in the johns and within twenty minutes the school was in a state of Ozymandias...round the decay of that colossal wreck, boundless and bare...the hallways were. And we teachers were in a state of shock. And all because the students wanted a new history book that had references to more Negro history. Maybe an oversimplification of the unrest, but sadly such violence was not a solution. Later, at the

faculty meeting, one of the assistant superintendents came over to our school to talk and to assure us teachers that the administration was behind us...yeah, forty some blocks behind us. What we teachers can't understand is that things have happened like this only not quite so badly before in other schools, and why there wasn't some prepared plan that the school should follow. I estimated that there was a least four hours notice that administration knew that something like this would happen. The student delegation, nit-wit leaders, stated that they would tear up the school if the administration didn't adhere to their demand immediately. Our library is choked with Negro texts. What a day. ...the Negro history book was only a pretext of the racial unrest in an urban society. Right now I feel as though the Earth has a skin disease and the itch for immediate reform would not come from a tube of Lanacane.

Eric Hofer[34] said the Negro revolution is a fraud...

It has no faith in the character and potentialities of the Negro masses. It wants cheap victories and an easy way.

Hofer seems to think that which corrodes the soul of the Negro is his monstrous inner agreement with the prevailing prejudices against him. On other occasion, Hofer said "It is thus with most of us; we are what other people say we are. We know ourselves chiefly by hearsay." Richard Wright parallels the thought in his short story "The Man Who Went to Chicago" in *Eight Men*. If you are interested in looking up this rather profound insight, the notation can be found on page 163, last paragraph, "color-hate defined."[35]

---

34   Eric Hofer (7/25/1902 – 5/21/1983) was an American social writer and philosopher. He produced 10 books and awarded the Presidential Medal of Freedom in 1983.

35   Richard Wright, Eight Men, New York: Avon, p. 163. "Hated by whites and being an organic part of the culture that hated him, the Black man grew in turn to hate in himself that which others hated in him. But pride would make him hate his self-hate, for he would not want Whites to know that he was so thoroughly conquered by them that his total life was conditioned by their attitude; but in the act of hiding his self-hate, he could not help but hate those who evoked his self-hate in him." This premise is also applicable to the homosexual. Examine behavior by the Christian right, and people like Pat Robinson, Bill Graham's son, etc.

King was assassinated on April 4,1968. And the world fell apart; at least, some areas were ablaze.

We here in Oregon with a population of less that 3,000,000 only read with dread about the events that followed in places like Detroit, Los Angeles, and Milwaukee, for instance. My brother wrote…

"In the final analysis all life is interrelated. All humanity is involved in a single process and all men are brothers."
MLK, Jr.

Dick DeMarsico, photographer[36]

If you can keep your head when all about you are losing theirs… you are a better man than I. On this Monday morning of 8 April, I threw out the regular lesson and asked my students to review several of our Victorian poets: Tennyson's In Memoriam, Ulysses, Kipling's "If" and the hypocrisy that can be found in Browning's dramatic monologues. The discussion was to deal with the connivance and duping oneself with irrational thinking, etc. The kids already had had a study of these poets so that the point was to relate these ideas with King's assassination and the effects. The discussion was becoming quite good when halfway through the first hour the Black Panther-type gang rushed down the hallways, yelled, marked up the walls, broke a few windows, pulled the shades off the spinners in some rooms and broke into mine and jeered at these advanced English students for not getting up and joining their hypocritical protest march. Not one of them moved. If they had gotten up and marched out, there would have been nothing that I could have done about it. Why didn't they? I don't know. With Washington, Chicago, Detroit and other places ablaze with what is termed Negro justice proves to me that King's leadership had certainly waned. I do not know what can be the cure of sick minds and the spiritually ill within the big cities.

---

36   DeMarsico took the photograph of King in 1964 while employed at NY World Telegram & Sun publishers. Reproduction rights were transferred to the Library of Congress through instrument of gift—ID, cph:3c26559. Many other photos are available at the library of Congress: MLK, Jr. NYWTS.

In the school year of 1968-69, came what I thought would be my last teaching post in Rainier, Oregon, on the Columbia and just across the river from Longview, Washington. After classes during the week, I was ready to drive back into Portland on weekends. After all, I had a house to maintain and most of my friends enjoyed doing all kinds of activities: horseback riding in the surf on the coast, there was a carnival at Janzen Beach, films, concerts and all were available to me. I even purchased a beach house in Lincoln City. There was this pink house restaurant that served marvelous fish and chips. It was always crowded and the inexpensive dinner fish plate was well worth the wait.

I met Dagmar Goe, who was the second grade teacher at Rainier Elementary. Her husband worked in management of a grocery store on swing shift. Daggie was free and I was not a great cook, besides cooking for one is a waste of energy; especially when there was superb fish-'n-chips restaurant in Longview. Daggie enjoyed fish there as well. She was a born-again-Christian and a dedicated teacher to her students. We became fast friends. I think it was Marlene Dietrich, who in one of her films stated, "'Tis the friends that you can call up at 4 o'clock in the morning." Daggie knew that I had been dating my friend Emil off and on since 1952. I met Emil, actually introduced, through his sister Josephine Riddle with whom I boarded while teaching at Lacombe Elementary School. Emil lived on his farm/ranch, cattle and feed operation in Scio, near what is now the fish hatchery farm. It was Daggie who helped me make up my mind to finally consider marrying Mr. Kotan. I was a little apprehensive when she informed me what the wedding rite was about. Sex education at my age is absolutely absurd I know. It's hilarious to believe that a woman of my age could be so naïve. And in telling you this, I hope that I don't meet you on the street and you give reference to my tale of complete innocence. I loved my job and I shared my joy about my forthcoming marriage. I told my class that he had purchased a horse for me so that we could ride the hills and back roads of this gorgeous part of the Willamette Valley (it's Wil-lam'-ette).

They were excited that my fiancé would buy me a horse, especially the girls.[37] My students wrote me goodbye notes:

"personal" Dear Miss Sheldon hope you and Emil have a goodtime together. Love, Monica P.S. I love you

Miss Sheldon I have enjoyed bring [being] in your class. Maybe you sat on me but now I'm glad you did. Hope you and Emil have fun Love Tracy

Hope you have a very dumb horse (not really) Yours Truly Write soon! Les

Minnie & me

I hope you like your horse and thank you for the ice cream love Duane Waggerby

By keeping these notes, I have fond memories of many wonderful children, hoping and encouraging students to be whatever they are by nature and whatever endowed talent they may have to spend it lavishly and in the spending develop successfully and happily. We teachers shouldn't be grading essays or writing assignments with the pen dripping red mark corrections. Whatever students write should be praised. If you want to give a grade, use "S" for satisfactory or "IN" for improvement needed. Find a letter to award the student an exceptional grade if that is your inclination; "N" for novel or uniqueness or perhaps "P" for peerless. And to be sure there is endeavor or effort made, I tell my student they cannot earn an "A" or "B" for the final grade unless they have attained a satisfactory mark in writing.

Suggestions for writing I would suggest come from the class reading assignments. Tell me you understand "cause and effect" by citing the part of the plot that pertains in such-n-such story. Tell me specifically

---

37   My 7th grade students thought Emil must be some great guy whose wedding gift to me would be a horse. I still chuckle in remembrance of their enthusiasm.

what the cause is and what the effect is. Likewise, the class could write on inferences. Whatever is assigned and accomplished the teacher should remember her charges are children and growth in writing ability will come faster with praise than a paper dripping with criticisms.

Chapter Nine:

Marriage—1969

I finally consented to marry Emil Kotan in February 1969, changing a unique friendship from a cocoon state into the beautiful butterfly betrothal followed by marriage. To explain our new status is to hint at a similar mutation, like mitosis. My hesitation certainly was an awareness of the difference in our ages. He was seventy, and I was forty-five.

Emil

Would friends and family think us foolish to embark on a "Cinderella syndrome" of living happily ever after? It took too many years to wake me up to the fact that here was a jewel and I would never meet another man as kind and gentle and loving person as Emil. I no longer cared what other people thought of our forthcoming marriage or the disparity of our ages.

Emil was born on 26 May 1899 at Howell, Nebraska, and the son of John and Frantiska (maiden name was Votropkova) Kotan. Both parents were born in Czechoslovakia; John in Rasovicion January 6,

1845, and Frantiska in Vrasovici on March 4, 1860, a farm suburb of Prague. At first, the family of John Kotan and his wife along with a

John & Frantiska Kotan

brother James Kotan, emigrated from Czechoslovakia to Cherokee, Iowa in 1886. A tornado destroyed their home and most of their belongings in 1889, and thus, they moved to a Czech community in Howells, Nebraska. John had been a Czech land agent for the government: a soil specialist and game warden. In 1899, John and Frantiska along with their children Emil, Joseph (1882 in Rasovici, Czechoslovakia), Anna (1889 in Cherokee, Iowa), Josephine (1890 in Cherokee, Iowa), and Mary (1893 in Cherokee, Iowa), moved to Scio, Oregon, where a number of other Czech people settled.

They purchased the farm owned by Alvin Gaines. There were four large bedrooms upstairs of the house that was built in 1852. It was remodeled by Emil Kotan and assisted by Joe Kotan and Jim Kazlowski in 1939. Joe, Emil and Anna lived here at the time it was repaired. John Hooker of Albany did the wiring of the house for electricity. In those early days on the farm, work was hard since machinery

Emil's sisters: Anna, Mary & Josie

was not available: hay was cut and stacked by hand; plowing was done with Belgium and Clydesdale horses. They sustained themselves with produce from their own fields and meat from their own livestock. A town trip was 20 miles, and it still is today, but roads are a little better today as well as vehicles/modes to travel. John and Frantiska had purchased from Emil and Anna Brodecky their 120 acre farm in Linn County, Oregon. This purchase expanded their farm acreage. Total price of the property was $3,000. At the time of purchase they were to pay an annual interest rate of 5½ %. At the end of two years the contract would expire which may or may not be renewed. To reduce the principal debt, the Kotans were permitted the paying on this note at any time with sums of $500 or more.

As one would expect, Emil did not have a high school education; secondary schools were not common in our area until the 1920s and even as late as 1930s. Yet farming for 50 years, one does learn something. With all my education, I would never know as much as he about grain and cattle operation, and I learned much.

And during those awful depression days in 1933, Emil paid off James Kotan's descendents for their shares of 132 acres located in Howells, Nebraska; to wit were Rose Kotan Holub and Emil Holub, her husband; Mary Kotan Holub and her husband Joe Holub, and Emma Kotan, unmarried. The sum was $3,000. The land was principally owned by John and Frantiska Kotan.

Before I married, I sold my house at 4135 N.E. 68th Avenue in Portland to Evelyn Luethi, who was a long time fellow graduate from Lewis & Clark College for the same price I paid for it with considerable improvements, and at the interest rate of 5%, with house payments at $50 a month. Property tax for the 1968-69 fiscal years was all of $292.85. I only mention these melodramatic financial matters so that my reader may chuckle over these unbelievable matters of inflation. Certainly, times have changed.

Joe and Emil, through hard work and Emil's inheritance from farm lands back in Nebraska, expanded the cattle/grain operation so that by the time I came into Emil's life, the farm (cattle/grain) operation had expanded to 440 acres. Joseph had unexpectedly died the year before in 1968. Josie or Josephine had married Joseph Riddle on Christmas Day in 1924, and it was they who introduced me to Emil while I boarded with the Riddle's on their farm just across the road from the Kotans.

At this time I was the principal/teacher at the Lacomb Elementary school.

Emil was a kind and generous person. I say some women find a lemon in the garden of love, but definitely not me. I married the best. When Emil would drive to Portland to see me, I often made dinner for him, which included a salad and broiled steak. Actually I never have been a superb cook as my mother and grandmother. They could take a cabbage and turn it into something spectacular. I never made a pie or cake in my life before my marriage. There was always a bakery somewhere near in my life and they certainly did better than I could ever do. If I needed a dessert, the bakery was the place to shop. And it was quite a shock to me to find out after we were married that he really disliked tomatoes, but never told me. Needless to say I never put tomatoes in his salad from then on. Another thing puzzled me. When he visited me in Portland, he never used my bathroom. I often wondered why as I assumed men had to use a bathroom as well as women. When I asked him "why", he said he was too shy to ask. All this narration is to reflect the man that I chose for my husband always had my happiness in mind. There was nothing that he wouldn't do to cater/coddle/indulge my wishes. I learned to do likewise my best for him.

While I was teaching in Verdun, Emil and I carried on a continuous correspondence. I'd write and tell him about my adventures and trip to Paris and he'd tell me about the time Joe, Josie and Anna went to Bessie and Jack's house to watch TV via the new channel they put in the valley and how the reception was excellent. He's telling me that the "things we want in life that money can buy really don't mean very much" for him. He's also telling me that "a gift from God is someone to love. You know I have been thinking this over so much." He's thinking in a round-about way that I'm such a nice woman; "You are honest, nice, sweet, kind and understanding. You don't smoke or drink (and such) good company. And when you find these things, I just can't keep from loving you." And then again, "So brace up Willie, here it is. Honey, I love you, won't you be *mine?*"

In 1966, he was writing to me about his pulling a muscle when he got tangled up with some root while cleaning a ditch stream, and added, "I do care for you very much, honey, and sometimes it seems like I'm pestering you all the time. Maybe it's not the right thing to do. Better close by telling you I love you dearly." Some of the endearing added notes from him may have been Hallmark kind of verses and who cares, but they reveal to me a man with sensitivity.

> "Sticks and stones may break my bones,
> But a hug and squeeze from you
> Will never harm me."

For Halloween he wrote me…

> There's a really weird character who can't wait to get you in his clutches!…ME!

And at Thanksgiving,

> Thank you for being a wonderful wife.

At Easter,

> I can't think of anyone I'd rather be 'cooped' up with.

Early in February 1969, Emil wrote again about the disparity of our ages and added while he was under duress of the flu season. "Well, honey, I don't think this is a lack of love. I am sure you love me as much as I do you….no one love could be any stronger….what I'm concerned about is that I'm a quite a bit older than you."

> In the innermost epitome of our being
>   lies God's greatest gift to us…
>   Love.

Love is not an easy concept to define.
It is a dimension of immortality
that links past...present...future.
Love is a universal need and all
Mankind search for it.
The breadth and depth of love is endless.
How much love can be contained in memory?
How much love can be shared in a memory?
How much love can grow in a memory?
It may be hard to find and it is easy to lose.
There is no monopoly on love as it is not limited.
Love gives a person the intensity for living.

At our next meeting, I accepted Emil's hand in marriage. "I'm engaged!" as I told my neighbor and flashed out my hand. "That's not an engagement ring, that's the wedding ring," she told me. I was a little shocked and blushed for my naivety for being the "show off." It didn't make any difference to me whether I wore the wedding ring for the engagement one. Anyway, I learned that Emil has mistakenly given me the wedding ring instead of the engagement ring, which was a Marquise diamond. His view was to give me the better of the two last: the moment of exchanging our vows. The next day I drove to Scio to see him and tell him I was returning the ring that I couldn't wear it. Before I could explain the situation, he blushed tomato red and professed that he was so sorry that I was breaking off our short engagement. Short? What do you call a

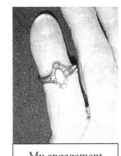

My engagement ring

seventeen year friendship? He was truly apologetic and embarrassed. Before another word could be spoken, I kissed him and said something to effect, "No, silly, it's only that you gave me the wedding ring instead of the engagement part of the set of rings."

In March he was writing and agreeing that circumstances were becoming complicated: "Hardly see how we can get married any sooner, sweetie. April is the time I have to get the crop in and then too all the stock needs feeding. By June some cattle will be out in the pasture and that way there won't be very much to do around here in the long run." Besides maintaining the cattle and overseeing the crops, he was building our house where we'd live after the ceremony: a three bedroom, two bath house. Anyway, in April he was writing that the foundation was in place and the well dug and complaining about not finding a plan for a fireplace that would suit us. Later he decided that the fireplace hearth should be made of Arizona flagstone and the kitchen would have a small connecting family room. And of course, my fingers were zipping through the yellow pages for arranging two receptions, a hairdresser appointment, shop for a dress, gloves, etc., meaning all the paraphernalia that goes into a wedding. One reception would be in Portland for my friends, like Mr. and Mrs. Oliver (Red) Johnson, who were ever so kind to me and my brother since our arrival in Oregon, my friends during my days working at the Bonneville Dam Administration, college people and fellow teachers.

I was finishing up my teaching at Rainier Elementary School. Amidst the thousand and one preparations, Emil and I found time to go through the solemnization of marriage rites as outlined from The Book of Common Worship printed by the Board of Christian Education of the United Presbyterian Church. We wanted that part that stated "Forasmuch as these two persons have come hither to be made one in holy estate, if there be any here present who knows any just cause"...etc., was stricken. And then the part where the minister asks Emil, "Will thou have this woman to be thy wife" was stricken and inserted my name Willette." And likewise the phrase "this man" was stricken for "Emil."

Early morning on June 14, 1969, my brother Jack flew in from Milwaukee. My maid-of-honor met him at the airport and drove him to the church. He met Emil and joked about the time for the ceremony.

A time to end Emil's long-standing bachelor status ended. I , too , had

Jack & Emil

anxiety: as nervous as a President to be out of the Iraq war...as nervous as a mortgage holder to be out of debt...as nervous as a farmer is to be out of a drought...as nervous as a patient to be out of the dentist's hands. Hey, I was nervous as any bride. I was getting married for the first time. I was 45 years old.

As any family knows, expenses of a wedding can be horrific. I hired a professional photographer and yet some of the family/friends photos were just as good as the paid professional's. Regardless whether amateur's or professional's the photos capture the joy of the day. Below is the prized bedspread presented to us by Emil's sisters. Hand/machine stitched head of a horse and our wedding date were inscribed at the far end of this bedspread.

The wedding took place at the Calvary Presbyterian Church in Portland. The Reverend J. Boyd Patterson officiated. Evelyn Luethi, my college peer, was maid-of-honor. My brother served as Emil's best-man, and they were both official witnesses on the marriage certificate. My brother walked me down the aisle, whispering how beautiful I looked. All went as planned. It could not have been better as far as I was concerned. The Portland reception was held at the Cosmopolitan Airtel in Portland. My friend Shirley Moore volunteered to keep records of gifts received. Then the second reception in Albany at the home of Mr. & Mrs. Lou Stanley[38] was for relations and friends and neighbors of Emil's in Scio and the surrounding area. The buffet was provided mostly by Emil's sisters and nieces. It was an extraordinary reception and their efforts were much appreciated by Emil and me.

Emil did not want me to see the new house that he built just for me until it was finished and all newly furnished. Emil's specific ideas about the floor plan of the new house and his ability in "homemaking" surpassed mine. His carpentry, mechanical, animal husbandry knowledge was amazing. His sister Anna would continue to live in the older, five bedrooms, and original home on the ranch which was built in the 1850s. John and Frantisca Kotan had first purchased this land in 1899.

After the wedding, off we drove to Nebraska where his Uncle James Kotan's descendants thrived. Emil was not the traveler. I suppose what kept him from ever leaving the farm was his constant attention to crops and animals alike. But he did thoroughly enjoy meeting his relatives and they welcomed us with open arms. The family, as I read from some Chinese philosopher, was the native soil on which performance of mor-

---

38   Mrs. Stanley is the daughter of Josephine Kotan Riddle.

al duty is made easy through natural affection, and then is widened to include human relationships in general. Ogden Nash stated at one time or another that the family is not only of children, but of men, women, an occasional animal, and the common cold. Ask Betty White or Oprah Winfrey if they consider their animals a part of their family. Anyway,

Descendants of James Kotan, Emil's uncle

everyone, speaking allegorically, wagged their tails in the joy of the reuniting the family even if it was for just a couple of days. If you don't already know this, I'll tell you that farmers are the salt of the Earth kind of people. Love abounds.

Since I got Emil away from the farm for a few days and probably wouldn't get another opportunity for a second honeymoon trip somewhere, we drove north into Canada to visit what I think is one of the more spectacular national parks in the world, Banff. A number of writers have taken their fingers and pointed at nature and stated, "See, God!"[39]

And if my reader is one of those who can sit somewhere and

Emil at Lake Louise

commune with the Almighty by just looking at his handiwork, then Banff must surely be added to your list. I knew that my husband had a

---

39   Emil, me, thousands of others embrace the pantheism view that in contemplating some aspect of nature we see the manifestation of the Infinite. Perhaps, unconsciously aligning ourselves to the Zen philosophy aspect of Buddhism of seeing/recognizing/ grasping a tint of Nirvana (for additional commentary see pp. 340-42.).

sensitivity on recurring events that appear in life, and now again gazing at Lake Louise with its mountainous background sprang just a little tear in gratitude for this amazing…gorgeous …spectacular…stunning scenic setting. For the moment he forgot all anxieties of leaving the farm. He was happy. I am inserting a photo of my husband standing at the roadside looking at the Athabasca Glacier. It was right at the roadside. Some fifteen years later on a return trip to Banff, the glacier had receded I would say at least three-quarters of a mile; a reminder of Al Gore's warning of global warming. And caused from some kinds of behavior I've seen by lunatics in this asylum of the Solar System.[40]

Athabasca Glacier

40   Samuel P. Cadman (1846-1946) held various ministerial position in both England and America. He is an author of a number of interesting religious books. In America, he is known as the first radio preacher.

Chapter Ten:

First Anniversary—A Trip to Europe 1970

Living on the ranch was a new experience for me. As I stated in my previous chapter, Emil bought a horse[41] so I could go riding on the ranch with him, especially when he was moving cattle to a different pasture. Roads in our neighborhood were not paved at this time and traveling on them was sparse of cars. Nearby was one of the better covered bridges found in Oregon? You will note that the Fish Hatchery Road is paved. Not always so. If you are a "nut," a person ardently devoted to covered bridges, and then Oregon is the place to visit. We have about sixteen of them. There is the joy of crossing such a structure that is a reminder of the past people who were concerned with matters not always of

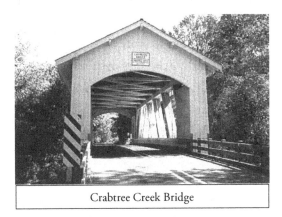

Crabtree Creek Bridge

---

41   My 6th grade students thought Emil must be some great guy whose wedding gift to me would be a horse. I still chuckle in remembrance of their enthusiasm.

just themselves. Our bridge here crosses the Crabtree Creek, which also borders the Kotan farm. We often walked or rode the horses near the creek for it was such a lovely spot to hear the water rushing over smooth granite boulders and gurgling a "hello" as it fled toward its designated destination, the Willamette.

We were living in a new house; we had a new horse and a new family routine. We also got a new Australian Shepherd pup. Their intense blue eyes search your face for a command to bring the cows to the barns; yes, we had more than one barn. And the dogs always knew which one was intended. Their welcome to see you in the morning or upon return from a city errand cannot be overlooked with just a pat on the head. A kneeling gesture was a signal for them to give you a kiss. Such loving companions man/woman have not had.

Australian Shepherds

My goodness the year passed quickly. June 14, 1970 was our first anniversary which is regarded as the "paper" anniversary. On the wedding trip to Canada, I learned that Emil did not and would not fly; he also would not go on any boat, yet he did everything to please me. For our first anniversary he purchased a ticket for me to go to Europe

I was excited about my returning to Europe, and yet saddened that Emil would not go with me. When you make your own travel plans, you run into many frustrations. Yet, all plans fell into place. My first stop was Lisbon, Portugal. And July temperatures here in Lisbon didn't help matters. I found that too many Portuguese think Americans are all very rich, and they, of course, needed to be told that we do not pick dollar bills off trees. While you're in a tourist spot, it is not easy to function like a native when you do not know the language. Lord Byron loved Sintra as well as an enclave of other Brits to spend some winter months there. The residential palace of King Carlos I is there as well as some remnants of crumbling Moorish castles. On July 4th, I was advised to visit the Statue of Christ, the Christo Rei monument. Directions were not as clear as I would have liked; I took a bus to the ferry and two more buses and finally wound up nowhere near where I should have been. Finally, I had to take a taxi to get to Christo Rei. The site gave the tourist a marvelous panoramic view. Afterwards, I walked the suspension bridge and then took three buses to arrive at the museum of coaches, which contains a marvelous selection of stage coaches, carriages, berlins and sedans of the 17th, 18th, and 19th centuries. Oh, how the very rich could exalt themselves by riding in such finery. In the Alfama district near the Targus River is the Castelo De Sao Jorge, which has a long

Car suitable for walled city of Óbidos

history dating back to the 5th C and rebuilt by the Moors in the 9th and then modified during the reign of Alfonso I.[42] The castle dominates Lisbon from atop the city's highest hill. At first I didn't think I would make it up the hill because the escalator/elevator to assist tourists was on the blink. But later it did function. The esplanade offers great views of the city. If one visits Portugal one should not miss Nasaré, a colorful coastal town with brilliant seascapes. Óbidos has a special simplicity as a Moorish walled town. Narrow roadways and small arches are fit only for the smallest of cars. The photo to the left is a car that would serve quite well in Óbidos. You can't help but be joyful about encountering a small town so different from others.

I wrote my husband to tell him how much I missed him and related how I was dissatisfied with my TWA flight and now switched to Swiss Air. I flew from Lisbon to Geneva, switched planes and flew on to Zurich, where Emil had arranged a rental car for me. It was easier getting onto the highway from the airport than trying to drive into the city. I was most anxious to arrive at Oberammergau and seek

---

42   Alfonso 1, called Alfonso el Batallador and ruled from 1104-1134; not to be confused with Alfonso I, who ruled Leon and Galicia from 739-757.

accommodations, which was not so easy a task. I did stay at the Hotel Klostenhof. I had extra tickets and since friends backed out at the last minute, I tried to sell them to hotel personnel or at the ticket office. I was not successful at first. Eventually two Belgium girls bought my ticket for 50 Francs each, a loss for me.

Again, I had great anticipation on seeing the 1970 production of the Passion Play here at Oberammergau, Germany. The scenes that were truly magnificent: one dealt with man's inner soul conflict dramatically portrayed in two dialogues: Judas in his yellow and black garments expressed and communicated completely to the audience his utter despair and remorse in betraying Christ and overwhelming

Oberammergau Passion Play

climaxed with his suicide. A comparable scene manifested itself when Peter seemingly emptied his soul in an emotional dialogue of guilt and realization in his denial of Christ. Garments were in vivid colors. Good drama is the absorption of the ideas by the characters and the dramatic force which the characters give to their performances.[43] To my view the Oberammergau production is good drama.

After leaving Oberammergau, I drove on to Innsbruck, Vadez and Wildhas, marveling at the fabulous scenery through eastern Austria, which included magnificent mountain scenes and pastoral valleys as well as flumes with rushing water. On July 12th, I arrived in Prague, Czechoslovakia,[44] and stayed in the Alcron Hotel. My observations of

---

43   Henry Becque (1837-1899) was a French dramatist. Wrote La Parisienne, which marked a rise of realistic/naturalistic French drama.

44   On 7/12, she wrote Emil: "All the towns look dreary. The roads are very bad; the worst in Europe. The country of Czech is not at all like other European countries in that everywhere things looked dismal and the people appeared sad looking. No gaiety or color anyplace. This was the kind of atmosphere you wanted to get out of right away."

driving here is that the Czechs lacked color. Many hotels in Austria and S. Germany displayed gonfalons. People dressed with panache. Somehow I felt my encounters seemed depressed. My imagination? I don't know. Before my purse was stolen while I was eating breakfast in the hotel dining room the day after my arrival, I had purchased this gorgeous Czechoslovakian crystal floor lamp as a gift for my husband. Other than this purchase I did not get to see much of Prague. I told the hotel personnel that I would be canceling my reservation since my purse was stolen. They asked me if I had more money. I did have traveler checks but I was seriously frightened and opted not to stay. They even wanted me to leave the car I had rented in Zurich, and of course I would not. Being in Czechoslovakia[45] was all I imagined of what living was like behind the "iron curtain." There was no sympathy for me about the theft. No investigative efforts were made on my behalf. Just, do you have more money? That day I packed and drove directly back into West Germany as soon as possible; it was a Sunday. It was a great relief to be out of Russian con-

Brandenburg Tor, over 200 years old; the Arch of Triumph of Berlin. It separated the West from the Russian sector.

trolled Europe. I had the car checked in near Nürnberg and arranged for a flight to Berlin; only $15. I met an American gentleman who had flown into Berlin fifty-five times doing business. One encounter with the Russians resulted in a severe bang on the head and he showed me his souvenir scar that occurred on this occasion. His experience with the Russians and along with mine reflects something is seriously wrong in the hiring of service people behind the iron curtain. The Golden Rule was not present and my thoughts ran along with the idea of what do we smite the evil doers.

---

45   Later correspondence revealed that she related her experience at the Alcron to friend James Pendleton, and he told her the same thing happened to him at the Regal Hotel in London, but he was entirely reimbursed. Conclusion was that quality in a hotel counts.

After returning from Berlin, I drove to Nürnberg, and from there north to Fynshav, Denmark. I ferried to the island of Aeroskobing for sight-seeing on an island with many 18th century homes and a museum of model ships; some in bottles. From there to Lolland Is, which takes me pretty much to the access road to Copenhagen. Regardless of island hopping, the ferry service was good; I didn't have to wait too long to arrive eventually in Copenhagen. The Mermaid[46] is here and Tivoli Gardens, which should be seen on a summer night rather than the day, for in the daylight it is akin to an amusement park while the fountains and lighted lanes throws an atmosphere of romance in the evening. Rundetarn, the round tower, dates back to 1643 and used by astrologists as an observatory.[47] Has any tourist come to Denmark and didn't visit Helsingör, a rather barren castle but related to Hamlet. "If thou hast any sound, or use of voice, speak to me..."[48] And so I too walked the rampart and visualized.

Ferrying from Helsingör to Helsingborg, Sweden, is just a jaunt. Sweden impressed this tourist as clean and progressive. Each city/town has its own unique television tower. It wasn't long before I arrived at Stockholm. I picked up mail from my husband at the Grand Hotel. Stockholm obviously has much water flowing in and about the city. The numerous canals and bridges lace this city and surrounding waters include Lake Malaren and the Baltic Sea. The old town is on an island in the center of the city. My father's mother, Anna Hegelston,[49] immigrated to America while still a teenager. Her second marriage was basically a failure. She could

Grand Hotel

---

46   Lille Havfrue is on the Langeline harbor promenade.
47   Among those were Galileo, who also was under house arrest by the Catholic Church for innumerable years because he would not recant his theory of the Solar System.
48   Horatio's lines in *Hamlet*, act 1, scene I, lines 128-9.
49   Some papers spell her name as Hegston.

not get along with her mother-in-law,[50] who all too well reminded her too much of her servitude on a landowner's farm. In my view her mother-in-law drove her son to drink and he, as well as Mary Ann, became physically abusive to his wife. While here I wanted to investigate the Boda crystal, Viking style. My brother had given us a beginning set of water and wine along with Champagne Viking glasses, and I thought I would expand our collection.

My next destination was to drive to Norway via Arboga and Karlstad and wound up south of Oslo at Drammen. I joined a tour bus to Larvik, which has an interesting 17th C. manor house, Herregarden. The tour also took me to Kongsberg, a silver-mining center and maintains a miniature train that carries tourists through the mining tunnels. In the town center are emblems of the monarchs of Norway, the Crowns, which are engraved on a rock. A tour of Oslo was mandated by my brother who has bragged about Oslo's Frognerparken, which is the site of the famous Gustav Vigeland sculptures. I think my guide book stated something like 200 sculptures. All varieties of love are expressed; yes, I did say all. This is a most impressive park. If you enjoyed the Rodin Museum in Paris, then you must make the trip to Oslo for the Vigeland sculptures. I marveled that cold, stone sculptures released emotions abounding with feelings of love expressed for family and friends. I think it was Chekhov, who expressed in one of his plays, that love is something that grows, and as time passes, into something enormous. And here you have these marvelous monuments giving expression of that enormity.

Eventually I drove back to Zurich. I was driving through Hamburg by July 22nd. What was going on, I didn't have any idea, but the autobahn was crowded. Everybody seemed on the go. I could not find accommodations along the way and had to continue on the autobahn until finally I parked behind a hotel near Garmisch and slept in the

---

50   Her mother-in-law was Mary Ann Hazen Sheldon, who was characterized in Opie Read's novel *A Yankee from The West* (Rand, McNally & Co., Chicago, 1898) and who was somewhat a superstitious woman and demanded loyalty and honesty from her servants; she also took a horse whip to any lazy or drunkard farm laborers.

car. For the next week I was the tourist in Bavaria and Switzerland. The scenery is so gorgeous; everything else is anti-climactic. By looking at nature and deriving a nearness of God is what some philosophers call his immanence and pushing the idea too far then becomes pantheism where God is lost in the world to which he is near. Methinks some eradicated men can bring confusion rather than clarity to an event encompassed by the sight senses. The week expired all too quickly. After checking in the car with an odometer reading of over 9,000 kilometers in Zurich, I caught my flight to Shannon, Ireland, via London.

My trip here was to tour the southern part of Ireland, particularly the Ring of Kerry peninsulas. When landing at Shannon, you're on the outskirts of Limerick, the nickname "City of Violated Treaty." Religious tolerances suffered when the Williamites attained victory over the Jacobites in the 17th C. On the coast road south of Limerick are the ruins of Mungret, a 7th C monastery and known as a center of leaning. Tralee is a small quaint town and the starting point for the trip to Dingle Peninsula, which hold superb views from a precipice over-looking the sea. On the other side of the peninsula

Dingle Peninsula

near Glengarriff, you will find other magnificent views of land and sea. Melville stated in his book *Moby Dick* that when the water and the mind meet they are forever married in meditation. And so it is with my standing on some precipice of the Ring of Kerry peninsulas. Wind came off the sea and caressed you and planted a wet kiss or two while tousling your hair in its fickleness to be gone.

While you are here, you must go to Killarney where an American donated something like 11,000 acres that eventually became Ireland's (Killarney) Nat'l Park. The Muckross estate has paved paths for cyclists as well as horse-drawn carts. It's a joy to jaunt about the park in this mode of transportation—a touch of romancing thoughts of yesteryears.

While I was preparing to leave Europe, my husband's last communication to me was a reprimand for sleeping in the car while there was plenty of room here on the bed for two. In writing that he just "quit a meal" of potatoes and baloney, the big news was that the neighbors Athtemius sold out

Dog-cart at Muckross Estate

to some California for the price of $100,000, and he thought that was a pretty good price. There was also the problem of Richy's bull getting out of the fields into ours and servicing our cows. Problems were resolved with understanding neighbors. I always give a chuckle when I think of Ambrose Bierce's definition of a neighbor as one whom we are commanded to love as ourselves, and who does all he knows to make us disobedient. It's not always true, but there is an element of truth within his version of a truth. Emil closed his letter stating that he had received all my letters as well as fourteen post cards.

On the morning of my return to Shannon, I had breakfast at a little guest house near Fermoy where I was staying. The young lady proprietor in her kitchen painted purple served me ham, bacon, sausage and eggs. Such a huge breakfast only a true farmer's wife would serve. At the airport, my agent as the car rental office handed our smart remarks because I turned the car in early. I was about to tell him off for his uncouth manner and lazy attitude in renting me a car with cigarette butts overflowing from the ash trays and general previous messy traveler's residue scattered about in the interior. I was about to expound to him my dissatisfaction but seeing a line formulating, I just told him that I would be sure to tell my travel agent about his company's lackadaisical agent at Shannon. I left. I was an early arrival at the airport terminal. After a sandwich lunch, we passengers boarded the 707 that would take us to Chicago. Delays for reasons unbeknown to us, I, with aprons, coin purses, glass vases, salt/pepper sets, candy, pewter gifts, wine—all gifts for folks back home—finally left the ground at 3:25 and I was on my way home: that part of the world where people know when you're sick, miss you when you die, and love you while you live.[51]

---

51 This is a Samuel Johnson (1709-1784) definition. He was better known as just Dr. Johnson, English lexicographer, critic and great conversationalist. He became famous through efforts of James Boswell's biography of him.

Chapter Eleven:

❦

Ranch Life—1971-1974

After an exuberant welcome home, life quickly settled into whatever chores we had in running the farm/ranch. I convinced Emil that we should try to raise sheep. A cosset is so cute, so cuddly, so captivating and so curly. This purchase was a big mistake. Our pasture lands are basically flat and our winters are with continuous rains. Hoof rot was a problem and Emil spent any profit on our herd on vet bills. And there were many. As with any of our cattle that were taken to market, they were purchased readily because Emil was strict about care for his animals. His cows were always prime. In my absence, Emil had a sheep agent come and look at the sheep and stated "too much money." When you think of the feed, care, vet bills, there was no profit and eventually had to sell at a loss.

a cosset

On the Ranch Emil was always trying to please me; whenever a holiday approached he would ask what I would like. He would not ask me once but many times, and I kept repeating myself "nothing" as I had everything I wanted. He would always call me "Honey," once I asked him if he knew my name, since he always called me "Honey". The little tit for tat teasing is how we communicated our affection for one another. When we went shopping for groceries, he would not let me pay, and I told him, as a cashier was listening, that if we were going to live together he must allow me to spend some of my money. The cashier did not say anything, but I am sure she did not hear those remarks often from customers and probably had some juicy gossip to report to family members at her dining room table. When we got married, he opened a checking account for me and he would deposit money when the account became low.

Into every life comes sorrow. In September 1957, my Aunt Ida Crapo died in Illinois, leaving my brothers and sisters and me a small inheritance. Due to various codicils and bequests made on conditions, the final disbursements to inheritors were not made until December 23, 1973. After I received mine, I would put money in Emil's wallet. When he discovered it, he would take it out with specific instructions that it was mine to spend not his.

One day while I was riding my horse and assisting Emil to move some cattle to a different pasture, my horse reared—a snake crossed his path—and I was thrown off my horse in such a way that when the horse came down, its hoof came down on my arm near the wrist area. Emil took me to the local hospital, and after a quick exam, they informed us that the injury was serious and we should go to a hospital to have a more experienced orthopedic doctor treat my arm. We drove to Portland. The specialist was not on duty when we arrived, and it was later that evening that I was in surgery and came out with a cast on my arm. After several trips to Portland to see the surgeon concerning the condition of my arm, which was not healing, I asked the doctor why he questioned me if I was drinking milk. The relationship of drinking milk and my wound not healing became a concern and we realized it was time to find a different doctor. I ended up with Dr. Ellyson in Albany. Dr. Ellyson had Bill Walton of the Trail Blazers as a patient, and I assumed that I had found the right doctor. He operated and placed a rod in the second bone in my arm and put me in physical therapy. It took about a year to get acceptable mobility for normal use of the arm. I never regained full use of the right arm. I hold my fork different from others and some may think it odd. It does not bother me as long as I can get food to my mouth I have it made. And I can not open my hand to receive coins in change for a purchase. Needless to say Emil had to do the entire house cleaning for several months. How many husbands would be so considerate about their infirm wife?

Life progressed. Animals had to be cared for, grains harvested and grasses combined and bundled and stored in the barns. Anna, Emil's sister, still lived in the original farm house with its large kitchen and she did just about all the regular summer canning. We didn't grow tomatoes but we grew just about everything else suitable for growing in our area of the Willamette Valley.

While I lived in Europe, particularly in France and traveled extensively in Switzerland, I was fond of fondue. There was a pretty good fondue restaurant in neighboring Millersberg and special celebrations were involved with fondue dinners.

We pampered our dogs and they were loyal to us, warning when stray cows either jumped or broke fences onto our property. I was always in awe of these blue-eyed, Australian dogs understanding our commands and wishes. Whistles from Emil were commands to be carried out immediately and enthusiastically.

The Easter basket

One Easter-tide and with the help of Annie Kotan, we prepared this gigantic Easter basket filled with eggs, marbles, suckers, pencils, puzzles, and other items for the Tharp family. Somehow we made the front page of the Albany Democrat-Herald.[52] We did things like this often.

---

52   This photo was taken by Stanford Smith of the Albany Democrat-Herald.

Besides my accident, 1971 will be a year that I will always remember for the L.A. earthquake and Apollo 14.[53] It was also the year my grandmother Mrs. Ida Crapo, Sr., died. Even though she was able to walk some, stairs were difficult. Her mind was not as active as it had been. There were times when she didn't recognize me or her closest family members; after all, she was 99. Her daughter Blanche, with whom her care was fundamental, was looking forward to having her mother's picture on the morning talk/news show after Willard Scott presented his weather report. There were those thoughts of Sir Walter Raleigh that come to mind about thinking of your "salad days" as a

Mrs. Ida Crapo, Sr. at 92

gift to remember when youth has forsaken you. Raleigh and I agree that while young we think it will never have an end, and yet we know that every day has its evening. Raleigh phrased it: we ought to sow all provisions for a long and happy life.[54] Life is not a rehearsal. Sadness comes when I think of our gobble-de-gook talks while shelling peas or husking corn. Forming tears now is a cause and effect of those remembrances.

Emil had good control of things on the farm/ranch, and he urged me to indulge in matters of education that I felt so strongly about. Reading was quite at the top of my list; another was doing more for the slow learner.[55] The federal government initiated ESEA Title III Project Vocational and Academic Education for the slow learners in rural farm areas. I wrote to Mr. Wold, Superintendent of the Scio School District 95C and requested that he review my finding as well as my brief outline of a curriculum that funds would be available from the federal government.

---

53 Apollo 14, manned by Alan Shepard, Allen Roosa and Edgar Mitchell, explored the moon's surface.

54 Sir Walter Raleigh (1552-1618) expressed his ideas in "The Nymph's Reply to the Shepherd," which was a reply to Marlowe's pastoral poem that begins "Come live with me and be my love." The point is a realist versus a romanticist.

55 She is not talking about retarded children, but those with below average IQ.

Ranch life: our farm life included caring for the animals, harvesting feed, hay rides for seniors and family entertainment, not quite as often as we'd like.

The curriculum was to intersect in three main areas: 1) academic, 2) vocational and 3) human value; the length of the school day will be approximately six hours devoting half the time to academic study and the other half to vocational learning. The school year for perhaps approximate 60 male students would operate more or less on an 11-month basis. I knew that I could get the funds, but I could not entice superintendents to persuade faculties to generate interest in such a program. *C'est la vie.*

> Statistics indicate that approximately 15 to 18 % of the general school population can be considered slow learners. Since they are a very large group and since they do not deviate markedly from the average as do the other groups of mentally retarded children, special educational provisions have not been considered essential. They do, however, provide one of the largest and most intense continuing problems facing the classroom teacher. They confront every teacher, with the possible exception of those teachers who instruct only advanced academic subjects. Because communities vary, the rate of incidence is even higher in some areas.[56]

Another disappointing experience in educational matters was that on April 1, I was interviewed for principal/head teacher position with School District #110C, Crabtree Elementary School. There were four teachers hired as faculty in addition to myself. I was the latter educationalist to be hired for the school year 71-72. After the interview, I was asked to leave the room while the board discussed my resume. Ten minutes later I was asked to accept the position as full-time principal as well as being a substitute teacher as needed and to handle some special reading classes. My husband was witness to the conversation that occurred between me and members of the board. Henceforth, I attended all the board meetings, presented the board with a policy orientation, and further prepared a Title 1 fund application, calendar schedules,

---

56   Many thoughts here were also expressed by G.O. Johnson in *Education for the Slow Learner.*

report card date schedules, and a Crabtree school policy all of which were submitted to the board. In preparation for the commencement of classes on September 7, I prepared an introductory orientation and workshop, which was held on August 30th; school was scheduled to commence on September 7th. On Friday, September 3, was my second contact with the teachers at which time we had an approximate 3-hour session discussing school policy matters. On September 4, the chairman of the board asked me to meet with the school board. When I told him that I had an out-of-town quest, he still wanted me to come as my presence was mandatory. Emil went with me as I couldn't imagine what was about to happen. When the members came in they were almost rude to me in their absence of friendliness and greetings. The meeting was called to order and the first ten or so words spewed forth were, "We have a problem and we are asking you to resign." Wow! I was stunned. I absolutely refused as I had nothing to resign about. I had been working since April and school would start in two days. They said they would give me three months pay, I still refused. Then they said they could buy my contract off. They also stated the teachers were unhappy, and they mentioned three reasons: 1) I asked for a biographical sketch. I justified this as I needed it when I introduced staff to the PTA. 2) Class schedule. This was justified because individual teacher's schedules must be in the county office by Oct 1. 3) My emphasis on use of the Caldecott books. I reiterated my good opinion of these books by emphasizing that these books provided a "floor" not a "ceiling" for our 1-6 grades. I still maintain that there isn't any reason why all youngsters (at least with a learning IQ) couldn't read all of them by the time they finished the 6th grade. I didn't mention IQ; just indicated my philosophy that they were good books. When I wouldn't resign they told me to stay in the teacher's room and not interfere with teachers as they would have an acting principal. When I appeared at the school, the acting principal came in and verbally told me to take the 3rd and 4th grades. I refused. I was hired as a principal, substituting when necessary and special reading instruction/class needs. On the 9th, I received an informal note to take the 5th & 6th grades. I still refused going because a hearing referee in Salem told me that I had a good case of breach of contract. He told me to sit tight, which I did. Then on the following Monday, I received a letter saying I was dismissed. I was angry. I hired an attorney and he was quite adept. He told me that the board had no grounds for dismissing me. He wrote letters, one to each member of the board with a copy to the Country Superintendent, stating he wanted to meet with the Crabtree board's attorney immediately.

What I could not rationalize is why the teachers turned against me. At my orientation Mary, Annie, Emil and I made a dinner with all the trimmings, and Mary and Annie made marvelous cream puffs. I made a gift tree so that each teacher could take a little gift home. I even asked the janitor to attend this dinner engagement. Prior to school commencing and at our school orientation, I met with the agent from Caldecott books and reviewed with the faculty my findings as well as required records filed with the County Office for matters that concerned testing.

I had to create the school calendar, pupil records forms, parent conference schedule, etc. I hauled supplies, texts along with a personal evaluation of our math texts. Another school policy was that I would compose a menu for the month, for then students could take a menu home and if he/she didn't like the item of that day he/she could bring his/her own lunch.

I tried to be pleasant to the teachers all during these first weeks of school, which was most difficult as I was seething with the board's illegal practice of firing me without cause. At my last meeting with the chairman of the board, I was not given any reason why the county superintendent or the teachers were not present when I was asked to resign. The board chairman told me that I should seek legal counsel, which I had done. Emil and I were on an emotional roller coaster and just sick with anxiety of wondering what or who had such hatred for me when I had basically no contact with any of the faculty until I invited them into my home and the one day of orientation.

I do recall being asked by the board, as their policy seemed to be, whether or not I went to church. My husband didn't, but here was a board asking such a personal question which had nothing to do with a position as Crabtree's principal. An inference is that the board members were supposedly Christian people, and yet they act with such dishonesty with these false charges: "inability to communicate and demonstrate leadership." To resign now would definitely hurt my resume in the necessity of finding another teaching job. Regardless of how the matter evolves, this was a no win situation for me.

My husband had attended school here: Crabtree Elementary. One of his teachers wrote in his autograph book

> Crabtree, Oregon
> January 18, 1910
> Dear friend Emil,
>   The talent of success is nothing more then doing what you can do well, and doing well whatever you do without a thought of fame.
>   Longfellow.
>   Your friend & teacher,   Rose Bierly

My husband may not have attended church, but I can assure my reader that he was more Christian in his deportment to man or beast than ninety-nine percent of any men I have ever met. He lived up to Rose Bierly's commentary. One acquaintance suggested to me that God was punishing me for some omission /commission act by either me or my husband's life. This is the same illogical reasoning as Jerry Falwell or Pat Robinson's logic that Americans have to pay for their sins through 9/11. It's a preposterous supposition that God punishes people. And yet I believe that there can be a death and a life in the power of the tongue[57] I believe that as a man thinks in his heart, so is he.[58]

---

57   Proverbs 18:21
58   Proverbs 23:7

One reason for my enthusiasm in taking on this position offered to me by Crabtree School was because my husband, brother-in-law and his sisters attended school here. My contract salary was for $8600 plus $600 for additional duties prior to and following after the school year. This is a step-down from what I would be offered elsewhere. There can be only one alleged supposition that may explain these times of extreme anxiety. One teacher had defamed my integrity and persuaded others to unite in an effort to oust me as their administrator.

Whether there was an element of personal dislike by one of the faculties, or whether it be another's expectations for my position will never be resolved. To make a long story short, I had made every effort to meet with the board or meet with the faculty to determine what was amiss. The board would not meet with me or with the teachers in the presence of the board. I finally relented not to do any further action in order to understand or resolve the problem. The greater the effort I made, the greater insult to my integrity. I sued. After two years in 1973, the Court of Appeal in the State of Oregon informed me that I won my suit. There is no glory in a victory that caused so much personal pain. Borrowing a thought is applicable: "Facing it—that's the way to get through! Face it!" And an appropriate axiom also works here: "He who increases knowledge increases sorrow."[59] And yet one can always find worse situations than the one you experienced. My brother wrote to me at the end of 1971 that someone (alleged teenager) had shot through his faculty window. This incident can hardly be called his thrill of the year. A pane covered with Venetian blinds deflected the course of the bullet enough so that no one was hurt. Derision of errors is not so funny when deriders err.

This was also the year that we all became literally tired of Jane Withers liberally sprinkling her Comet around, whitening the path for other movie stars to supplement their incomes. But never did I ever

---

59   This is actually a translation of an idea coming from the Tamil (Indian) religion and primarily located in S. India. Basically Hinduism and closely aligned to Shiva, the third major deity (Brahma, Vishnu and Shiva).

think the day would come when I would see Betty Grable[60] on TV commercials advertising Geritol.

In the interim of our farm days, we included castrating the pigs so that they'd sit on their haunches and fatten up for market. Yes, even those male pigs attained a castratos "oink, oink." Sheep had to be attended to, especially during those very wet spring days for rotting hoofs. The cows needed care; they don't always just eat grass. We saved by installing feeding sheds. Fields had to be cut, raked and combined and bales brought into the storage barns. Fences had to be constantly mended. Draining ditches had to be cleared as well as two gentle brooks kept clean. There was the joy and pride in purchasing some new equipment for use on the farm/ranch. Besides these farming tasks, there were birthdays to celebrate, have a hay ride for seniors and other family celebrations.

The plight of the small time farmer is serious business; I tried to convey my thoughts in an editorial, which got published and received sympathy as well as empathy from as far away as our Albany neighbors. As I wrote:

> I do not know what profit the middleman receives, but I am fully aware of the profit as well as what is involved when my husband places 20-30 choice, grain-fed Herefords on the market yearly. Weather permitting, and it plays a significant role, he 1) plows the ground, 2) cultivates the soil, 3) plants the seed, 4) applies fertilizer, 5) applies weed killer and 6) harvests the grain; each one is a distinct and separate operation involving fuel, labor and machinery. The costs of seed, fuel, fertilizer and weed killer have almost doubled in price the last six months. After harvesting the grain, he must grind it to feed cattle three times daily for six months as a finishing process. During this time, he must clean barns daily of manure. In early summer, Mother Nature permitting, he will cut, rake, bale and stack hay and straw

---

60   Betty Grable (1916-1973) traveled vaudeville circuit with Jackie Coogan, her first
      husband; divorced in 1937. Later married band leader Harry James; two children,
      Victoria and Jessica.

to feed and bed cattle year-round. These eight operations again involve fuel, labor, machinery and twine, which incidentally has tripled in price? He must pay taxes, insurance, utilities and buy supplies, as well as pay for repair and maintenance of machinery. This year it meant purchasing a $6,395 used tractor since new ones are almost unobtainable. He pays Social Security taxes on net income rather than gross income, this means his retirement benefits will be much lower than other blue collar workers. Six months ago he received 53¢ live weight for his choice, grain-fed beef, resulting in the consumer paying approximately $1.10 per pound and include packaging and wrapping. A 900-pound choice grain-fed Hereford dresses out 55¢ with about 495 pounds in steaks, roasts and hamburger. If my husband could receive the $2 minimum hourly wage for fifty, 40- hour weeks, his labor cost would be $4,000 yearly. Unlike the middle- man, the farmer works every day including Saturdays and Sundays, and he is on call 24 hours every day. At a bank one can expect at least 5 percent return on his savings investment; my husband received 1 percent yearly return on his capital investment (land, machinery, supplies). My husband cannot add his labor (middleman does) to his production costs, nor does he receive 5 percent yearly return on his capital investment, both of which indicate dramatically that the consumer and middleman are being subsidized by the farmer and his labor. Inevitable conclusion is that we are living in the twilight hours of a great colonial era of farming, since it is becoming increasingly impossible, economically, to raise grain-fed beef at the present market prices.

The days do fly by. The 1973 Christmas came with the joy of finding that the courts had exonerated me in my confrontation with the Crabtree Board of Education as I previously stated. Christmas, more than any other time of the year, is the time the heart has its chance to revive itself. In God's Holy Word—Proverbs 4:23—we are to watch our hearts diligently...

> BECAUSE from it comes all the issues of life…
> Our deepest feelings pivot from the heart…

Hardening one's heart evolves from compassion without understanding,
 a conscience without honesty,
  forgiveness without tenderness,
   friendship without harmony,
    sympathy without empathy,
and hope without faith...even distorting wrong into right.
 One can have sight but not necessarily vision[61]
  dramatizes vividly that the heart has essence but
   not necessarily soul literacy...
 Soul literacy implies
  surrendering...yielding...submitting
   one's soul to be placed
    in an attitude of a kneeling position.
Literacy is disciplining for a clean heart...speech...imagination.
  It is re-affirming God's existence and re-dedicating one's heart
   to become an instrument of
    Christ-like wisdom and understanding...
It is searching deep within the heart to give a prayer with
 creative thankfulness
  a smile with natural warmth
   kindness with humility
    trust with faith
My Christmas wish is that during the Holy Season
  you and I will become both giver and receiver of gifts
   which revive the heart.

Haven't you sat there in your chair with a bundle of cards, address book and pen 'n paper in hand, and then apparently for no reason at all become, with fixed eyes, one as the dear light of sense and thought have fled. I stare at this bloody typewriter and hoped that my vague thoughts crystallize before they stream shapelessly through my mind. Some thoughts pierce me like thorns on some Christmas wreath

---

61   See appendix C for illustration of the thought.

decoration. This vast blank page must be filled with some summary, some capitalizations, and some rippling letters trickling forth to form some message of good cheer. The typical banners on "trim a tree" sections of the local department store says "Season Greetings"; "Joy" is said by making a small purchase of a giant, old-fashioned Christmas tree ornament. "Noel" is spirited via twinkling lights attached to shopping centers, apartment buildings and neighboring homes. These luminous sculptures reflect the abstract. The Christus Rex dominates our culture in which we live and is a mosaic of cosmopolitan life, complex and flowing. And yet "it" all reminds me of the warm friendships that are being renewed and formed among us all as we share a moment or two by writing a brief line of Christmas cheers.

It's amazing how the tempo of living has quickened. I can vividly recall the importance of such men as Ex-Presidents Truman and Johnson, who died at the end of '72 and early '73. Noel Coward passed on in March and W.H. Auden, whom I enjoyed, meeting on one of his circuits of universities, also died most recently. With their passing, my middle age status is underscored. And another sign of middle age is when the phone rings on Saturday night and you hope it isn't for you.

It was a season when farm work was not at its peak that my husband and I took a trip to the SF Bay area to visit my brother who lived in Kensington, the bedroom community of Berkeley, CA. Our plans were to attend the S.F. symphony: John Mauceri was the guest conductor; they were to play a piano concerto as well as Sibelius Symphony No. 2. We had gone into the city early to have dinner and were confronted by a disheveled, dirty, apparently drugged hippy-type character. He approached us with the flattering remarks on how nice our clothes looked. I didn't like this and was about to tell him my slacks costs $7 at one of the leading department stores and certainly not much more than his dirty, infamously patched crotch, seat, etc. pants. But he immediately began raving about the new revolution in which our wealth will be shared by the poor people of the world, and such what we had would be taken from us. He added that "we" still love you, in one breath and cursed us with another, using the foulest language. Since we were near the opera house, there was no way to reach a phone to call the police as he blocked us from proceeding to our destination. There were three men in our party and not being able to walk-away, moved forward attacking him verbally to move away and, probably to his thinking "this" will lead to a physical tangle, he ran off. But what a frightening experience, especially after the messages printed in the S.F. Chronicle from SLA in the Hearst kidnapping.

In February of 1974, Emil purchased a new Dodge Sport PU. We had looked for several weeks and the best buy we could find was at the Beaverton Dodge Auto Sales outside of Portland. Emil had a new canopy put on and as soon as we can get away, we will take the Chippendale table down to my brother Jack in San Francisco. Emil really liked his new pickup even though we had a Chevrolet truck to carry stock to the auction markets or whatever. The pickup was a means for him to go to town in style. We should never put off matters that are important to the living.

When we farmers heard about the possible creation of a nuclear power plant on the Brewster-Lacomb Road five miles northeast of Lebanon, I became irate and fired off an editorial for the Albany Democrat-Herald, which appeared on Feb 21, 1974.

Opposes Nuclear Plant Proposal

Keep Oregon green. Keep Oregon livable! I hope this will be the first of many letters that will voice strong opposition to the proposed Pacific Power and Light Co.'s nuclear power plant on the Brewster-Lacomb Road five miles northeast of Lebanon.

Paradoxically, across from the same site, if not feet from it, are existing towers transmitting electricity from hydroelectric dams in the Northwest. It would seem obvious that Willamette Valley users of electricity could receive their supply from existing dams. If not, then why not through new hydroelectric dams which can harness our abundance of water, rainfall and snow much more safely environmentally than by building nuclear power plants.

It also would seem apparent that our PP&L rates could be considerably lower. PP&L must be an extremely profitable business since PP&L is willing to spend $700 million dollars (our money) for the proposed plant.

A very basic fact that I learned in science as a youngster was man could not survive without water or air. Mother Nature has provided an abundance of oxygen via the miracle of plant life. Each time you drive by and through the Willamette Valley, you will see evidence of this perpetual miracle. Inch by inch in this rich fertile farmland, the farmer is assisting Mother Nature in its work to keep Oregon green and livable via the trees and plant life, which are recycling/purifying our breath of life. Man must have this to keep alive.

Yawing each year our planning commissions literally give away, not inches mind you, but acres and acres of this precious farmland to sub dividers and industries. These acres will never be reclaimed as farmland again when such areas should be the necessary participating factor with Mother Nature to recycle our air and water. Nuclear production of energy involves a chemical change which ultimately can be much more destructive of air and water systems than man can possibly comprehend.

All residents near the PP&L proposed site are water users via a net-work of wells. The harm that this nuclear power plant will have on our underground water system must be seriously considered. Again, each year, realtors sell land which is not adjacent to existing water and sewer systems, and each year new taps and demands are being made upon the underground water supply. Man must come to realize before it is too late that this underground system is not an inexhaustible supply.

The proposed PP&L power plant will mean further tapping into our underground water systems by a work force during construction and by an operational work force during maintenance of the proposed plant. There is the questing of seepage of extremely harmful chemical waste products into systems. One might well consider the harm geothermal exploration might do to our underground water systems.

Lastly, man can discuss, debate, argue, and verify the needs why a nuclear power plant should be built, but this rhetoric will not change the established miracle of recycling air and water.

The quality of air and water available for our use will depend dramatically, categorically and simply upon the pollutants we keep out of our air and water systems. It is as simple as that!

This quality will depend upon combined efforts of you, me and the Oregon Environmental Council to prevent potential pollutants from entering and impregnating our air and water systems, and by so doing will sustain Mother Nature in her in her never-ending miracle of recycling our air and water systems in keeping Oregon green and livable.

Willette Kotan,   2/21/74   Scio, Oregon

For extra money, I purchased three day-old Holstein calves to raise by nippled bottles. When I learned that their mothers would not nurse them—I'm guessing at the reason that they hurt her too much in giving birth to them— I couldn't resist them and brought them home. Regular nursing schedule had to be established and with Emil's help, we saved them from immediate slaughter.

On the morning of August13th, 1974, this five year marriage ended. It was usual for Emil to get up first and put the coffee on. This particular day this did not happen. When I awoke he was still in bed. I touch him to wake him and was shocked beyond belief in feeling his cold body. Amazing unrealistic thoughts ran through my brain. I knew I needed help and I called my sister-in-law and an ambulance. My husband was gone; I could not believe it. I was a robot functioning on automatic pilot. Calling his sisters and then my friends who came down from Portland to assist me in making some decisions that had to be made—ones that you don't ever think about until the event has arrived. I called my niece Marrae who lived in Beaverton. She came down and was absolutely wonderful and took over the matter of informing my family who still basically lived in the Waukegan area.

In every life comes a sorrow. The embankment holding back a flood of tears broke and can logically be explained with Tennyson's "Tears, idyll tears, I know not what they mean." Oh, yes, Tennyson knew what they mean, for tears can only flood forth as a measurement of the joy you have received. The tears are the tangible measurement of that joy. Emil's death reverberated an endless rush of sadness that took hold on me.

Chapter Twelve:

The Grieving—1974/1975

My husband was gone. The hardship of life abounded at this time. I had come to love this section of the Willamette Valley with its foothills to the west and Mt. Hood and Three Sisters Mountains in the background to view on clear days. I had come to love everything my husband thought dear, and I would do anything to perpetuate his philosophy of protecting Oregon farm lands.

I had the funeral service on the 15th. Dr. Morton Booth officiated the service held at the Fisher Funeral Home. It was a clear, sunny day and an August Thursday when friends and family paused briefly and made their condolences before going into the white framed chapel in Albany. The organist played softy songs of reassurance and comfort. The auditorium was well-filled. Many beautiful floral tributes filled the front auditorium, making it almost a mass of varied colors. A beautiful bouquet of gladioluses and chrysanthemums spray represented my family.

My brother Jack was at the Hellenic University in Athens and presently somewhere with a study group touring the antiquities of the Cycladic Islands and didn't know of Emil's passing. I had a cross of white chrysanthemums to represent him, which I know he would have wanted. There were a total of fifty-two floral offerings of which the Kotan family was well represented. I had a small bouquet of roses placed on the casket as a token memento from our Australian shepherds. Dogs are family and they were an important part of my and Emil's life. There were other beautiful bouquets representing a line of others in the Kotan, the Stanleys, and the Holubs families. I was so overwhelmed with grief, I cannot remember all those who were so thoughtful with their flowers. The soloist sang "In the Garden." Its message was a source of consolation. The minister spoke fittingly of Emil Kotan as an affable, winsome, and gentle man, a man who loved the soil and the work required to maintain it. A specific instance of his respect for all life was illustrated in the time he opened a bale of hay to free a snake that was trapped inside it. Biblical examples of those who lived from the soil were given. The minister's message centered on John 14: 1-3: let not your heart be troubled for in my Father's house are many mansions; if it were not so, I would have told you. I go to prepare a place for you. And if I go and prepare a place for you, I will come again, and receive you unto myself; that where I am, there ye may be also. And because I live, ye shall live also.[62] The solo "How Great Thou Art," was in worship of God, an affirmation of His eternal greatness.

It is odd that certain moments during stress that are recalled that have no great significance and yet a word or two spoken are forever etched on this slate of experience. Dorothy Vachter came up to me and gave me her impression of the service and said that it was "nice." I hoped that she did not detect that I was perturbed by the praising "nice." If you get my meaning, no funeral can be "nice." Although I appreciated her effort to commend the service, I hardly think "nice" is a consolation. The service was to reinstate beliefs that we are so well indoctrinated in Christian faith. In this sorrowful moment, I gained time for composure, and stated the idea that we as a group had high respect for Emil; that in this moment in time we paused to claim Emil's noble stance in life

---

62   John 14: 19

and that his death was not the end of everything, but a new beginning. The deepest message of Easter is and always has been the promise that this life here on earth is only a beginning for all of us and that the here and hereafter are merely different aspects of the same thing. The verse in John 14:19 and the promise therein means that eternity does not begin with death, for eternity is the living now and death is but a change.[63]

Commitment of Emil's body was at Franklin Butte Cemetery, Scio. Inevitably there were people who were late learners of Emil's demise. Rather than a casserole dish or flowers, they sent money and such amounts were donated to the Oregon Heart Association in memory of Emil Kotan, and I asked the association to send appreciation acknowledgement of their monetary gifts.[64] Fisher Funeral Home attended to my wishes for Emil's burial. Cost amounted to over $2,400. I suppose a reasonable cost compared to the like at the present funerals. If you listen to commercials, it's a wonder that some celebrity hasn't been paid to testify there are terrific savings with so-n-so.

During our life together, he told me that he carried a special knife given to him by Scott Stanley. Although he continued to use his old knife, he was reluctant to use this special one because he wanted to give it back to Scott at the appropriate time and not because he didn't cherish it, but to return it with his love. Think of it as a thought/feeling gone to seed.

Some time after the funeral and in memory of Emil, I gave copper milk cans to Anna, Emma, Mary and Josie. Copper milk cans because they were chosen as appropriateness as farm items for durability and uniqueness as an heirloom. And inside the cans I had placed exceptional photographs of Emil that were taken in 1953 when we first met and then in 1969. I included a note that if his sisters did not want them to go-ahead and sell them and donate the sum to the American Heart Association. No one needs a material object to remind them of a

---

63   Willette's thoughts here come from Dr. Norman Vincent Peale's "Easter: Day of Glorious Hope," Guideposts, 3/75, p. 8.

64   Elda Lowman and Mr. & Mrs. George Rice were just two examples.

departed love, but a tangible object that can be touched or seen may be that silent, consoling manifestation of that existence.

In running back and forth from the city, I would stop off at the cemetery and visit Emil, and I mumbled to him my woes of the day, week, whatever. At one instance I noticed tire tracks across his grave. I thought of putting up some flower barrier to keep this from happening again. Have you noticed many drivers making left hand turns who turn too quickly and come all too close to your front fender. Well, there are apparently no qualms about cutting the turn short and running over graves and in my view serious ruts began to appear, especially after a rain. I became incensed; irritated as all heck. As a result, I decided to

As I walk through the valley of the shadow of death, I will hear you say to me, "I love you."

bring Emil home to the land that he worked all his life, the land of his father's...his family. This final interment came in September 6, 1975; Mr. Heggis dug the grave. Oregon Historical Society now has the register of the Gains/Kotan Historical Cemetery, and having Emil moved there was a considerable expense. I had all the nine tombstones, relations to the Gaines family, refurbished. This cemetery sits on the down slope on the higher point of Kotan ranch/farm.

At first I thought that the entrance to the cemetery should have a notation in Czech, and my brother had an inscription translated for me: *Hospodinova jest zemê, a plnost její, okrslet zemê...Žalm 24:1*[65] Eventually, I decided on the memorial stone, and I made a drawing of the one I wanted placed there. Capitol Monuments in Salem would complete the headstone. Even though it was inconvenient for family or friends to visit the sight, I wanted it to be impressive and express my love for the man who unfortunately had only five years of marriage, but twenty-three

---

65   The Earth is the Lord's, and the fullness thereof. Psalm 24:1

years of friendship. On the side of the memorial stone I had inscribed "As I walk through the valley of the shadow of death, I will hear you say to me, 'I love you,'" and on the reverse side, the inscription reads, "Love survives a physical death." Birth and year of death were sufficient that we existed for one small moment in time.

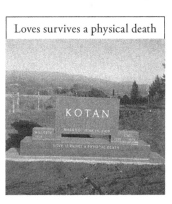
Loves survives a physical death

As you may or may not imagine from my words, I had great spasms of depression. In the early evening hours, I would walk up to the cemetery, sit myself down under the pine tree with Snoopy's[66] head in my lap and meditate—unraveling bitter thoughts about my forced dealings with the world. Eventually, with the passing of time, these bouts were as Thea[67] felt while attempting to sing an aria from Wagner's opera. It's taking the physical notes of the composer and bringing that combination of notes into harmony of their intent. Thea draws upon her own personal strengths of her life in such a way to crystallize a unique expression of deep passion, and it's her passion, not some famous contralto/soprano who is striving for the emotion that is significant of the moment. It's completing a catharsis. My thoughts gave birth to words:

> I have had a wonderful and exciting life
> and love but something now is missing
> and now I know it is the
> unfulfilled passion of love...
> How does one explain love...
> and its depth
> its breadth
> without discovering...
> passion.

66   My Australian shepherd
67   The heroine in Willa Cather's novel, Song of the Lark, 1915.

Passion is a word and within itself
contains no meaning
as it is only a formation
of a group of
alphabetical letters
forming the word which has two syllabic sounds.

Passion is filled with emotions
distinct from reason
as they are deep...stirring...intense...
and, yes, ungovernable.

Passion is what the artist
feels and tries to express
in his paintings...

Passion is what a composer
feels and tries to express in his music...
Each trying to express
the deepest feeling
that have an unfathomable depth...
a depth without a ceiling or a floor.

Passion too has its unique place
in the expression of love.

Passionate feelings
cannot be expressed in words...

Passion must be felt
it cannot be passive
it must be expressed.

Passion was ignited in me during our first kisses…
And it took the book by Willa Cather to pinpoint
the missing link in the love
of my life.

How do I describe love?
Saying "I love you"
seems so inadequate
as it is a deep emotion.
Can it be compared to clouds…
Clouds…
in their unique shapes
are always moving within the sky.
We observe their whiteness
as they intermingle into the heavens….but
if this infinite movement
of the clouds
could be heard…
the movement would emulate sounds like a
great musical composition…
such grand music expressing
in harmony and rhythm
a beat…a tempo…a melody
that only hearts
can hear and understand…
for words cannot describe the sound
nor the movement of the clouds…
nor can words describe…
express the deepest feelings
of love.
How does one keep in tune with love…
understanding relationships…
tasting the tender consciousness

in the search for love.
This is the search in life...
    for love
        There is no monopoly on love
It is not limited...
    nor is climbing to the top of one hill
        for you will find another
            which will even take you higher...

There is no conditional claim
    on the immensity
        on the intensity
           of love
              in life.

To love is to live forever
    as tomorrows can unfold
        that which will elevate
           one's dreams
              to a vivid anticipation
                  of exploring love

    and the real meaning
        for living in all of one's todays.
Love truly permits you to leave
    the external world
        and scale the hills
        to arouse the uppermost emotions.
Love is a universal need
    which is searched by all...
Love has a dimension of immortality
    that links the past...present...and future.

Now that I reflect on the importance of missed passion, I might as well include here my monologue that I call "Lip Conversation." At my age and as for all women I know we still have desires. Our husbands may not be here, but at least I think my thoughts into words:

Tenderly I will embrace you in my arms
   And gently place my lips upon yours.
      With great tenderness our lips meet
         And move ever so slowly in unison.
      In this movement
     Our lips communicate
    Tender feelings...of love.
The moments are breathless
   exciting...sensual...
     The sweetness
       the warmth...
         is sustaining us
           as our lips caress.

Instant communication
    passes between our souls...
       The touching of our lips
          becomes quiet communication...
Lips apart leaves vivid memories
   of a love shared.....
      nor is there anticipation
       nor an expectation....and
         again...again...again a recitation
           lingers on...and on....and on.

I think the quote from Anne Frank's diary[68] is appropriate here:

> I don't think of all the misery, but of the beauty that still remains... My advice is: go outside, to the fields, enjoy nature and the sunshine, go out and try to recapture happiness in yourself and in God. Think of all the beauty that's still left in and around you and be happy!

I marvel that such a young girl had such wisdom. Such lessons in times of despair are not easily learned.

---

68   Annelies Marie Frank (6/12/26 – March 1945) was a Jewish girl who was born in Frankfort and whose family moved to Amsterdam when the Nazi gained control of Germany. She gained fame posthumously following the publication of her diary (Diary of a Young Girl), which documented her experience hiding during the German occupation. Of her immediate family, only her father survived the concentration camp internment.

Chapter Thirteen:

The Job Years—1974-1976

The book of Job in the Old Testament has been classified as "poetical," even though Hebrew poetry does not have meter and rhyme as poetry is taught in schools. Job is a book of parallelism of thought rhyme. One thought is expressed and then repeated while a second thought is contrasted and maybe climatically of the first. I called this chapter "The Job Years" as it invites a comparison to Job's never-ending problems; his destiny and God's way with him. With all of his suffering, Job never waivers in his faith. Not so with me. I questioned the injustices of human sufferings, particularly to those who did not deserve these afflictions. Existentialism, in part, is a philosophy that relates to matters on hand and they have some particular purpose or design; these are the second parallel thoughts of Job's companions, telling him that his afflictions have some cause because of Job's behavior. But I'm belaboring my point of calling this chapter as I have. You decide whether it's valid or not.

The hardships in life come to us all; every cloud has its silver lining. Trouble came with the flood of tears, and it was most difficult to visualize a rainbow at an end of continual storms. Yes, we all have troublesome storms in our lives, but to learn to dance in the rain is not easy.

Once in Persia reigned a king
Who upon his signet ring
Graved a maxim true and wise,
Solemn words, and these are they,
Even this shall pass away.[69]

And so it came to be, but let me tell you my troubles; in retrospect, there are lessons to be learned.

The morning of Emil's death, I walked over to Anna's, a matter of crossing our driveway, cross a creek (generally dried up during the summer month) and a hundred yards to the original farmhouse where Anna lived. I related the matter of what had happened and thought I had better check with her about funeral arrangements before going to the Fisher Funeral Home. I wanted her to know of my wishes and intentions and to ask what hers might be. All she could think of was to ask me to locate the twenty dollars she had given Emil the previous day to buy groceries in town. Oh, it's far more difficult to leave unsaid what was tempting at the moment than to say something derisive at this time. It's good to keep your mouth shut when you are in deep water. I was in no mood or frame of mind to look for twenty dollars.[70] In the moment she asked me for her $20, an over-whelming wave of dander flashed over me; tears of sorrow and anger mingled, camouflaging one another. In a flash came this feeling that there was never any great liking/love between Anna and me. No affection for her that I felt for Josephine and the other sisters of Emil. I know that my husband had integrity and he had paid all bills on the old farm homestead, did all the chores, took care of such matters as property taxes, utilities, and assured that SS taxes were paid for her and Joseph both prior to their

---

69   Theodore Tilton, American journalist; on editorial staff of the Independent, a Congregational journal (1856-71); also one of central figures in famous case of Tilton vs. Beech (1875), in which he sued Henry Ward Beecher, pastor of Plymouth Church, Brooklyn, N.Y., for criminal conversation with his wife, Elizabeth Tilton, and demanded large damages; trial result was a disagreement of the jury.

70   Later in the day, I sent either my niece or a Portland friend over with the $20; I found the $20 bill and grocery list in Emil's truck many days later.

retirement age. Annie had been dependent on Emil and Joe for her entire subsistence. It was a year after our marriage that I learned about an instance of her frugality was a broken, inoperative sink in the house, making it necessary to carry and wash all dishes and cooking utensils on the back porch. When I learned of this burden, I told Emil we must call a plumber to have it fixed. The cost was a meager $30. Prior to our marriage he had considered a tenuous partnership of his earning with Anna. Yet Anna was unyielding, inflexible, and demanding person who would not allow my husband to exercise in some important matters his own individual decisions in operation of maintaining the farm. Her behavior was so uncompromising that Emil and Joseph's life became so intolerable that he and Joseph moved into a deserted shack on the farm and lived there for 10 years before he moved into our home. It was this former treatment of her brothers that sheathed an acridity that now struck a sore that I cared not what followed.

Her dislike of me came forth in actions that I would not have expected, for she moved out of the farm house shortly after Emil's death. and into the city to live with her other widowed sister Mary Holub and spinster Emma Kotan, who lived at 727 E. 4th Avenue, Albany, and yet Anna maintained her private mail box at the post office. By November 6th, Anna had stripped the old house of its furnishings for which she had every right, but "strip" here means taking the light fixtures is a case of throwing me into darkness with a fuming antipathy.

Unfortunately, and as I see it, Anna became frightened with Emil's passing. Although Emil had a Will designating me as executor and beneficiary of his estate, Anna sued me, contesting some aspects of Emil's Will. She claimed that I had no right to inherit eighty acres that were a part of Frantiska's estate, as widow of John, and had been designated to Joe Kotan, the eldest born, and upon his death, Emil became sole beneficiary of the land. There were accounts initially listed in Anna and Emil's names and then my name was added to these accounts upon our marriage, as Emil's name became joint owner of my real estate and bank accounts. But because my signature was not on his bank's original records, Anna was permitted to withdrew the total sum of over $19,872.19 without me being told, and yet this account was listed in the assets of Emil's estate for which I was to pay an inheritance tax.[71]

There was also an account at the US National Bank in the amount of $6,773.83 that was turned over to Anna. Anna sued me for partial landholdings. Annie's lawyer was Mr. Reid and it was his office that sent me papers to sign that I was to release this land to Anna. I look at this threat as a lawyer trying to take advantage of Anna because he should have known by looking at the county records that she had no chance of this matter happening. I stood my ground with legal papers of my ownership. The suit went on until early '75 when her suit was dismissed by the court for no legal basis. I can well understand her frightened financial status, for I believed that all matters could be ironed out in due time. Eventually I paid her an additional $10,922.80 from the value of US Saving Bonds. I had to withdraw all monies from my California teacher's retirement fund to meet these threats of holding my right to Emil's farm. I was determined to preserve this estate as part of Oregon farm land.

Anyway it was now up to me to run the ranch of 440 acres. Even though I had learned much from my husband about animal husbandry, grain operation, why burning of fields is necessary and farm financing, I still had to learn much. For instance, could I keep emesis in check on castrating piglets or bull calves? Learning how to run a ranch meant first learning how to use the tractor; and this my husband did not teach me. If you are chuckling about how dumb I can be, then I say after the age 50 I am permitted to be myself, because the people who matter don't mind and the ones who mind don't matter. So, an agent at the farm vehicle agency instructed me correctly on tractor methodology, I forgot to ask how to put it in reverse, so I had to make a second trip into town to learn how to back it out of the shed. It is always better to

---

71   It was Frantiska's will that designated Joseph Kotan as the beneficiary of the farm land and upon Joseph's death Emil was the designated inheritor. I assume that Anna's suit for 80 acres derives from Franciska's death, meaning she was actually claiming 80 acres from Joe's estate. This is the only logical conclusion I could come to.

play it safe than later regret any chance of stripping the gears or creating other damages.

Fortunately, I knew how to drive a 1 1/2 ton truck so I could get supplies from town; but there was a whole gamut of other things to learn. I can honestly say I enjoyed the ranch life. To run a ranch of that size in the Willamette valley takes skill and knowledge I did not have. My friends kept telling me to sell the ranch. My brother wrote…

> Your latest letter has arrived reflecting your independence and hard physical work to complete the harvesting and carrying on with the farm chores. That is admirable. I know that you must feel totally inadequate at times, yet your struggling by treading water is keeping you above board. You seem to be in command of things rather than them commanding you.[72] Emil's Will, leaving everything to you, is what Anna and maybe some of the other relatives feared from the very first and now Anna's suit is vocalizing what she/they have long thought. Such was inevitable and this trial and tribulations cannot be avoided. I feel very foolish giving you advice or rather very incompetent, but since you asked, I'll ramble out my thoughts. First, you must be realistic. You know not what life has in store for you. What you may decide now may not be what may be in ten or twenty years from now. You feel strongly about keeping the farm in tact, yet you must see the time that you just may have to sell it and buy some other property within a city or town, at least nearer a shopping area. This whole matter of the Annie-Emil relationship sounds too complicated for me to comment, but it appears that you are being more than generous to Annie. Time will resolve matters; the angel on your right shoulder tells you so. Believe her.

But I firmly believed that it is farmers like Emil who keep the valley land productive in farm products. And this I set about to do.

Problems during these close years after Emil's death came readily one after another. One ludicrous instance was in dealing with the

---

72   A stoic philosophy: I cannot control events in my life, but I can control my attitude toward them.

ambulance/emergency service. Upon waking up and finding my husband not up and about, I called 9-1-1. An ambulance was sent out to the farm. Medicare refused paying for such service because it was classified as nonessential emergency service as Emil was dead before the arrival of the ambulance, and thus I became responsible for this billing. One never reads the fine print for what Medicare will pay or not pay coverage clauses.

Then there was this man named Jerry Wallace, a tentative renter who bargained for a good 2/3 parcel of all tillable soil. I told him to check with ASCS[73] office in Albany on what was grown and to receive a map of the land before he offered me $11,500 for the rental figure on Oct. 20th. On the following Monday, the 21st, he walked the land and reduced his offer to $9,000, which I accepted in good faith and considering the soil condition and the time already spent preparing the land for planting and since it was getting late for a crop to be planted, I told him that I'd have the attorney check over the lease. His remark was that we'd have no problem as we were both honest farmers. When the time came to sign, he reduced his offer to $4,000. In expectation of his signing, I had installed a private entrance to the far acreage of the land plus four culvert-bridges for his convenience. My anxiety grew with this encounter of renting the land to whom I thought was a forthright farmer. I was over a barrel so to speak. Lateness of year and harvesting were matters of concern and Wallace took charge of just the 300 acres.

When he failed to make the rental payment in early '75, I filed a suit against Wallace at the Linn County Court House. I was rather taken aback when I was called to the trial proceeding in Marion County Court House on February 28th, which turned out to be only a hearing, not a trial. In May there were more delays and misrepresentation by Wallace. I never did know what he had told his lawyer or the court, but such was an aggravation with all these delays. I was strapped for money,

73   Agriculture Stabilization & Conservation Service, which keeps records on land use, etc.

so I placed my beach lots property up for sale, which sold quite readily. Time passed and in March 1977 I noticed that Wallace had advertised a number of farm machinery for sale. On July 19th, my lawyer called and told me I had won the suit and later in the month my lawyer and I went through the settlement papers, and it wasn't until November that I actually signed for the check in the amount of $5,100. With the court cost and lawyer's fee, I was left with $3,331.47. Here is a modern day example of a pyrrhic victory. This hassle consisted of too many days without sunshine and produced too many nights with the idea of "Oh, no, not learning experience!"

In late September 1975, I drew up a lease for Wilbur Hewitt and his wife to rent approximately 400 acres for the sum of $15,000 per year. The lease ran from September 1975 through August 1978. It was also agreed that they would pay $41.08 per day should there be a need to complete his harvesting due to weather conditions. In my inventory included in my inheritance tax forms I had an IM 101 combine, Ford twine baler, IN DC-6 tractor, hay and grain elevator, grain hopper, hammer mill and 40 ft belts, a 3-bottom plow, disc, corrugated roller packer, John Deere hay & grain elevator, side delivery rake, E-Z Flo spreader, 20 ft. auger with motor, fanning mill, cultivator, 3X8 hydraulic remote cylinder. As an incentive for land rental, I agreed that the renter would have the use in part of my farm machinery, such as the manure spreader, the combine and grain hopper during the time of his leasing my land.

Regrettably, Hewitt over-extended himself and did not keep to the signed lease, and initially I filed a suit, but an agreement was settled for his use of 200 acres for grain in 1976 for $7500. He was using my land and he had advantage of some assets of equipment in the lease, and yet he failed to comply with our agreement. As I see it, he was lackadaisical and not as industrious a farmer as Emil was. I was fortunate to rent part of my grazing land to Perry Roth for $1,600, which income helped me to exist. He had 10 horses feeding in the pasture by the old farm house, which was not a part of our original agreement. This was just another little aggravation by some who were taking advantage of me.

We farmers are not in any sense of the word rich. Yes, the land has its value and must be considered the thing that will provide for our bread and butter, so to speak. And yet in these days of gloom, days of dark cloud and the stormy weather times, I came to wonder how bad things eke out, seep through, and predominate my thoughts in thinking of the worst that pertain to farming tactics. It was a time of my life that strikes at a memory on how Haile Selassie must have felt when he stood before the League of Nations requesting aid for his country against the Italian invaders. His plea was in vain.[74] So were mine to a man named Fleury, who took possession of two lockers full of beef. How in the world did I lose two lockers of prime beef? There had to be a fluke in the legal system. Emil had always been attentive to his obligations; for instance rental fee of the meat locker. Fleury had taken advantage of my situation; he was another companion of Job who interpreted my plight of events as legally his advantage. It was the middle of 1976 that I came to an end of encountering an unbelievable amount of devastating inheritance problems along with poor legal advice; especially matters pertaining to the federal and state taxes. I considered myself smart enough to go through the federal and state income tax form and a whiz when it comes to taking deductions on schedule A. But taking on federal tax form 706, inheritance taxes with its many appendages and schedules, was a Herculean task for minds to unravel the Gordian knot[75] or who would ask why there are interstate highways in Hawaii. With a duly officiated Will, Emil and I had covered each other. In this matter of one's demise, there was willing care for the one surviving. Should I have preceded him in death, he would automatically inherit my inheritance from my Aunt Ida, the beach lots,

---

74   Haile Selassie, Emperor of Ethiopia, at the time of the Italian invasion in 1936 (the same
      year my mother died in a drunken driver accident) was a statesman, he helped establish
      the Organization of African Unity in the 60s, deposed in 1974, and assassinated on
      August 27th, 1975, coinciding at a time of great turmoil for me.

75   A rather complicated story of Gordius, who upon being chosen king of Phrygia,
      dedicated his wagon to Jupiter, and fastened the yoke to a beam with a rope so
      ingeniously that no one could untie it; whoever could would rule all of the East.
      Alexander came along and gave it a whack with his sword. Thus the Gordian knot
      became a symbol of getting out of a difficult situation.

my US Saving Bonds, teacher's retirement funds in both Oregon and California as well as the mortgage payments coming forth from Evelyn Luethi on the house at 6817 N.E. 68th Avenue, Portland, as well as a bank account in my and his name. I had previously been misinformed by legal advice in completing my federal and state tax returns. The tax office for the State of Oregon stated that I would need to pay a federal estate tax as well as for the state regardless of having filed the 1040 for the year 1974 for myself and my husband. During my interviews with attorneys, a federal estate return was never mentioned, nor was it in my many contacts with the State of Oregon when they assisted me in filing the state return in 1974. What a maze was the federal form 706. It reads that every citizen or resident of the United Sates whose gross estate as defined by the Statue exceeded $60,000 in value at the date of death must pay an estate tax. What a rip off for the American farmer. Our adjusted gross income for the years 70, 71, 72, & 73 never came near $10,000. And now I was to pay both federal and state inheritance tax, not only on the farm/ranch that we owned, but also on half of everything that I brought to our marriage financially. Had the farm been a part of Howells Cattle Company of Nebraska, there would not have been a tax because the CEO would have drawn only a salary and no tax would have been paid upon his death as another CEO would have stepped in as replacement. A capital gain tax would have to be paid upon the selling of the company, but not because of a death. No farmers, widows or widowers are excused from taxation when the value exceeds $60,000.

Now I was confronted with verifying what I inherited. What a mess! Tangible things to be taxed were such things as the cattle, US Saving Bonds, bank accounts, motor vehicles, farm machinery, IM 101 combine, Ford twine baler, IN DC-6 tractor, 50 ft. hay and grain elevator, grain hopper, hammer mill and belts, 3-bottom plow, disc, corrugated roller packer, side delivery rake, E-Z Flo spreader, 20 ft auger with motor, fanning mill, cultivator, 3X8 hydraulic remote cylinder and other tools. My inventory of things amounted to slightly over $107,000. The land including my beach lots was valued at $115,000.

The social Security death benefit of $255 also had to be included for inheritance taxation at this time for the state because this lump-sum death benefit qualifies for a part of the $20,000 state exemption. I was allowed up to 50 percent of the land value as part owner, thus reducing the taxable amount from $115,220 to $57,610. Now the task was to find what was deductible to reduce the sum for estate taxation; these included property taxes due for me and my husband, funeral expenses, medical expenses that pertain to his death not covered by insurance (i.e. Lebanon ambulance service). There was a choice of either taking the $50,000 automatic deduction or apply for the Homestead Act deduction, which in my case was far more financially beneficial; the withdrawal of 198.31 acres from estate taxation. The end result was that I had to pay an additional $1,608.23 (previously paid $749.92). For the unpaid balance due the state amounted to $6,088, which included inheritance substance tax owed by Anna Kotan, but there was obvious faulty computations here; eventually I paid $5,118.23 to the State of Oregon in inheritance tax; it was later reduced and a refund was due me which I requested such a refund be sent to Anna Kotan.

Obviously Emil's Will was my saving grace to inherit the land. But now a problem arises. What will happen to the estate upon my demise? A revocable Will becomes irrevocable at the time of my death and will automatically transfer such and such property to so-n-so upon my death. Once executed it takes precedence over anything else. Such will take care of tangible property. Bank account—and this is where Emil and I failed to have in place TODs— transfer on death beneficiaries for bank accounts, stock, and the like. Live and learn. Every farmer knows that you should shear the sheep, not skin it.

Walnut trees

In October 1975, I picked up the last of the walnuts in the old farmstead yard. The trees were old and I thought/knew they probably have to come down before the winds took hold of some branches and they come crashing down on the verandas on both the first and second floors. I cut the trees down with Emil's McCulloch saw. Feeling rather proud of myself I went to town for a pizza to sort of celebrate this achievement, and this time as with others, I met a stray black bear that wandered into Albany.[76]

But I stray from my point. After making repairs and restoring some features of the original farm house, such as a new well and electrical improvements, I tried to rent some of my acreage along with the old farm-house. I was not successful, and I'll deal with those problems in the next chapter. Maintenance was in continual operation. Obviously I had to hire laborers for certain tasks; i.e. putting in culverts from the draining ditch along side of the road to give access to the north tillable land for grain, had to get the drill in the shed, and fix fences, particularly by the middle pasture; fences were a continual replacement job with having an ever increasing herd.

It was in May 1975 that I first returned to our bed since Emil's death. What makes a widow hold onto memories that a simple reminder of your shared bedroom can bring the shadows of sadness? In my college English class I did a paper on Tennyson's "Ulysses" and recall the sense that we are all somewhat like Ulysses; although… "Made weak by time and fate, but strong in will…" this despair will eventually pass. And so it is with me; I returned to our bedroom.

A bright spot in my life came in August 1975 when my elder sister Ruth and her husband Michael came out to visit me. I decided that I'd have a party and invited all the Kotans I could think of and celebrate with a dinner. I'd be 51 years old. It's a reason to celebrate. My brother Jack said that he'd come and cook for the occasion: a ham, a turkey, and

---

76   Albany is situated on the Willamette R., and during this time there were considerable forest and park areas in and about Albany.

the whole smear of condiments to go with the buffet.[77] I invited about 30 people, but for various reason only 22 accepted the invitation. All the Kotan sisters attended, except Annie, plus my friends from Albany and a few from Portland. I planned a variety of parlor games and gifts for winners and included a hay ride through and about the farm area.

A senior hayride

My sister-in-law Josephine Riddle died 15 November 1975, and the funeral was on the following Tuesday, which I attended. It was she with whom I resided while I was principal/teacher at the Lacomb Elementary School and of course through her met Emil, Josephine's brother. Since her husband was a WW11 veteran and was interred at the Willamette Memorial Cemetery in Portland, she too was interred there next to her husband.

My major problems were dealing with renting the old farm house, my suit with Annie and my suit with Wallace, which didn't come to an end until 1977. I was plagued with expenses; i.e. wiring for old farm house, and outbuildings for farm machinery, a well dug, bridges/culverts, stove for old farm house, and besides the inheritance taxes already mentioned in this chapter. Uses were all undeserving acts of vexations. With 1975 ending, I failed to received the joy, Noel, and all those other ring-a-ding sounds of Christmas signifying good fortune, incredible resilience, goodwill prevailing over the tattered tempers; in other words I was failing to put the Christmas spirit altogether.

In May 1976, I invited my mother's sister, my Aunt Blanche, to come and visit me. I paid her airfare, for she was retired from Abbot's

---

77   He worked in a variety of restaurants during his undergraduate and part graduate studies; restaurants included such as House of Steele off route 41 in Waukegan, and Union League Club in Chicago, the Alpine Village in Milwaukee, etc. He is accomplished working with food.

Laboratories, and, as all seniors, surely felt the financial pinch in those remaining retirement years. My mother and her other sister, Ida, are worlds apart. My mother, Ida and my grandmother attended the same church while Aunt Blanche has a much different idea on how a Christian's life should be conducted. For instance, one permitted dancing while the other suggested it was a cause for improper behavior. One permitted a congressionalist to smoke in the kitchen/dining area of the church while the other strictly forbid it. One church favored loving the sinner while the other prayed for redemption for the sinner even though

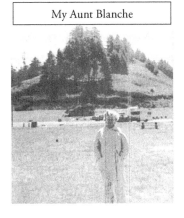

My Aunt Blanche

God already knew of events to come through predestination. I still cannot accept her fundamental and literal interpretations of her standards. There was conflict. I had to take her to Corvallis to a church there which coincided with her beliefs. It wasn't just for the Sunday service, but she had to return for the evening and mid-week services. I finally had to say that her Biblical adherence was taking a toll on me and that God would surely excuse her adherence for strict attendance. Even after she left, I was amazed when some member of the congregation came to visit me and proceeded to give me an over-all church indoctrination. This I had to put a stop to in the most kindly way I could think of doing—"Please, do not return to my house. Thank you!"

Emil lived the 13th Chapter of 1 Corinthians[78] more than anyone I know. Every breath of his life was to make his family comfortable and happy, never thinking of the cost physically to him or emotionally. Living in the shack for ten years without even holiday dinners, yet not

---

78   Corinthians is a testament in the form of letters of Paul's philosophy dealing with the premier teaching of Christianity, and parts deal with the perfection of human character and the essence of God's nature. You may do all kinds of benevolent things, but you are nothing without doing them in the spirit of God...love. Emil possessed it; we all may possess it.

one complaint amazes me. By going into raising Herefords I can make this farm known by cattle buyers. And to do this, I must have capital and realize that by selling the acreage annexed to Crabtree Creek, I can do this.

Crabtree Creek

My expenses at the close 1976 were breaking the bank: land clearing of underbrush $360; seed for tillable soil areas, $81.84[79]; advertising $85; legal fees $530, machinery repairs, $422; maintenances, $326; vehicle repairs $417, truck repairs, $163, and medical costs for me $877. I haven't included utilities or food. 1976 was a year when the national conventions took over. The political scene included several presidential candidates' hats having been thrown into the ring; none for whom I had any preference.[80] Hopefully, someone more presidential would appear on the scene and change. The successful politician ought to be one who can get in the public eye without irritating it. The price for eye medication like Murine and Visene rose, but maybe prices will go down if the sales are up. Food costs went up--and by the way apples were so expensive now you might as well have the doctor. Unemployment, inflation, crime, etc. were all points of concern. I understood, at the time, that now nine out of every ten criminal cases nationwide are settled in chambers behind closed doors by plea bargaining. Is John Doe becoming the loser: the guy who goes for a walk with a German shepherd inevitably meets a mugger with a rhinoceros? My mind created more afflictions to be dealt with, and so that is how I felt as this year ended.

---

79   Through necessity I accepted the idea of sharing cost of planting and then taking a percentage of the harvest. This suited both renter and me better.

80   1976 was the year that Jimmy Carter barely defeated Gerald Ford for the Presidency.

What I had failed to realize during the years of this chapter and chapter 14 is law of attraction.[81] Thinking too much of your despair expands that idea; it is as if the person is a magnet...like attracts like. One Chapter of *The Secret* discusses the idea of asking yourself what brings you joy. As you commit to this joy, you will attract other joyful things because that is how the law of attraction functions. Lisa Nichols[82] is an advocate of *The Secret*. She writes...

> When you think of the things that you want, and you focus on them with all of your intention, then the law of attraction will give you exactly what you want, every time. When you focus on the things that you don't want, thoughts manifest the things that you're thinking of and so it's going to show up over and over and over again. The law of attraction is not biased to wants or don't wants. When you focus on something, no matter what it happens to be, you really are calling that into existence.

So my despairs enumerated here and again in chapter 14 were thoughts creating more of the kind. Companions of Job followed me. Glancing back I see that this chap-
ter seems to recite the decantation of life's "little" problems will seem mundane.[83] But I assure my reader that I felt the equal of Job; so many afflictions undeservedly mounted to a state of unbalancing reason-able thoughts to questioning my faith and my God. Yet presenting these problems to my reader, re-gardless of how serious they were during this time of my life, I can now add some humor to take some of

My driveway

81   Rhonda Byrne, *The Secret*, Atria Books, Beyond Words Publishing, 2006.
82   Ibid, pp. 13-14.
83   Little/small whatever, but at the time, four law suits meant great despair.

the bitterness about life that I was experiencing. I can chuckle about them now as I keep trying to remember that years wrinkle the skin, but lack of enthusiasm wrinkles the soul. I still can recall that when I walked this land, the sole of my feet sent happy messages of contentment to my soul. It is as if I were living a life with senses of smells and sights abounding of heaven.

Chapter Fourteen:

The Interim—1977-1985

Everyone knows that an interim is an intervening period of time, but some reader may have forgotten that the definition infers that the period is temporary. I thought my main crisis following the death of my beloved husband was over. My law suits described in Chapter 13 found resolutions with a cost to my well-being. The law according to John Dryden[84] can be an instrument of happiness, but I found that in this happiness of winning it's, more generally than not, a smile that burst. I concluded that a law suit is a convulsion arising from the sudden transformation of a strained expectation into nothing. You can't go through four law suits and come out unscathed. All of this—and near financial ruin—was behind me, so I thought.

Each year or generation we lose great men and women in our society; society has erected monuments to these people. They have named airports, streets, buildings, etc. after them. Emil was the greatest man or person I ever knew, and it was my intention to make this farm a tribute to him. The farm is becoming the endangered species; more farms are taken out of farm production each year and never to be

---

84 John Dryden (1631-1700) was a Norhamptonshire poet and dramatist. He was involved in all sorts of political issues of his era; he was at one time Cromwell's chamberlain.

reclaimed as farms ever again. It is my intent that the farm will remain as a farm, a paying farm even if it takes all my emotional, physical and financial costs; it will remain a paying farm.

It was always a joy to see wild deer cautiously coming out from the woods, and at times with a fawn and meandering through my pastures and at times helping themselves to my feed. I had caught hunters on my land at various times even though it was well posted that no hunting was allowed. I told them that this was private property and to shoot pheasant or deer or whatever was unlawful on my property. Some wanted to argue the point that I may own the land but I don't own the deer. My view is that once on my property they have sanctuary, and I replied, "How would they like it if I came to your property and camped, picnicked, skylarked, shot off guns on your property." I had the sheriff out once when a hunter actually shot a deer. And my worst encounter with hunters was on New Year's Eve when some obnoxious hunters mistaking my Australian shepherd for an animal of game shot Snoopy. I supposedly thought that once they realized their mistake, they would do something honorable rather than just running off and leaving Snoopy lying there. When Snoopy didn't appear when I came outside, I searched and found his wounded body in one hay field. I quickly drove the PU to his bloodied body and holding his head in my lap, I rushed him to the vet. His spine was shattered and he'd not walk, romp, gaily wagging his tail expressing his happiness to see me ever again. On advice from my vet I held him while the vet injected a sleep potion and I gave the promise that he'd be with Emil soon. I buried him in the Gaines/Kotan cemetery on the hillside.

Three weeks later I had an opportunity to obtain a female Australian shepherd that was 14 weeks old. She was a frisky pup and I hoped that I could live up to her tail-wagging happiness to see me mornings and every time I returned from town. I named her Tammie.

Tammie

One of my worries in those years was to rent the old farmhouse. I thought a retired couple may have interest if the rent was cheap enough. I kept asking myself isn't there someone out there who may want and enjoy living in a large farm house as much as I want someone here. Can God answer two people at the same time, helping both people? Better yet, was to find a couple who wanted to take over the operation of the land also. This was much to be desired. Such a lease would give me an opportunity to get away from my responsibilities for the animals, etc.

My niece's husband Chuck Virgil came from a farming family, and they thought they might be interested in taking over the old farmstead to live in and utilize the land to make a living. The matter of ownership eventually could not be and two households making a satisfactory living were highly unlikely. They decided that the eventuality of becoming a reality was not there and declined.

About this same time and through advertising, a Mrs. Anita Paech and her son wanted to go into raising cattle. I sent money for her fare to come to Oregon and tour the land before a commitment can be made. From what I understood at the time, became something quite different. My supposition was that she wanted to raise about 50 head of cattle. She expanded her idea to over 300 head. But allowing cattle to graze on grain during the winter will only damage the ground severely since they are heavy animals and dig sod or surface dirt to a different level, changing the fertility of the top soil. I quickly changed a supposition and related an offer/intent was to rent the house and 20 acres and use of loafing shed for $100 a month which she would not accept. I was thankful, knowing that if ever we came to some kind of agreement, we'd come to confrontation eventually.

Another niece, Terry and her husband Ray Zilisch came to see what Oregon was like as well as the farm and of course the original house on the farm. Large rooms with a huge kitchen and five bedrooms of which three had access to the second floor veranda. All this became attractive to them. They had contemplated taking charge in overseeing a cattle operation on the ranch of which I was perfectly willing to do, with sharing the income. But I was barely making ends meet, and I was in no position to sponsor financially their venture into farming. It would mean that Ray would have to take outside employment until a sizeable herd could support another household. So their venture into farming/ranching was not to be.

Besides the law suit in chapter 13, I found myself with four more law suits during this year. One was during 1977; my friend and peer from college days Evelyn Luethi sold her home for which I was holding the mortgage at a very low interest.[85] Interest rates were escalating and VA house loans were highly desirable. In certain areas of the country, a house buyer was lucky to find a mortgage at 12 %. She received thrice for what she initially paid/agreed for the property. Her

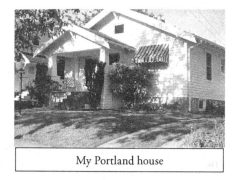

My Portland house

buyer paid her off and attempted to carry on monthly payments. Her contract clearly stated that if she ever sold the property that I was to be paid off entirely from the sale. She didn't do this. When I learned of her duplicity—actually I think it was her real estate agent who gave poor advice along with her naivety—I threatened a law suit. Initial contact did not produce results and I had to contract a lawyer and insist on payment within 30 days or take steps to reclaim the property. Such an aggravation ruined a friendship. She was a college graduate in business administration and should have known better.

Another involved my neighbor to the west, Stuart, who was clearing his land. He cut down giant firs and uprooting stumps and piling such together. My sister Dorothy Lossman was visiting me at the time. When she came running back to the farm house and related that a bulldozer has come through the fence, and men were cutting down my giant firs.

---

85   Sold for what I paid my neighbor: $9,000 with 5 1/2 % interests.

I thought this unbelievable. In confronting them, I demanded that they stop. They didn't and thus a law suit followed. Matters went onto the middle of 1978 when I settled for $2,000 plus expenses for installing a new fence. This event was settled with money, but in the stealing of my trees, they took my well-being. The long process for justice created in me another anxiety and made me physically ill. This was another instance of my equating me with Job.[86] I asked myself when will these "slings and arrows of misfortune"[87] cease. It was in November 1977 that the theft of not only the gate to the southeast pasture but hinges as well, I became so despondent and, surely unlike Job, questioned my belief in God. Are we brainwashed? Is a belief in God only to be a cushion? I was searching my brain for a logical conclusion for all these despairs.

Dorothy taking measurements

At first the neighbor Millers thought that their sister-in-law might be interested in renting the old farm house, but a prospective renter came not to be.

There was a fellow Williams who agreed to purchase 79 acres that I offered for sale, for I found myself without funds to carry on my costs. He made initial interest payment, but then came and told me in August 1981 he could not make "it," meaning many farmers were having a seriously bad time surviving.

I rented 65 acres to Vince Harris. In March 1980, he failed to make the $1,000 rent payment. By October I had to file another suit. These matters were taking a toll on me, for I had worries about making payment of expenses also. Property tax alone can be over-whelming. Not to denigrate some of my renters, but some were poor farmers and basi-

---

86   Job 4,5 deals with Eliphaz, one of Job's four friends who come across with the idea who ever perished, being innocent?

87   Hamlet 111, i, 5

cally over-extended themselves and had worn out equipment, while others were down-right cheaters, as Gus Raynard did on naming one price on cattle feed and then cheated me on delivery. All of these kinds of troubles were basically involved in one way or another with the worst of times, an age of political foolishness, an epoch of incredulity, a farmer's season of darkness and a winter of despair.[88] It was the time for farmers like me who were having a bad time keeping afloat. The 70s and 80s were not a flourishing time for farmers; absolutely not! The machinations of politicians, at least in the view of the small independent farmers, abounded. If one looks briefly at history of agriculture in the U.S., he'd find that between the years 1900 and 1910, farm prices rose between 200 to 300 percent, which is all very good. We were changing from an agrarian state to one of industry: the Industrial Revolution. New farm implements were being introduced: the tractor, the combine, etc. By the 20s there was a decline of farmers and yet over-all production increased. A surplus of farm harvest was hurting farmers. President Herbert Hoover provided government means to buy domestic surpluses at a price higher than the actual market price, which surpluses were sold on the world market. This helped, but by the time of the deep depression, this tactic was abandoned. Roosevelt created the Agriculture Adjustment Administration. From them information was disseminated about upgrading livestock, scientific cultivation, improved methods of fertilization along with uses of insecticides.[89] Slowly but ever-so-much in dominance was the growing agribusinesses[90] or cooperative farms. In the'50s, Congress created soil bank program which was certainly a stimulus to agribusiness, for in some instances this program took entire farms out of production. And congress denied benefits to farmers who

---

88   These phrases are reminders of the opening lines of *A Tale of Two Cities* by Charles Dickens.

89   In 1962 Rachel Carson wrote Silent Springs that highlighted mutual hazards backed by some agribusinesses of pesticide uses.

90   In clarifying a difference between usage of agribusiness or cooperative farms from commercial farm terms is essential; I am a commercial farmer. Independent farmer trying to raise and sell a product while agribusinesses own vast lands and hires laborers to do corporative business.

did not comply with the conservation element of their program. But what actually happened was that those who did take certain lands out of production purchased more land with the money Congress benefited them for their abstinence of farming and the cycle began. American farm lands were changing; agribusinesses were much more commonly seen. New or young farmers had no chance of beginning to farm and survival for those in the business had a hard time to succeed. As a result small farmers' life style, for the most part, worsened. And this was happening during the time of my marriage and after Emil's death.

Polled Herefords

Emil's 137 acres in Nebraska was taken over by a Nebraska agribusiness titled A Cattle Feed Company (a Nebraska Corporation) for only $50,000 in 1971. This agribusiness paid out $9,375 per year for four years with interest, six percent. They paid $12,500 down payment. Out of this mega agribusiness rose newly formed agricultural entrepreneurs by using government loans and subsidies to expand their operations. With farmers

abundances whether coming from commercial farmers as myself or from agribusinesses, there were definite benefits that came to the general pubic; these included food stamps for low-income families, school-lunch programs, food for the elderly and Indian reservations and an increase in nutritional levels for the general populations.[91]

---

91   For a more detailed account see "Agriculture: Since 1920" in *Oxford Companion to U.S. History*, Paul Boyer, ed., Oxford Press, 2001.

According to my final estate inheritance tax for 1976, schedule D; my livestock was valued at $6,000. The herd was less than 60. By the end of 1975, I sold 31 heads (12 were calves) to the Corvallis Auction with an income of $3,675. My aim here in the later part of 1977 was to specialize in just Polled Herefords. Emil's herd was seemingly always sought after; he fed them well and took personal care of his animals, and not sold at any great profit. His animals were thus sought because of Emil's reputation. We were making a living. And I set about improving my herd with Polled Herefords. Beginning my search I learned that a good line of Herefords could be expensive; i.e. a bull with good bloodline could run $500. Cows bred takes 18 months before you can realize an income. It takes nine months to have a calf and then another nine months before selling the calf as a feeder. Heifers won't be sold because they will become part of the new herd. A heifer must be at least fourteen months before being bred. A prize steer may bring thousands depending on pedigree, but this isn't all profit. The animal must be fed and cared for. And so this project began. By the end of 1984, I had two young steers that I purchased for $350 each. Bull 20M was priced at $900.

I loved cows. My interest in them was passed on from my husband, for I had no affection for cows at the time I was placed on Leo Sheldon's farm, my father's second cousin, in Rollins. I disliked it so much that I got up at four in the morning and rode back to Waukegan in the Brumand's dairy truck to escape my environment. An antithesis changed to pietism. Anyway, I never minded the muck in cleaning out the barn for cows now. Since I was going to use the northwest pasture for

Josie with twin calves

expanding the herd, I installed a loafing shed, which was easier to clean than a barn mess. I named the cattle and they wore earrings for identification/registry. Troboy, mostly white, came in May 1979.

Others were Anna, Mary, Kelly, Heidi, Collene, Little Willie, and even St. Helen[92]; named after the May 1980 eruption of Mt. St. Helens in Washington state. I even named one heifer "Victories" for successfully

Little Willie & her twin calves

winning all my law suits.[93] In the spring Little Willie bore two calves. Sara had a steer bull as did Sally; Kelly bore twins: a calf Maryanne and a steer named Bob; Kim missed becoming pregnant and there was no issue from her ever; Emily bore a steer George, and Josie had twins Annie & Rosie. And as years succeeded one another, I changed to numbers.

In the five years following Emil's death, I was rather proud of the fact that I have kept my head above water, surmising that the land is in good condition as much as any woman alone could do. As I worked the ranch, I had been having trouble with my hands and the doctor told me to cut down the use of my right hand or else suffer dire consequences of losing more use than it is handicapped since the horse accident in 1972. The photo

Hay harvesting

shows that I am driving the tractor while one of my hired hands stacks baled fodder onto a loader to take to one of the two barns for storage.

---

92   From May 25th through August 7th, 1980, St. Helens erupted 5 times, none as severe as the first. On the first eruption, it shot ash and steam 6500 feet over the peak of St. Helens at over 9,000 ft. The May eruption sent smoke and ash 12 miles high and the blast made havoc and destruction for more than 200 miles. Yakima to the east of Mt. St. Helens had to remove 600 thousand tons of ash. The death toll of those in the vicinity numbered 62, mostly smothered by ash. If you come to Washington state, it is well worth the trip to the park headquarters for the film on the eruption and talk by the rangers there.

93   Total were now seven.

My efforts to succeed have some fruition. My adjusted gross income at the end of 1976 was $1,473. Not bad when I think I had learned to act as a farm business accountant. In the early years of the 1980s, my gross income increased to slightly over $10,000.

Kotan fields

I had installed a 13X20 foot loafing shed; installed a cattle chute and when needed, a new well. I learned to be aware and to list my depreciation write-offs, which totaled to more than $2,000. The land was valued at $84,000 in 1977 for tax purposes, and I paid a property tax of $1765. Selling my lots in Lincoln City on the coast, the 5 acres bordering Crabtree Creek and residue coming from interest holdings obviously supplemented my needs. And I learned to keep accurate records that permitted my deductions in the operation of the farm; these included items of farm labor help along with SAIF,[94] feed, veterinary fees, breeding fees, gasoline as well as fuel oil, insurance, land clearing, vehicle licenses, advertising, surveyor and office supplies.

Speaking of office supplies, postal rate changed from 15¢ to 18¢. I was spending more than $120 for various ads: farm machinery, bales of hay, renters etc. About the time of the royal wedding of Prince Charles and Diane, I found a puzzle, badly warped, in the old shack where Emil lived 10 years before our marriage. A reminder of even just a puzzle he had forgotten to give me was a reminder of happier days that jolted my emotions. There were many jolts during these passing years that I wished for his physical rather than spiritual presence.

Other matters of maintaining the ranch was having had to put in a new well: $2,000. It seemed that there were numerous breaks in fencing. I realize that much of the fencing had been standing a long time and decided

---

94   SAIF is a cooperation that deals with worker's compensation in case of being injured
      on the job. All farmers who had hired hands were required by Oregon law to enroll in
      this insurance program.

that "this woman" needed lessons on fence repairs, including post hole digging. And while doing it or having it done I might as well put in new gates. There was also placing culverts to cross over drainage ditches and these had to be cleared periodically.

New fencing

This was also a year to put up the Kotan Ranch sign. In December 1981, I had to put a new roof on the barn: $1,150. Adversities lessened when I changed tactics from renting arable land to a limited space. For instance one renter put 40 acres in grain. We were to share the profit after expenses.

New roofing

This method of finding renters was more satisfying than a written contract. Farmers Cox and Brunen paid me $3,000 for a 1/2-year in shared profits in 1977/78. McGill rented 40 acres for $2,000. With income I was able to make various improvements. Putting in a load of gravel for a 50 yard driveway was $116. The photo here shows my sister Dorothy Lossman and me clowning at our accomplishment.

New sheds to house machinery

Clowning after spreading gravel for driveway

There had to be electrical installations when I had a 24X24 foot shed with doors built for $2500. This additional building was to house some farm equipment, especially if my renter needed to make repairs in a dry and lighted facility.

My electrician had to shoot a woodpecker that was making a nuisance and interfering with his work. And it was during this time that I shot a rifle for the first time in my life. Installing flood lights became a necessity for $179. Cattle grazing by the house kept breaking the fencing and obviously I had to install something better. With hired help in digging post holes, I was proud of my accomplishment.

Emma and Mary, my sisters-in-law, were great at quilting. I purchased three of their blankets for $75 each. I was glad to get them and they were glad to sell them.

Emma and Mary's quilts

The folk art of creating colorful home necessities I suppose is now passing into history. Surely you will see them at state fairs and they will have a fancy price on them. I'm herewith showing off my sisters-in-law's craft as well as my new fence gate that I was installing all over on the farm property. And, as I previously stated, can you believe that someone had the gall to steal the south gate, including the hinges. Dirty crooks!

I decided in 1981 that the old original farmhouse must come down. It had been vacant from 1974 until now. There were monthly utilities, heating and general maintenances. A big concern was mice. I'd swear they had grown and were more daring with their infestation. I had picked up kittens and cats ad-

Original farmhouse

vertised in the newspaper and brought them to the farm; I specifically housed them in the barns.

My brother was nearing retirement and I offered them the land where the old farmhouse was because I had installed a new well in the hopes of eventually renting it to someone. The years passed and no one had an interest. My brother thought he'd retire and we'd mutually benefit one another. I'd have someone to help maintain the animals and thus could get away from it all and he'd be able to build his dream house without having to purchase land. He sold his house, and brought in a mobile home for temporary use while the process of obtaining permits to do so. I failed to tell him that I couldn't break up the farm in lesser allotments than 40 acres. By the time he got lumber and permits, etc., he was naturally upset that he could not own the land where he intended to build. All agreements were cancelled. We were both upset; I because I thought I'd have a dependable person to help me care for the ranch, and he irate because he would not build without ownership of the land he intended to build on. Such circumstances became the banana peel of a bad situation.

Eventually, I found a carpenter who was willing to take the farmhouse down. Much in building of the house contained redwood, which was priced much above general lumber. I took the knobs off the stairway and created hors d'oeuvre holders for shrimps or other condiments of delight. In taking the wall boards down, I was surprised to find this note buried within the walls:

> This house was built in 1852 by Alvin Gaines. Upstairs was remodeled by Emil Kotan assisted by Joe Kotan and Jim Kazlowski in 1939. Joe, Emil and Anna lived here at the time it was repared [repaired]. John Hooker of Albany did the wiring.

It was such a surprise to read a note from my husband in the past. It was as if he took hold of me and squeezed tears from my eyes. At the same time of taking the old farmhouse down, I decided to take down the shack that Emil had lived in during a period of 10 years prior to my marriage. I even placed an ad for the antique two-seat outhouse for $25. It sold for $6. Waste not, want not.

Emil's cabin

We all went to the movies in the 30s and 40s, for 10¢—oops...11¢; President Roosevelt introduced a luxury tax.[95] One of my favorite actresses was Ethel Barrymore. I remember her as the Czarina in *Rasputin and the Empress* and in *The Spiral Staircase*. One of her quotes in her life...

You must learn day by day, year by year, to broaden your horizon. The more things you love, the more you are interested in, the more you enjoy, the more you are indignant about--the more you have left when anything happens.

It's in retrospect that I wished that I had this point of view in these years I'm calling the "interim." But—there is always a *"but"*—life had a downside for me. Adversities ruled in these years and I became quite despondent and maybe my reader can see an analogy elucidated in a story via the internet about a professor who was trying to teach his students matters of relativity. The instructor held up a glass of water and asked his students how much does this glass of water weigh. For practical purposes my glass of water weighs 450 grams. Now hold it at arms length for 5 minutes. No problem, hold it for an hour. Does the water weigh any more even though you feel as if the weight increased? Hold it all day if you could, and you'd probably have to be taken to the hospital for recovery of an injured arm. The whole point of the instruction was that you must lay down weighty anxieties for a time.

---

95 There was an exception; we had to pay 25¢ to see *Gone with the Wind* in 1939. The wealth tax was introduced in 1935.

Get relief. Change your *modus operandi*. I did not get this point until after me so-to-speak retired from the ranch/farm. At the end of these interim years, I found my gung-ho attitude to maintain my status on an Oregon producing farm began to wane.

Chapter Fifteen:

Decision to Sell—1985-1990

They kept on saying that you can't equate time with money. I dillydallied with the idea of selling out. After all, I wasn't getting any younger. I rather thought of myself as a person who jumped at opportunities that equated with fun, besides Peanuts taught me that there is no problem so big that it can't be run away from.[96] And I'm afraid my present state of mind kept inching toward a change. After all, by the time of a serious sale becoming a reality I was sixty-six years of age, which means that I had been running the ranch alone for about 14 years. Deciding to sell was not an over-night revelation.

Besides the keeping records about my anxieties and about mending this and that, I kept records of how many times I was eating out; sometimes brunches, sometimes lunches and then early suppers. I never went specifically to go eat, rather it was a matter of an event following an errand or something related to the farm. To get a repair part for the tractor, I had to drive to Corvallis. So, in all this business of buying and selling Herefords, etc., I found myself gaining weight. With all this exercise demanded by farming, I ate on the demands of the belly

---

96   Charles Schulz (11/26/1922 – 2/12/2000) was the most widely known cartoonist in history. I think it's Linus who gives these terse words of humorous wisdom.

and looking down at the scale became another worry. My renter in 1985 spread the word about my heifers, which in that spring I had nine calves born. I sold two bulls to a fellow named Terry Innis for $425. Little Willie gave birth to a dead calf; sad as it was, it is a chore to bury a dead calf.

In the fall of 1986, I hired one of my faithful and dependable laborers who was available for hire to take care of the animals while I dashed

Banff Hotel

off to Banff. I wanted to visit the place again, for it was one of the destinations of my honeymoon. I was always affectionate for fondue; Emil enjoyed it also. Returning to a place of memories, I ordered two fondue dinners. The waiter asked whether he should wait to place the order for I was sitting alone. I told him he could give the order to the cook, for I was ordering for my husband who would not be here, for he died in 1974. I stopped him from further inquiry and told him to humor me, for you just met a crazy, old lady who is celebrating part of an endearing memory.

> Be now for ever taken from my sight,
> Though nothing can bring back the hour
> Of splendor in the grass, of glory in the flower;
> We will grieve not, rather find
> Strength in what remains behind;
> In the primal sympathy
> Which having been must ever be;
> In the soothing thoughts that spring
> Out of human suffering:[97]

---

97 *Ode, Stanza x,* by William Wordsworth. Wordsworth was looking at a picture of Peele's castle in a storm when he wrote these stanzas.

The gist of Wordsworth's lines matched my feelings that nothing can bring back the density of my relationship with Emil, and thoughts of that relationship will live in constant memories suggested like those of Banff. I quote it because I think that we are all Romantics at some time or another. To receive by inspiration of the real nature of things, the human mind must concentrate on the object to glimpse at the inner life. It's as if you are rearranging the Platonic thought that everything has a primary and a secondary nature. What you see is the secondary nature of, lets say, a flower, but it has a primary nature in that it grows, carries on photosynthesis and osmosis, its energy, etc. The object in a Wordsworthian case can be as simple as a daisy. Within the examination of a flower and through imagination, Wordsworth comes to terms of connecting the physical with intellectual, moral, aesthetic and spiritual insight into its significance and come to understand that the "feeling" is never bereft of love.

While searching to quote correctly Wordsworth, I see that I have noted in my text that Wordsworth's thoughts were akin to Lord Byron's.

> Is it not better, then, to be alone,
> And love Earth only for its earthy sake?
> …
> I live not in myself, but I become
> Portion of that around me; and to me
> High mountains are a feeling, save to be
> A link reluctant in a fleshly chain.….[98]

But surely my reader has had enough of this proselytizing for the Romantics. I can never adequately explain how and what I feel in the sight of such awesome beauty as seen in this Canadian National Park.

Lake Louise

---

98   *Childe Harold's Pilgrimage*, Canto 111, stanza lxxi & lxxii.

There are times when I think I'm odd to recall some aspects of my life that are not a part but tangential. Danny Kaye, Jackie Gleason Randolph Scott and my Aunt Blanche died in 1987. Danny Kaye is remembered for his, at times, slap stick humor, and Randolph Scott had multiple leading roles with multiple leading ladies, but I remember him for his roles as the handsome cowboy in western films. Jackie Gleason entertained me many a lonely night with his enactment of leading the life of a bus driver; he also was a magnificent musical arranger. My Aunt Blanche, regardless of all her horrid outlook as the fundamentalist view of a religious life, was a woman who purchased for herself complete riding outfits in her salad days and was an excellent horse woman; she played the jazz on her saxophones, bobbed her hair and smoked Chesterfields when her father frowned upon woman being so rascally independent of society dictates. In my view of her now, she followed Scot Fitzgerald's characterizations of the 20s. She was a smart dresser and enjoyed dining at the best places. She worked for so many years at the Snow White Laundry, shaking sheets, etc. before they were swallowed in the mouth of this giant ironing machine. To pick up extra bucks while vacationing in California, she worked as a maid in the once grand Grant Hotel in San Diego. She also took summer jobs as a parlor maid for the more affluent residing in Highland Park and Lake Forest. She worked in a place that was neighboring Shirley Temple's estate which had stately evergreens in perfect alignment down its gated driveway. An opportunity appeared to work for Abbott's Laboratories, and she took it and labored in the assembly line until she retired. She had the gift of gab and several marriage proposals; one was a childhood school chum who just recently divorced his third wife. She did enjoy his company, but rejected anything that hinged on a closer, more intimate relationship. I sort of regret that she lost that spontaneity for life in her later years. I don't know about you but to me there is a pleasure to have that backward glance and meditate what changed from what was then to what it is now living in my memories.

During the latter part of 1987 and not doing so well financially, I tried to sell my innovation of what I called my educational device/

cubes entitled "CISE."[99] In a cursory examination, the device/method may appear as an esoteric approach to explain the reading process. It didn't do well. But my brother presented a methodology on reading to his faculty and parents that reading is not any one thought going on in the mind at any one time, but a conglomeration of stimuli; for instance, his presentation was showing of two films: one of a Parisian woman who takes a seed bean and plants it in the Tulleries gardens and another film about a small boy being bullied by peers in the streets of Paris and all the balloons of Paris come to his rescue. A slide session was also presented of various students activities at the 7th/8th grade levels and every other slide pictured a classroom activity going on in various Micronesian schools. A classical score of Beethoven's Fifth Sympathy and himself reading excerpts from my text *Reading is "human awakening."* All these processes were going on at the same time. The whole process took approximately 25 minutes. At the close, several questions were presented to those in attendance, and all correctly identified the main ideas of each media presentation. This CISE schism is a presentation to explain what is happening in the thinking process, and a trained teacher may assist illiterate students or adults into the reading activity. Should my reader have an interest is the process of a one-on-one teaching of this reading process, I have enclosed a deeper explanation as appendix B.

While at the University of California, Berkeley, my professor approved of my concept and I implemented the CISE devise in promoting literacy while temporarily employed at the Oakland Adult Day School as well as the Oakland Technical School along with the Catholic Diocese School in Oakland. I wrote to several publishers for marketing. Included among those contacted was Bill Cosby, SAH Enterprises located in Santa Monica. Bill Cosby,[100] because he impressed me with his sincere and logical approach for the need to stay in school and obtain an education. He was most kind and wrote me a letter wishing much success in my pursuits and that unfortunately his "extremely hectic

---

99   For a more complete description and explanation of CISE, see appendix B, pp. 333.
100   Mr. Cosby's letter is dated 12/10/89.

schedule" prohibited him from involvement in my interests to educate the illiterate.

By the end of 1987, I was finding myself in financial difficulty. My property taxes for this year were $2,931.29. I certainly needed my property lines defined again and Udell's survey cost me $1,180.14. My

New calves - a growing herd

expenses were barely being covered. Symbiosis between me and the ranch was not happening. By the end of the year, I had at one time or another 23 new calves. Again, heifers must be twelve months old before being bred or 21 months passing before calving. I sold three bulls and two heifers for $1,475. I was not getting rich.

My thinking process was earnestly leaning toward selling out and retiring to Terrace Lake Manufactured Home Park. The process of selling my herd did not bring any joy. I sold Little Willie for $510. I cried. So by June 1988, the last of the cattle were sold. This was the first time since 1899 that no livestock were on the ranch. With the last of the cattle gone, it thundered and in the sky lightning, a symbolic happening of my failures.

I doubted fruition of my placing ads in various newspapers of major cities, but I did it anyway. Who knows who may be out there who is looking for a ranch or farm for tax deductions? My results were rather poor at the start. I had heard that a Japanese family will take on a piece of property and mortgage it through for three generations. So, I sent letters with photos to three cities of Japan. Somebody has to have money and want to purchase my farm/ranch. I had three calls from

An aerial view of farm for sale

California from an ad placed in the *S.F. Chronicle* and one even from Grass Valley. All came to naught. I also had calls of inquiry from Idaho, Maryland, New Jersey and again, others from California.

I thought that since United Airlines flew into Medford, Eugene, and Salem before it disembarked passengers in Portland for other places; then there is a possibility that one of the more affluent passengers would see my newly, 16-foot white painted, fence posts spell out

PLEASE BUY
OUR FARM
503-658-8765

My efforts of placing the logs into the sign did attract attention; well, not the very affluent but a United Airlines pilot. The "cause and effect" were something different than I expected, and my efforts were not in vain and eventually led to unusual experiences. The UA pilot saw the 16 foot, painted white fence posts and reported such to KOIN television channel 6. Mr. Ray Summers,[101] reporter-at-large, reported my efforts on a segment of his human interest news. I wrote and thanked him for airing the segment on "Woman Trying to Sell Her Farm," which appeared for the first time on October 11th. It appeared a second

---

101 Ray Summers had a unique ability and friendliness in interviewing people. I thoroughly appreciated his kindness to me.

time when Susan Hauser[102] for *People magazine* saw the segment, wrote and stated she wanted to do an article on me and my interest in selling my ranch. She came to Scio on October 25th and took photos on the 27th. The story appeared in November 21, 1988, issue of *People's Magazine,* page 134.

The photo to the right reflects that I can't spell the word "our." As Susan's article states, the switch of a 16-foot fence post was the work of pranksters, but as far as I am concerned the misspelling backfired on them in that the sign drew

more attention with the misspelling. And it did. Beginning on November 18th, 1988, I received phone calls from all over the states; people mostly wishing me luck in selling the farm. However, on November 21, 1988, I received a person-to-person call from someone who identified himself as Donald Trump. He wanted information on the farm and asked me to send such to him by Federal Express. He also asked me if I could meet him in Portland on December 5th. I sent the photo and letter to New York via Federal Express on November 22nd.

By December 5th and after waiting two weeks with anxiety, I came to the conclusion something was remiss. Of course, I was extremely disappointed as it all unfolded as a hoax. There are some despicable people who relish playing pranks on others. My December 7th letter response on the 15th confirmed by Mr. Trump's secretary that, indeed, I had become the butt of someone's warped sense of humor. Mr. Trump showed that he/his office had a concern for me. He was most kind and his secretary added that Donald Trump would autograph my copy of his latest book. And he did.

---

102   Susan Hauser came with People's Magazine photographer David Falconer, who took this collection of pictures.

Since the hoax involved a recognized personality, Donald Trump, and *People's Magazine*, I thought I would write some letters to see if I could make the hoax backfire on the caller who impersonated Donald Trump. I wrote to people who might find interest in the scenario: Dan Rather, Diane Sawyer, Charles Kuralt, Tom Brokaw at CBS, Phil Donahue, Sally Jessie Raphael at NBC, Ted Koppel and Oprah Winfrey at ABC, and finally a letter to Ellen Goodman, a writer for the *Washington Post*. No one can say that I wasn't determined to sell.

On December 2nd, 1988, Anna Kotan died. I sent flowers, but I did not attend the funeral. I sent a sympathy card to Emma. I visited Annie's grave site and said a short prayer. What's the saying? Carrying around hate is like taking a cup of hemlock and hoping that your adversary dies.

But I stray from my thoughts. I subdivided the ranch in 3 parcels. Two parcels less than 100 acres would be easier to sell than the main parcel which included the main barn, tool sheds, garage for machinery, loafing shed and feeders plus white fencing.

On May 1, 1998, Mr. and Mrs. Peoples[103] purchased approximately 77 acres for $90,000. I asked that I have life-estate access to the Gains/Kotan cemetery and permission to be buried there next to my husband. Purchaser also agreed not to log the property for twenty years accept for the portion described and marked as the Timber Tract. The south border was already fenced along Fish Ranch Road. The purchaser also agreed to erect a fence which completely borders the east and north sides of the property by July 30 of that year. Since the land has an odd number of acres, it insures that it cannot be subdivided by Oregon law.[104] We were to share other costs for the selling of this land.

On April 30th, 1990, Mr. and Mrs. Ronald Garris purchased approximately 178 acres that included my three bedroom home with double garage and most appliances for $225,000. Of course there were document fees, prorated taxes, removing my underground fuel tank and

---

103   Linda People's mother and brother would be involved in this sale.
104   Oregon subdivision cannot take place less than 40 acres.

pump and refill the hole. Another expense was insuring the erection of the east boundary survey fence on the north and south borders. All of this amounted to well over $1,000. With all the additional addendums to the sale contract, I required a substantial deposit and earmarked non-refundable as I had thought I had previously sold this area and the purchaser backed out of the deal. Since I had already purchased my manufactured home in Salem for placement in Terrace Lake, I was madder than a red hen in the story book about the sky falling. Such is the matter of business. The land was sold as farm use and thus eligible for a reduced property taxation. This property was assessed at $116,610 for tax purposes. Money market accounts were giving as much as 5.5 percent, a far cry from the present day listings. A fixed rate could be as much as 8.32 percent. So I should be able to live comfortably and travel extensively if I watched my dollars carefully. I would not place my trust into any bank that did not have FDIC[105] insurance up to $100,000. Losing any part of my financial status would mean disaster for me.

The binge of selling was depressing. I sold 214 bales of hay for $1 a bale. The tractor went for $5,000, the PU for $1800. And on and on went sales of so many items that I obviously could not take with me to Terrace Lake. With April ending, it became a red letter day for me, for it was the final sale of the land and house that Emil had built for me alone and now I must give it up. I have wonderful memories here and as the day approached to vacate there was this haunting, depressing, lost feeling. It's a feeling that only time can heal, yet knowing that living here on the Kotan ranch to date was the highlight of my life, even with the arduous tasks of maintaining it. Love is hard to find but easy to lose; love is the one thing that makes life worth living. Nothing could be worse than to live a life unloved. Closing this chapter on my life was one of the hardest things I ever had to do. There is some homespun philosophy that says something about remembering the turtle; he only makes progress when he sticks his neck out.

---

105   Federal Deposit Insurance Corporation.

On September 14th, 1990, the last acreage sold was approximately 62 acres, which also contained a barn that Emil built. It was sold also as farm land and therefore entitled to farm land rate of taxation. My payment for the land after "this" and "that" documentation and taxes, etc. was $74,608. Settling in Salem at Terrace Lake Manufactured Home Park had covenants and other rules, most of which I approve: 1) no hanging out of the wash; 2) sidewalks and building of a two car garage is mandatory; 3) owners of their respective manufactured homes are responsible for maintaining the landscape of their respective lots regardless of not owning the land. Water, garbage service, and television line utilities are a part of the monthly rental fees. In living in this park, I also had a swimming pool, sauna and hot tub available for use including the club

My Terrace Lake
manufactured home

house for personal use when available. So, living here fit my idea of home, one that I could manage and be free to travel. It was my intention to roam and take my fill of the world and its beauty before the day will come when I must quit it for good. I immediately planned a trip to Europe, taking my elder sister Ruth to Switzerland. Besides my brother gave me this stitched and frame home axiom: "Housework doesn't kill you, but why take a chance."

Chapter Sixteen:

Switzerland—1990

Abridge your hopes in proportion to the shortness of the span of human life, for while we converse, the hours, as if envious of our pleasure, fly away; enjoy therefore the present time, and trust not too much to what tomorrow may produce.[106]

It's been twenty-one years since I made my last move from Portland to Scio. How do you pack up those many years that make a sum of a fourth of your life? My husband has been gone now sixteen years, and nine months. Methinks I have done well, but there isn't any point of carrying on when the inevitable age will arrive when I can no longer maintain the physical strength of performing the duties and responsibilities of running the ranch. I'm sixty-six years old, and it's time for a change.

After I received the last payment on the ranch sale, I began packing and moving to Terrace Lake retirement park in Salem and was completely moved by the first of May in 1990. Having the use of a hot tub, sauna, and swimming pool helped me accept my transplant. With larger plots of land than most manufactured home complexes, residents created

---

106   Quintus Horatius Flaccus, (65-8 BC) and Roman lyric poet and satirist; "Fleetness of Time," Od.i.II

beautiful park-like surroundings. A continual flowing creek broadened out on the premises and formed a small lake and the meandered onto

My new Dodge Caravan

other places. Wild ducks and other aviary found temporary refuge and added to this pastoral setting. To meet new surroundings I needed a new car.

I've always loved to travel. Drop a geographical name and I'm ready to go. I have wisely invested in most conservative investments: Certificate of Deposits that brought in an interest and US government bonds that would support my living habits. Of course, I had social security which was a menial income as my social security tax contribution was minimal, but it paid for my monthly park rental fee which included some utility services. I was covered under Medicare, which means that my supplemental health insurance was more reasonable than a premium if I were under sixty-five.

It may seem silly to my reader but I operated on a budget of $10 a day while running the ranch; this was being frugal, but also my income was a frugal sum. Now that I was in a retirement mode, I changed my budget from $10 a day to $20 a day. If I spent more than $20 I would stay home the next day, or if I stayed home 2 days I could spend $40, 3 days, $60 and so on. I told myself I would always try to maintain the budget to $20 a day. And of course I was saving. Saving meant making an old lady happy by traveling. This strict budget was not used when I went on a trip. In visiting and evaluating particular costs of a place I was visiting, I would adjust the living allowance necessary to fit that particular trip or country.

Beginning in the fall of 1990, I planned a trip to Switzerland; since I had extra funds from the ranch sale. I persuaded my sister Ruth to join me. She had never been to Europe and this could be a special trip for both of us. I volunteered to pay for her transportation and hotel ac-

commodations since she also had limited funds. So, in late fall of 1990 when tourist season is clos-
ing down, I flew to Chicago and met her at O'Hare airport where we took the evening flight on Swiss Air to Zurich. Upon arrival I rented a Sedan Opel and we headed for Schaan, Liechtenstein, where we stayed two days.

The drive to Wildhaus

This is an area I had visited previously and I wanted Ruth to see the unique Swiss scenery. It was

Wildhaus

a short drive to Wildhaus and we stopped at the Hotel Bellevue to have coffee and pastry in the Konditorei. We sat on the balcony to have our coffee and gaze at the mountainous countryside. Ruth was so impressed with scenery she had tears in her eyes and remarked that it was so beautiful; this showed me that she really appreciated the scenery more with her heart than her eyes. And I say this figuratively speaking because I still lingered in the age where the heart was not just a troubled muscle at times, but the center of control or uncontrolled emotions. South African cardiologist Dr. Christiaan Barnard changed people's con-

Coffee stop

cept of the heart when he performed the first human-heart transplant in 1967. Anyway, here we are both carried into realms of Switzerland's beauty and through our tears of joy, a way of expressing our emotions as becoming a witness to this great beauty of a natural setting.

From Schaan we drove to St. Moritz,[107] which again is a beautiful drive; after finding a room we made plans to take the Glacier Express train to Zermatt. The Glacier Express is an exciting experience all by itself; you see magnificent scenery on this train ride through Switzerland. As we were leaving the train station I noticed that I had lost my currency; yet I still had traveler checks that I could cash later. When we arrived in Zermatt we rode to our hotel by horse and buggy as cars are not allowed

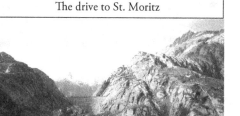

The drive to St. Moritz

| Glacier Express dining | Glacier Express scenery - the Matterhorn |

in Zermatt; it was somewhat foggy so we did not have a clear view of the top of the Matterhorn[108] at this time. The next day we took the Glacier Express back to St. Moritz where I checked at the hotel about my lost

---

107　Eleanor Roosevelt married her distance cousin Franklin in March 1905, and part of their nuptial celebrations were here at St. Moritz; costs here for such celebrations are definitely more than the usual fare for Switzerland.

108　Matterhorn is 4,482 meters, which makes the elevation approximately 14, 700 ft.

money, and I was informed to check with the police as they believed someone had turned in some money. Blessedness! Success! The money was returned to me. It was Seneca[109] who wrote...

> If you are wise, you will mingle one thing with the other
> Not hoping without doubt, not doubting without hope.

Obviously, there was some Swiss soul who held fast to honesty and resisted temptation. I would have survived had it been otherwise, but there was enough joy to call for a celebration for my unknown benefactor.

From St. Moritz we had planned to drive north through Austria to Garmisch in Germany. Our intentions were right, but I took the wrong turn and we ended up in Italy in the little town of Chiavenna. When we tried to get directions back to Switzerland, I could not immediately find

Swiss Mt. Road

anyone who spoke English; and finally, we found a man who had been driving a motorcycle who led us to the right road to Switzerland. This was only the beginning of a most harrowing experience as we were on the Splugen Pass, which has the highest gradient in Switzerland and reminding novice travelers, such as us, that the Alps are a very high mountain range. The road was curvaceous and narrow, and higher up the lights of the homes and villages became smaller and smaller. Needless to say we were both scared as we saw no guard rails to keep us safely on the road, which parts of the road were under repair. The trip back become more challenging to drive and we did it slowly and with extreme caution.

---

109   He was born about 1 A.D. Educated in Rome and rose to praetor ship and tutor of Nero. He later became Nero's chief minister, but eventually fell into disgrace. Suffocated himself in 65 A.D.

Late that night when we finally arrived in Splugen, Switzerland, we found a hotel open and were able to get a room. The next day we were on our way to Garmisch, a destination many Europeans visit; it is unique and colorful, as the residents paint the outside of their homes often times to show the occupation of the owner. While in Garmisch, I took Ruth on the cogwheel train that takes you up to the Zugspitz,[110]

| Zugspitz | View from Zugspitz |

highest point in this part of the Germany and part of the Bavarian Alps. After a cogwheel train ride, you still must take a cable car to the top where you have a tremendous view of the snowy mountains even far into Austria.

This trip included a side trip to Oberammergau. I had already attended the Passion Play there in 1960 and 1970. It was a treat for Ruth to browse

Schloss Linderhof

in the attractive shops. Driving to Oberammergau also made it possible to visit the famous Monastery at Ettal; and we also took time to tour the famous Schloss Linderhof[111] surrounded by gardens and fountains. Linderhof was built in the style of Italian Renaissance and

---

110   Zugspitz is 2,963 meters, approximately 9,721 ft. The 1936 Olympics were held here and an American Black athlete Jesse Owens won four gold medals and thus put holes into Hitler's idea of a super race.

111   Built by King Ludwig 11 of Bavaria; his father Karl August Wilhelm Ludwig 1 ruled from1825-48, but actually died in 1868.

French rococo, and it is well worth your time to visit. I was certainly impressed. The area is known for its fine wood carvers as reflected in the 18th C. church and I found great souvenir gifts of little men with open mouths as toothpick dispensers.

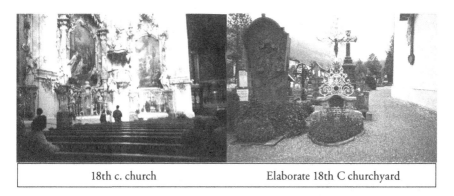

| 18th c. church | Elaborate 18th C churchyard |

From Garmisch we returned to Switzerland to visit Meiringen, which embraces the fictional stories of Sherlock Holmes and displays a statue of him in the town. It is in the nearby mountains that Sir Arthur Conan Doyle decided that he was tired delivering stories of the famous detective and ended Holmes' life in a struggle with Professor Moriarty.[112] The painting was done by Sydney Pacet in 1893.

Sherlock Homes

Pacet's painting of Sherlock's death

112   "The Final Problem" appears is in *The Memoirs of Sherlock Holmes* (1894).

Among the scenic spots of Meiringen is the Aare Gorge. This is nothing that you drive through, but for a small fee you walk along the Aare River on a specially constructed footpath with sheer-faced sides and jagged eroded rock, which all makes a truly enhancing experience.

Aare Gorge

From Meiringen we visited Interlaken, which is located between two lake areas: Thun and Brienz. Interlaken has all the charm of a rustic village and I understand that since Interlaken was founded by the Augustine monks in the 12th Century, the town has been a popular resort area, especially after the 17th Century. Once in the town, you can see the

Jungfrau view

Jungfrau Mountains, a matter of 4100 meters high.[113] As I said, it's an attractive town, and we had no problems securing pleasant accommodations near the center of the town, even though the place was crowded with tourists. My sister Ruth was somewhat surprised to see cows with large bells hung around their necks so close into town.

Cows in Jangfrau

These neck bells tell where the cows are if weather does not allow a visible location at any particular time. Often you have to stop on secondary roads as farmers are walking their

---

113   This is roughly 13,450 ft elevation.

cows back to individual farms, which are times to add to my photo collection of cows, for after all, my living was made from raising polled Herefords for about fourteen years.

We took the tour of the Jungfrau on our own. In order to reach the top you take three levels of transportation. After arriving at the end of

the first level, Ruth was a little apprehensive of this means of travel and decided to stay at the end of the first level while I took the cable cars to the top level where I had a spectacular view of the Jungfrau Alpine area.

Jungrau alpine area

While staying in the Interlaken area, we decided to take the train to Bern; Bern as I remember is a truly Swiss town. It is a busy place and we decided to leave the car at our hotel and ride the train as it would stop in the center of town; the station was huge with an underground shopping area as well as the usual town center above. It was getting close to the end of tourist time and we both were interested in purchasing gifts for family and friends to take home with us. A solution of carrying around packages was to rent a locker and return each hour with items purchased. And this we did, and after a pleasant lunch near Bern's famous clock and clock tower, we browsed some more in the stores. I was a mini car collector and I saw a white limousine

The Bern clock

in a window in one of the shops and knew this had to be in my collection. I first started collecting cars when I was in London; I bought a Mamod Steam Roadster that was made and engineered in London and even ran on fuel; it was about 20 by 8 inches in size. It was just one among my prize collections.

Some of my mini car collection

Our last stop was in Zurich and we had no trouble finding our reservation hotel. With the extra time before our flight home, we took a short drive to the border of France via Baden and Basel. It was an opportunity to just view the countryside and my intention was crossing the border and returning, so Ruth could say she had been in France. It turned out to be one foolish idea as our venture turned out to be a costly decision. When we drove thru the border we had unhooked our seat belts to visit a border business area and jumped back into the car. As I was making the U-turn to return to Switzerland, we were stopped by police. I was fined for not having my seat belt on. It took all of Ruth's Swiss Francs to pay the fine, which we thought quite unreasonable after a logical explanation. I can remember that I was irked and once back into Switzerland and at dinner we laughed about the circumstances. The lesson was to avoid any behavior at all costs that reflect that you are a tourist. So this, an unconscious act, joined so many other fine memories of beautiful and mountainous[114] Switzerland.

A typical Swiss view

114   Lord Byron called mountains the palaces of nature, and I agree.

Chapter Seventeen:

New Zealand—1991, 1993, 1994

With the ending of 1990, my father died. My adult relationship with him had been at a minimum. To save herself his mother abandoned him at an early age by sending him to live with neighbors. Taking her youngest child, she fled to the Chicago area and thus rescued herself and child from the abusive relationship not only by her husband but also her mother-in-law. My father was born in an era where farmers' sons were kept from schooling to complete the thousand and one farm chores. With a minimal education, he was fortunate to work for the city of Waukegan as a laborer, more often than not, accomplishing road repairs. Talk about coincidences in life, here is one: my mother was killed in an automobile accident on December 20, 1936, and he was killed by an erratic woman driver head-on collision on December 23rd, 1990. The span of fifty-four years interim is a reminder every day should be lived as if it is our last one. I received a small inheritance from him and celebrated his remembrance by purchased a set of Evesham Vale English dishes that I fancied. I have done this often, meaning making a purchase that is a reminder that this person was a part of my life and the article then is a reminder of the good happenings and a sort of a perpetual celebration reminder. Anyway, I had a little extra money now and I planned on taking in a part of the world I have never been: New Zealand. In fact, with the urging of my brother Jack, I should also venture off to Africa; thus this chapter will be a boring narration relating my experience here in New Zealand and followed by a chapter pertaining to my adventures on Africa.

One reason I chose New Zealand was that every brochure related to and suggested, at least to me, the beauty an eastern version of Switzerland. Among the facts that New Zealand is a composite of many islands, the two North and the South Islands are where principal population is located. New Zealand[115] is the about the size of Colorado and from my reading has about 1,000,000 more in population. Looking at a map you'd get the impression that N.Z. is just a stone's throw away from Australia when actually it is 1,200 miles southeast of Australia. There is actually a sea between the two countries: the Tasman Sea. What I think is so admirable about the history of N.Z. is that it was the first country to give women the right to vote, and to provide old-age pensions and social security for all citizens. There is also a law that required workers and employers to settle their differences by arbitration. Oh, how I remember the violent strikes in the various factories of Waukegan. These strikes turned into rock throwing situations with high density. It is too bad that Illinois didn't have such a law in place in the 1930s.

Anyway, On March 4th I flew to Los Angeles and then to Auckland,[116] New Zealand, and arriving on the 6th of March. When you cross the International Date Line, you lose a day, a first time for me. From L.A., you can fly to either island or then take the ferry at the south end of the North Island to the north end of the South Island, or vice versa. I chose the north island, and once at the airport, had a rented Lanser sedan waiting for me. I drove north as it was getting late and secured accommodations at Owera, which is on the Hauraki Gulf. The agent at the motel gave me directions to the nearest RSA Club, of

---

115 It was Captain Abel Tasman, an employee of the Dutch East Indies Company, who named it "Nieuw Zeeland" after the Zeeland province in The Netherlands.
116 Auckland is pronounced much like our "Oakland" city of California.

which there are many located throughout N.Z. in many cities. These Returning Servicemen clubs were established during WWII and still exist; I suppose much like our American Legion Clubs, etc. And since I was a Veteran of World War II, I was welcomed and yet I surmised that not many American women visit these RSA clubs. I was probably the only one visiting here. I used their facility not only for the food, which was good, but also the prices were even better.

My drive the next morning skirted water as I headed for the Bay of Islands to Piahia, where I rented a self-contained unit at the Abel Tasman Hotel. The accommodations included a balcony with a fabulous view of the countryside as well as the bay.

Russell's sloop

Although a little tired, I was compelled to see the area: beautiful, attractive and phenomenal scenery. Literally, it took my breath away. By taking a ferry to Russell, I, along with a few other tourists, chartered a sloop. This 6-hour plus sloop sailed with a pace of eras past about the islands. What a wonderful way to see the beautiful coastline. The skipper, Jim, loaned me a jacket as weather was cool and windy. Jim also allowed me to take the helm to get a feeling you are steering the sloop. It's true that there is communication between the water and your feet. Don't ask me to explain but the surging of waves communicates your steerage via the feet to your hand. Don't I sound so salty? The deck hands served us hot coffee/tea. On this adventure a larger yacht passed by and Jim called them "cattle ships" because they carried so many more passengers than Jim's sloop. The Bay of Islands is a location dotted with so many islands, and the water is clean and a deep, royal blue while continuous waves rush to plant kisses on many a sandy, blonde shore. The islands here are basically uninhabited and yet cared for by N.Z. Maritime Parks, which are kept all so beautiful. When we docked I was back at Paihia again.

Now, after two days, I left here to drive south to see more of the North Island.

In New Zealand, cars are driven on the left side of the road, and it took a little time to orientate oneself to drive on the left side of the road as well as adapting the use of the rear view and side mirrors—let's say all of one minute; after all, on-coming traffic must be avoided and learning for this sixty-seven year-old lady takes a little longer than someone younger. Driving in the rural area was not as bad as driving in the larger cities and on the freeway, especially with these circular intersections. And a tourist driver exercised caution when there are these flashing lights that granted permission to pass-over these periodic one-way, rural bridge crossing roadways.

Rotorua was my next destination, and since I was a tourist, I wanted to take an opportunity to view/experience all that was offered to a tourist. Locating a motel was easy; shopping was a different story as they did not give you bags to carry away the item your purchased. Residents knew to take their own bags. Of course, bags were available and sold at the cashier counter for a very nominal fee. I quickly learned to carry a bag when I entered multi-use stores for lunch groceries.

Among the many things to do in Rotorua was the use of thermal springs, but the one that took my attention was taking the "luge," a kilometer ride on a small toboggan apparatus to ride down a hill. You go up the hill in a cable car where they rent you this luge. I boarded this sled thing. There is no snow, just a dirt path. By pulling the handle back and forth you can adjust and brake accordingly. This sport, if one may call it an athletic adventure, is popular with the young people; however, one can be easily hurt on this steep sloping roadway. Ah, from somewhere came this urge for this sixty-seven year old lady willing to take the challenge. You could even go down this slide more than once, but once was enough for me.

Luge slide

Staying in the motels here was exceptionally pleasant for a number of reasons; one was that the agents always had facilities for you to make your own tea or coffee; a half pint bottle of fresh milk was provided with your accommodations. The cost of the motels was very reasonable because the exchange rate was around 50-50. In other words a New Zealand dollar would cost you fifty cents in American money. If a motel room charge was $60, it would translate to 30 American dollars. There is a joyous feeling about cutting costs of everything in half.

My accommodations here in New Zealand were basically on or near the water. I can testify to the braggadocios who say fishing here is the best in the world from my ordering the fish specialties listed on menus throughout New Zealand.

Departing Rotorua I headed south for Wellington, the capital of New Zealand and it is located on the southern tip of the North Island. There are some aspects of Wellington that remind me of San Francisco.

Lighthouse - Wellington Harbor   Terry Channel & Arapawa Isles

For instance, at the port Nichalson, there is an electric trolley that carries passengers up its steep hills. My primary reason to be here in Wellington was to take the ferry across the Cook Strait, and then travel south with the Pacific Ocean on the left and the Tasman Sea on the right; it's all the same water and names like Cook and Tasman honor New Zealand's early western explor-

Road to west side of S. Island

ers. On leaving Wellington, there came into view this lighthouse that I'm told is the oldest in New Zealand.[117] My first impression of the South Island was through the Torry Channel, which is a perfect marriage of land and sea. Again, the shoreline is gorgeous. The far northern point of the South Island is called Arapawa Island. It was here that Capt Cook's first landfall involved a killing of a Maori, and then on his second voyage in 1773, ten of his men were killed and eaten here. Makes you shudder.

The ferry port for the South Island was Picton. I can't say too much about a quaint and picturesque docking point. Nearby is Bluff, it's characterized by its name. Driving south to Christchurch was a very delightful excursion as scenery was beyond expectation. And while here I decided to drive across the Arthur Pass, and it was during this time that I saw my first Kiwi in the wilds. This is unusual in that this flightless bird hides itself during the day and hunts for its prey during the night. Its feathers look like real hair and its crazy sound is like saying its name elongated with emphasis on the first syllable: "KEE-wih." The inclines of the pass are steep, innumerable and followed by downward curvaceous roadway. I could tell my brakes became hotter than blazes while making these kinds of declines.

Driving along the west coast near Greymouth was as delightful as driving along the east coast from Christ Church to Dunedin, where there

Sheep - Dunedin area

were hundreds of sheep pastures. I watched some of the dogs guide flocks of sheep, and they reminded me of my own Australian shepherds who were so helpful controlling my Herefords. In viewing any map of New Zealand, you

---

117   First built in 1859 and located on what is called Pencrrow Head.

can tell that the South Island is more rugged incasing many mountain passes that give panoramic views of land and sea. If I were to vote which is more scenic, I'd choose the South Island, and besides it is far less expensive than the North Island where most of the population reside.

On the Otago Peninsula there are these unusual round Moeraki boulders that sit on the beach. I was reminded of our own Cannon Beach on the coast of Oregon, which are much larger. These appear to be unique in that I did not see them elsewhere on the eastern coast of the South Island.

Moeraki boulders

My time was expiring for touring New Zealand, so it was necessary to make the drive back through Christchurch and eventually back to Picton where the ferry service returned me to the North Island. I wanted to spend more time around Lake Taupo, where I took time to charter a boat to sail on the Lake. While doing so I talked to the skipper about other exciting things to do in this area. He suggested why not take the tandem jump at the Taupo Airport.

This intrigued me as I did have at one time my pilot license, and I did routine work around fighter planes, and I did have flight skins while in the U.S. Navy. Somewhere back in my mind I always wanted to jump from a plane and now I had my chance. After visiting the airport and talking to the personnel in charge, I made arrangements for the tandem jump with Mark, who would accompany me. Mark gave me careful instructions and then we took off in a small plane with another couple who were making the same kind of jump. It was cloudy that day and at 9000 feet, we were ready to exit the plane. Before leaving the

Harness for tandem jump

plane you are instructed not to try and grip the door, you must go. You have no time to hesitate. In those initial moments, I had thought even with my eyes now open that we descended slowly; yet the ground seemed to be coming closer and closer. Actually you are numb with fear and all your senses are really responding to an abnormal situation. You do not register everything in the way of coming in contact with the ground. The scenery was overwhelming and the sensation of falling in the air was a thrill in itself; one can never describe the experience as there is no comparison. Needless to say, I was scared but thought nothing could happen until I hit the ground. At 6000 feet, Mark pulled the cord and we were sailing down to earth. The view was spectacular. I had my camera to take a picture but all I got was this one view and one of the chute.

View from tandem jump

My heart was pumping like mad even though I tried to appear calm on the outside. Mark told me that he would place his fingers in front of my face when the chute opened. He did not have to tell me this as I surely felt the thrust when chute opened. I think one would have to take a second jump to really get the extent of the experience. But, by the time I got down and realized what I had done, I was too smart to try it again. Mark gave me a certificate to verify the jump. When I told my brother what I had done, he scolded me, saying something to the effect that I was a sixty-seven year-old woman and if by chance I landed breaking a hip, leg, ankle, whatever, I would not be healing all that well. There would be unnecessary suffering. When it all comes down to it, of course, I do not have the desire to do it again.

In all my travels, I have never come across basically my name sake. As I said my mother originated my name, but here in a shop that manufactured cottage furniture was my name. Of course the final "e" is in omission, but there it is, my name. No one was available to give any insight of the name here in N.Z.

Willett's cottage furniture

The city of Taupo will be long remembered. I took two thermal baths when I got back to my motel as my body felt stiff and bruised; both thighs were bruised when the chute opened because of the thrust on my body. Regardless, another detail has been struck from my bucket list.[118]

In 1993, I flew from Hobart, Tasmania, to Christchurch for a second tour of New Zealand South Island. My intent was to revisit my favorite spots plus see/visit Fiordland National Park, which is one of the largest national parks in the world. Anyway I drove south from Christchurch and over the mountain passes via Lake Wakatipu. Queenstown sits about half-way the length on the shores of this lake. In my view Queenstown is a top tourist town. Many young people go there to commence a backpacking walk.

Parasailing views

---

118   Oxford English Dictionary: usage stems from early 19th C. when a criminal was hanged...1890: G. Allen, Tents of Shem, "Sir Arthur...will do the right things in the end before he kicks the bucket.

Hiking trails abound and these trails with grand scenery attract the very young. Hey, I'm sixty-nine now and the place attracted me although I am not able to go backpacking. But I did go parasailing. The agent takes you out in a motor launch and they hitch you up in a harness with a chute and with the aid of speed, the wind pulls you up in the air. Oh, do you get a grand view of your surroundings. When it is time to bring you down they use a crank to pull you back into the boat. I asked the personnel to please bring me down into the boat. The lake is nowhere near bath temperature—brrrrr, but it's cold. And if you look closely at the boat there is a ramp, a pad, for you to land, and they do it with panache by catching the sail, me in harness and dropping of speed; it was a thrilling experience, but I'm not sure that I would try it again.

Also in Queenstown there is the Skyline Gondola, which takes its passengers high above town to gawk at the magnificent scenery. Having been formerly a gold-mining town, mall buildings are built in preserving that part of its historical past. It's a

Queenstown gondola

fascinating place and should my reader have the opportunity to visit New Zealand, be sure to include the more western part of the South Island.

I continued my drive west and eventually arrived at Milford Sound, the very north part of the Fiorland National Park. You must return the same way you entered the park at this

Fiorland National Park

point, meaning you should have a reservation as Milford accommodations and cafes are basic and limited. If any of you have taken the mail run from Port Hardy, Vancouver Island, to Prince Rupert, British Columbia, you'll know the reason why. And remember winter here is from June to August. I had made a reservation for a tour on the Milford Sound. Many tourists and backpackers hike the area surrounding the town, but I opted to join a group who did their sight-seeing via a boat or was it a cruiser. No matter, the scenery is superb with its high, steep sides and many waterfalls. This you don't see hiking. What I'm trying to say is that this old lady needs to give excuses for not climbing over hill and dale for such marvelous views.

Fiorland waterfall

In driving back to Christchurch, road signs indicate you haven't strayed off the main road with CHCH indicators. And of course, a driver sees many slopes and meadows filled with sheep.

Sheep near Christchurch area

Before arriving back at Christchurch, I passed through Oamaru, where you may purchase a most delightfully delicious, white cheese at the Whitestone Farmhouse Cheese Factory. They'll even prepare a packaging so it will keep until you arrive at your destination. Oamaru is the place where I saw my name on a furniture manufacturer place in 1991, and now I see the name outside a bake shop. Business has seemed to have expended with the Willett's family.

Willett's Bakery

Having arrived back in Christchurch somewhat early before my
scheduled flight home, I drove up to Hammer Springs, which is a
resort where people from all over come to bathe in the hot springs. It's
an attractive area, and I took time to drive about the surrounding area
besides bathing in the hot springs. In this scampering about, I came
upon an area called the Oregon Estates, which turned out to be a new
residential subdivision. I'm always carrying about a book or two while
traveling. Waste not your time, for there is always something new to
learn, to see another view, to meander in minds more advanced than
mine. Do you remember the required reading of Sir Francis Bacon's
essay "Of Studies?[119] I'm sure you do.

> Some books are to be tasted, others to be swallowed, and some
> few to be chewed and digested; that is, some books are to be
> read only in parts, others to be read, but not curiously, and some
> few to be read wholly, and with diligence and attention.

And such is true with this book. Books are my friends and they
never disappoint me. I took what I was traveling with and dropped them
off at the Christchurch—do I dare say Old Folks Home? Anyway, they
appreciated my gesture of friendship. We seniors appreciate whatever
attention given us. Our library at the South Salem Seniors, Salem,
Oregon, has good collections of DVDs and videos besides up-to-date
popular novels as well as puzzles that have all been donated by various
members of this organization.

My flight home first stopped over at Auckland, and I was able to
shop at the duty free shop. I was later to discover that one of the better
souvenirs that I could give my friends was a tin of New Zealand butter.
Texture and taste is excellent. My brother Jack says that he always bought
New Zealand butter because it was the only butter he could purchase
without it being putrid while he lived in Micronesia for two years.

---

119   Sir Francis Bacon (1/23/1561 0- 4/9/1626) was the one who introduced the essays to
      England and through this form of literature wrote prodigiously on a wide range of
      subjects of which many deal with his scientific experiments.

On this third and last trip to New Zealand in 1994, I arrived at Auckland, rented a car, and headed north to the Bay of Island. Oh, my, it was hot. I called Avis to request an air-conditioned model and my request was rejected—there were none available. Since I had been here before in 1991, I noticed that there were considerably more people who have discovered the Bay of Island as a wonderful place to vacation. On the shores of the bay are three more popular towns: Kerikeri, Russell and Paihia. Kerikeri is full of citrus-fruit orchards and a number of craft workshops. Russell is New Zealand's first European settlement, and from what I read a place with a violent past by whalers who obviously angered the local Maori people. In the Russell Museum there is a one-fifth scale model of Cook's ship, the *Endeavour*. My main purpose here now was to take a tour to the furthest northern point on the North Island, Cape Reinga. I was somewhat surprised that our tour bus rode, at times, right on the sandy beach coastline with sand and water splashing on our windows, which made visibility difficult to

Cape Reinga Coast

see outside. Cape Reinga is about 150 miles from Paiha. Only buses are permitted to do this as I think we were told that there are spots of quicksand near some stream-bed. And in my view, the drive to the destination was one of superior scenic beauty than at the Cape Reinga destination. Legend has it that the Cape is the departure point for Maori spirits returning to their legendary home of *Hawaiki*. This northern point is so beautifully unique; I don't know why any spirit could possible elect to continue on to another place called heaven/Hawaiki.

While spending time in Auckland, I was directed to a suburban area called Parnell Village. The person from whom I made inquiries told me that even the Kiwis go there for shopping. "Kiwis?" I asked and then was told some New Zealanders refer to themselves as Kiwis, named after the flightless bird native to New Zealand. Anyway, Parnell Village typifies colonial-style buildings, older homes were turned into shops. Along Parnell Road there are many restaurants, cafes, craft shops and boutiques. There seems to be parking space near the cathedral and then I could walk about the area.

On this 1994 trip, I flew from Auckland to Christchurch, one of my favorite towns in New Zealand. I rented an A/C car and began my trip to the Marlborough Sound area in the very north of the South Island. At Picton, I joined a tour on the mail boat which takes passengers and groceries to residents who live in out-of-the-way places. The mail boat visits Torea Bay and Lockmana Bay. The Marlborough Sound has truly magnificent scenery.

| Picton mail boat | Marlborough Sound mail run |

I had reservations in Blenheim[120] with accommodations that I truly enjoyed: waterfront view of the ocean or bay, it's not crowded, the scenery gorgeous and restaurants/cafes serving good food. I've concluded that most Kiwis spend all their leisure time on or near the water. I spent two days here before driving across the island to the west side of the South Island.

Once reaching the west coast, I was not disappointed with the drive south, for the road skirted Tasman Sea. And again land and water found a perfect marriage as the scenery invoked my thoughts of the line that

---

120   The town is named after the battle at Blindheim, called Blenheim by the English. Duke of Marlborough's army joined by Austrians and Bavarians on August 13, 1704.

comes from the *Color Purple* that paraphrases into earthy words that stick in your mind: "Wouldn't God be pissed if you didn't appreciate all this

beauty." I still found Greymouth and Hokitika most interesting coastal towns; I was in Greymouth in 1991. Still farther south is the Franz Joseph Glacier. I enjoyed the coastal drive so much that I went on almost until the road ends and then turning left drove east on

Franz Joseph Glacier

the Haast Pass. The road followed a river, not steep but windy. As I went merrily along I recall that the road suddenly changed: steeper and parts of the road were washed out making driving difficult. I even thought of turning around but that was not possible because it meant driving too close to the edge of the road and I don't think I saw an AAA recommended garage anywhere. An on-coming car meant that in spots one of us had to back up; at other meetings I pulled over as close to the edge of the road as I dared and waited for my encountering driver to take the initiative to drive pass me. Oh, did I say that regardless of the condition of the road, the scenery was all to my liking: unparalleled gorgeous.

A typical N.Z. church

Reaching the east side of the South Island, I drove north which allowed me to revisit the town of Oamaru. This is the town that had the Whitehouse Cheese Factory where I, of course, purchase more cheese. This is also the town where I visited the Willett's Furniture Manufacturer and a bakery shop with that name. The family businesses were still flourishing.

When I arrived in Christchurch, I could not find any place to stay. I learned that the

Floral Festival was in progress and rooms were at a premium and not available. One motel agent was kind enough to call around to various places and found accommodations in Culverden, which was 100 km away, which meant a long drive. On the next day I was able to find a room in Christchurch at the Garden City Motel. Again, while waiting for my departure date, I made a quick run up to Hammer Springs, a popular hot springs resort area. Christchurch is the largest town on the South Island and it has multiple places that are well-worth a visit. As I previously stated, this was my third visit, and I

Floral Festival display - Christchurch

still haven't seen it all. In the city center is the cathedral with its Gothic unique architecture. Its steeple is high enough to pinpoint my direction in coming and going in and about the town. The Avon River runs through part of the park area, and one may rent a canoe and paddle in the river. I stayed away from renting one; I could paddle down stream, but coming back would be a different matter.

There is a cable car to the top of Mount Cavendish where there is a marvelous view of the Canterbury Port on Lyttelton's Inlet. I also visited the Antarctic Center, which displayed much information about the Antarctic. Christchurch is the embarkation site for personnel/tourist who may wish to fly to that continent. I thought about such a visit, but time and money prohibit further thought.

The Arts Center is within walking distance to the Christchurch Cathedral. Here there is a display of British and New Zealand art, and also space for many diversified vendors to sell their own handmade crafts.

What more can I say about New Zealand? With only three visits, can I say I love the country? Some critics may say there is an absurdity about loving this country only after three visits. But I think love, no matter what the circumstances, is the only thing about which it is impossible to say anything absurd.[121]

---

121   In her collections of axioms there is a note on this thought made by Sébastien Roch Nicolas Chamfort (1741-1794), who was a French man of letters. He also wrote in 1796, "The poor are the Negroes of Europe," which is an interesting observation to be made so early in our history.

Chapter Eighteen:

Africa—Fall 1991

I t was during the Eisenhower administration that he implemented the Eisenhower Doctrine. It was this doctrine that came into play when the Egyptian Premier Gamal Abdel Nasser, who instituted his policy of nationalizing the Suez Canal, which then sparked the Anglo-French military assault on Egypt. It was years before the Suez was reopened for shipping traffic. The incident elevated Nasser and discredited Britain and France, which were the traditional protectors of western interest in the Middle East[122] and elsewhere on the African continent. Anyway, there were many advocators not to support European countries whose vast colonial holdings were on this continent. North and South Rhodesia became Zambia and Zimbabwe; parts of French Equatorial Africa became Chad and it goes on and on. The brutality among African tribes has been well-recorded, especially now in Somalia and Sudan, where there is all too much Muslim struggle for control. But my purpose is not to give a recitation of African history even in a briefest possible summary. My

---

122   If my reader has an interest in the Eisenhower years in the White House, I can
       recommend The Oxford Companion to U.S. History, which can enlighten any reader
       on nebulous facts.

point is that I had been warned to listen carefully to advice of when and where to travel on this continent.

In the fall of 1991, and after much researching, especially about the Blue Train, of what and where else to go in Africa, I set out on this extended travel. It's always been my habit to do much research and learn as much as possible so that my trip becomes absolutely enjoyable. I also found that while in large cities, it is always better to act like you know where you are going. Gawking as a novice gives attention to those professionals who are capable of ripping you off—stealing your purse or purchases. You never know who is watching you. In my September travel plans, I had the option of flying to Union South Africa either via South America or via Europe. I opted to fly by way of Switzerland as I would be granted travel miles to my United Airlines travel card even though I would use Swiss Air. I arranged matters so I would have several days there before and after my tour to parts of Africa. I have always been fond of Switzerland. Having a couple days

Geneva — Nairobi (7.25 h)

Dinner

Air-dried beef
and tomato filled with shrimps

Sauteed veal escalopes
Spaghetti with tomatoes
Leaf spinach

Cheese

Vanilla custard and red currants

❑

Early Tea

Nairobi — Johannesburg (3.55 h)

Brunch

Fruit cocktail

Pancake filled with creamed spinach
Chicken and vegetables on a skewer

Cheese

❑

Refreshment

Swiss Air menu

in respite of long trans-Atlantic flights was giving me another opportunity to visit Switzerland. On September 3rd, I took a Swiss Air flight to Zurich; there is a small hotel in Kloten, which is near the airport and provides a regular shuttle to and from the city. There was also a convenient train at the airport to take me and other tourists to downtown Zurich. On the 6th, I was on a Swiss Flight to Johannesburg with a fuel stop in Nairobi. I've copied the dinner menu of my Swiss Air flight from Nairobi to Johannesburg. I thought the flight provided marvelous food.

Facilities inside Nairobi airport were very primitive, meaning that there were no toilet tissue or toilet seats. It was a bleak and depressing experience, and glad I was once aboard the Swiss plane heading for Johannesburg. Henceforth, my advice is that one should always carry their own small packages of Kleenex for such emergencies.

Once arriving at Johannesburg, I was informed by Swiss Air not to go into the city alone, and respecting their advice I found accommodations at the Holiday Inn adjoining nearby this Jan Smut Airport. Later that day I took a short sightseeing tour of Johannesburg offered by a private tour operator. During this short tour of the city I noticed huge mounds of yellowish dirt; the tour guide told me that these were remains of mining gold in the city. No one lived in Johannesburg 100 years ago except Pygmies, and with the discovery of gold, the city of Johannesburg had its start. I don't know about this elaborate explanation of the yellow dirt. It will have to do until something better comes along.

I was somewhat surprised at the condition of the town as it appeared unimpressive. I did notice at every large store or business there was guards. Since the warning not to go downtown, I spent the rest of the time browsing in the airport or watching TV and preparing myself for the excursion on the Blue Train. A pre-arranged taxi took me to the Blue Train station. As I got out of the taxi an African man came by and picked up my suitcases and was about to rush off with them, but my taxi driver interfered and carried them to the platform of the Blue Train.

Bloutrein agents

I was probably naïve enough that, for a moment, I was being robbed in board daylight or else he was a self-assertive non-union porter. It's a guess. I just didn't know. With my travel voucher schedules, I had no trouble boarding the train. A group of people were already there and entering their respective compartments while other train personnel were taking photos of the passengers. Oh, I was excited. Actually, I had been favoring this trip since 1951 while I was teaching in England.

Bloutrein crystal

Everyone who told me about the trip stated it was a luxury personified. Anyway, after my picture was taken, a porter directed me to Car #5, my private compartment which consisted of a separate long seat to be made into a bed that evening and a small attached table on which was a lead crystal glass and half bottle of Nederburg Champagne.

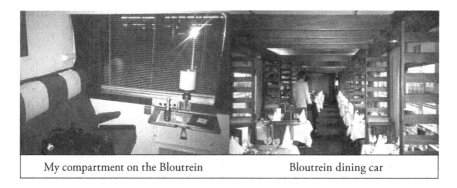

My compartment on the Bloutrein   Bloutrein dining car

This was a sure sign that I was about to take a train ride above all other trains, even superior to the much publicized Orient Express —Paris to Constantinople. My compartment included a complete bathroom with a separate shower. This was a luxury, indeed. I have no regrets spending the extra costs to feel that I'm worth every penny of these costs. There is a Persian proverb that says that in my going I have woke up my luck.

At noon I was instructed to go to the dining car for lunch, which turned out to be a six-course, fabulous meal. The train stopped several times, once in Kimberly and I got off just to look at my surroundings. At other times the train stopped to allow other trains to pass. I did see a rhino and flamingoes from the train.

For the evening meal, again I was thoroughly impressed at the quality and quantity of the cuisine, and again served in courses. One does not eat on the Blue Train, one dines; the cuisine was impeccable. I felt like I was dining in the most expensive and luxurious restaurant in the world. There were two sittings for the evening dining. I understood the second sitting required more formal dress, and since I did not have a formal dress I opted for the first sitting.

Coffee was delivered to my compartment at 5:50 a.m.; I got up and got ready to go to the dining car for breakfast. Again a multi-course breakfast meal was served in the same style as the dinner served last night.

Upon arrival in Capetown my car rental was awaiting my arrival. It was not automatic, and I declined acceptance. I was then driven to a hotel and the car agent stated they would contact me when an automatic car was available.

My accommodation in Captetown was at the Surfcrest Hotel in Seapoint; it consisted of a large room with two beds, bathroom, and an enclosed balcony. The view was beautiful and my room was on the ocean side with only a green

Surfcrest Motel at Seapoint

lawn and street between me and the Atlantic Ocean. The one drawback I discovered about the bed was the fact there weren't any springs under the mattress; just a flat board underneath, which was hard on my back. But I have been in worse situations and this was certainly not any great inconvenience, especially when I figured out the room rate was 85 Rand a night, which also included breakfast and dinner; when translated into US dollars, it turned out to be $30.

There were stores within walking distance from the hotel, so I took time to browse in the shops. Budget car rental called to apologize and tell me the car I asked for was in an accident on the way to my hotel and there would be a short delay until it could be replaced. The evening meal consisted of soup, salad, peas, rolls, chicken , potatoes, cheese, and pudding and a fresh fruit to take to my room to eat later.

The next day I made arrangements to take a structured tour of the area, including Table Mountain, however it was too foggy to view the sight this morning. It became visible later on in the afternoon. The rest of my tour was to the Cape of Good Hope at the southern tip of the

At Cape of Good Hope

peninsula where geographers call the water to the left the Indian Ocean and the water to the right the Atlantic. I included a picture to see whether you too can tell a difference. Methinks my jocular humor is failing.

Budget finally delivered my rental car. I drove it along the coast on N-1 highway, and noticed the change in the scenery and how beautiful and green the countryside was. I stopped in Stellenbosh to get gas and to walk through a small shopping mall where I did purchase a change purse. This area was dramatically different from Johannesburg and its environs. I stopped at the Nederberg Winery[123] but it was closed on a Saturday. I was very impressed with the way wineries were land-

Stollenbosh winery

scaped with entrances of long driveways lined with stately trees. All the

Nederburg winery

buildings and farmhouses in this area were painted a snow white and showing a predominance of Dutch influence.

I drove to Franschoek to view the Huguenot Memorial; it is a tribute to the Huguenots who settled in this beautiful area more than 300 years ago. What actually brought me here is that my brother has a steel engraving on six panels and framed together creating a 4.5X5 foot picture. Cardinal Richelieu commanded the leading steel engraver of his time Jacque Callot to depict the annihilation of the Huguenots at

Huguenot Memorial at Franschoek

---

123 My champagne furnished by the service of the Blue Train came from this winery.

La Rochelle, France, in 1627-28. It's a most interesting library collection of prints that illustrates the horror of war, for Callot has incidents of rape, cattle being slaughtered, men being hanged, women followers of the camp washing and animal sodomy all taking place to define for any student to study this harsh moment in time. The brochure explaining this memorial states that the three arches represents the trinity. The figure of the woman has a Bible in her right hand and broken chain in her left, symbolizing their strong religious belief and freedom from oppression they received in Europe. From France some fled to The Netherlands, England, to several American colonies. I also noticed the fleur-de-lis pattern in her dress is the same as in the glass in windows in Sainte-Chapelle in Paris and representing her nobility of spirit and character. It's an interesting memorial and it sits in a gorgeous setting in this countryside of wineries.

Upon returning to Sea Point I noticed an open market at the sports complex; the name of this area was Bloubergstrand, and it was a high point of my day to peruse so many vendor stalls in one location.

On the third day in Capetown, I had booked a short flight on SAL to Durban, where I rented a car and planned to drive down the southern coast. I found a delightful and convenient hotel called St. Michael by the Sea in Margate. My room was on the ocean side with a sun room to look out over the Indian Ocean.

The next morning after breakfast (which was included in the room rate), I rented a canoe so I could paddle in the lagoon, and later I waded in the warm Indian Ocean. I discovered many places one could shop, and since I am a shopper I continually took advantage when I had the opportunity.

During the next three days I drove south to Point Edward where I stopped at the country club. I had been looking for a driving range but it seemed nothing

Point Edwards Country Club

like that was available; however, personnel provided an opportunity to exercise this activity at this golf course. They loaned me a bag in the shape of a bowling bag filled with golf balls, guided me to tee #1, where I hit the balls, and a native African was down the fairway picking up the balls and returning them to me in the bag. This was an extremely cheap driving range experience; it cost 3 Rand which translated to $1.25 US Dollars.

While in Margate I did buy a new putter and golf bag which I later used to pack some Nederburg wine to take back to the states.

From Durban I returned to Johannesburg by SAL, staying in the Holiday Inn and prepared for the next leg of my trip. By this time I had accumulated many extras which would not fit into my luggage, so I made arrangements to leave some items stored at this hotel until I returned from the safari tour.

On this flight I only took items that I would need; it was only a two hour flight to Zimbabwe (formerly Southern Rhodesia). It was a package tour which included viewing the Victoria Falls, a Cruise on the Zambezi River, and accommodations at the Victoria Falls Hotel. The land around the Hotel was brown, dry and barren. It took me a day to learn how to operate the air conditioning. If you read *When Hearts Were Young and Gay,* you will know that it operated something like a "geezer."

| Victoria Falls Hotel | Victoria Falls |

You can walk to the falls from the hotel, which I did and took some pictures. On the way from the falls, I saw a native sweeping the path and learned later it was to keep the snakes off the pathway. Believe me,

I tipped him and he swept any fear that by chance I would meet up with Eve's enticement to sin. No, no, no, I would not even take the slightest chance. The convenience of walking to the falls was possible and thus

A slithering side view of Victoria Falls

different stances on the rim for the enthusiastic photographer. It's not like our Niagara[124] in that the precipices have guard rails; you walk only where you are sure of footing. The falls were immense and I walked down different pathways to take photos near the rims; on my walk to take a side view the temperature was warm and the mist from the falls was wet and cooled the air somewhat. This jaunt urged by my brother Jack was well worth the additional expenses in coming to this area of Africa. There is a bridge that connects Zimbabwe and Zambia but I did not walk across; it was a different country for which you had to use a passport.

The Sundowner Cruise was lovely with furnished drinks and snacks. The Cruise on the Zambezi River was to allow passengers to observe African animals in their native habitat. The water was calm and reflected a quiet serene atmosphere. I did see an elephant along the shore. The cruise was designed to have guests see a scenic view of the countryside with the sun going down and the moon

Zambezi River cruise

---

124   Niagara Falls runs from 186 ft. to 193 high; Victoria Falls runs from 256 ft. to 355 ft. at center.

coming up. This was not quite the *Moon over Miami* setting, but it still was beautiful and the warm breeze on the water caressed you. I thoroughly enjoyed this jaunt onto the river and sighting some animals in their native environment.

African dancer in outside theatre

In the evening the hotel management also provided a show of African Dancers in the outdoor theater for their guests. The dances were highly representative for success in a hunt or for overcoming some adversity. Costumes were colorful and fascinating; better than MGM impersonations.

When you come upon a bronze statue in unexpected places, you can't help give wonder about the life of Dr. Livingston, who dedicated so much of his adult life to Africans, and his chance meeting of Sir Henry Stanley,[125] which happened on Oct. 28, 1871. Livingston refused to return with him to the coastal area and later died near Lake Bangweula in April 1873. The statue commemorates that meeting and Livingston was buried here.[126]

Site of chance meeting
Dr. Livingston

From Zambezi I flew back to Johannesburg for a day of rest and to organize the last part of my trip in Africa. Via Com Air the next day, I flew to Skukuza, close to the border of

---

125   Stanley was born at Denbigh, Wales and baptized John Rowlands. Orphaned early he became a cabin boy on a ship to New Orleans, La., where a merchant Henry Morton Stanley adopted him and gave him his name Stanley. As a journalist, it was the New York Herald that sponsored his search for Livingston.

126   Actually Livingston's body was taken and placed in Westminster Abbey in London later on.

Mozambique and yet in the realm of Kruger National Park in the upper northeast section of S. Africa. I was met by a representative guide from the Rattray Reserves, and he took me in a Land Rover to Harry's Kamp, just one of three such safari camps. I was the only guest arriving at this time and pleased with the prospect that my tour into the wilds would be with a small group of tourists.

Harry's Kamp

It was about noon when I arrived and was directed to my accommodation, which was a small cabin with one room with twin beds, a chair, a table, a closet and a bathroom with a tub. There was no suffering of any inconvenience here. At this base camp, lunch was served at 1:00 p.m. I was also given a packet of malaria pills and told to take two now and two more each week thereafter for three weeks. In the compound in the center of the cabins was a small swimming pool.

All the meals were served at a picnic type table except at the evening meal where we ate in an open thatched roof area in a semi circle seating with blazing flares all around the inside. The compound consisted of several cabins, a swimming pool, and the main lodge, which held a bar and a lounging area.

Lunch setting at Harry's Kamp   Harry's mode of transportation

The schedule for each day was very similar except for the specific animals we were seeking that day. There was a system to this safari business. There were scouts out to direct us to an area where such-n-such animal was seen. Two Land Rovers were used and in the one I was assigned there were five guests and a driver/guide. The guide packed an ice chest as we were in the bush for about three hours at a

Hyena

time. There weren't any roads to speak of except dirt pathways, and often we were driven into the bush to view certain animals. The guides in each Land Rover had communication contact and would let each other know where some animals were located. The guide hoped and wanted each of us to see the big five animals in their native habitat; these included the buffalo, lion, leopard, elephant, and a rhinoceros.

On our first outing we were able to see giraffes, elephants, buffalo, and lions. They hide in the grass and bush foliage. We are also warned not to make noise to attract the animals; when spotted, our driver would get as close as possible allowing us to take our photos. We saw all except the leopard or jaguar. This was not a great disappointment for me. The jaguar was noted for his speed, maybe up to sixty miles an hour. I cannot visualize our jeep under these conditions out-running one of them. So, basically we were in the Land Rover 6 hours a day; three hours in the morning and three hours in the afternoon. Riding in the bush without paved roads was a bumpy situation and if you do not have posterior padding, I suggest you bring a pillow as I often braced myself for a rugged ride each day.

There is no Albertson's or Kroger's nearby the camp, so many of our evening meals included meat from the impala. Our guide informed us that they kill a hundred a month to be used in preparing the meals in the three different Kamps. I didn't mind; preparation of this kind of meat was well cooked, but Koby[127] beef it was not.

Time did not seem to have green leaves, and much bark was eaten away by the animals. I understood that the most vicious animal was the hyena and his aggression is well-known among our guides and natives.

Each evening before dinner we were taken in the Land Rover into the bush where an African native would set up a table so we could watch the sun go down; we were served a drink of our choice along with an appetizing snack. The liquor served was not any of those cheesy brands as far as I could notice.

---

127   Koby beef refers to the practice of massaging the cow before slaughtering to ensure tender pieces of beef. Special markets carry this product.

On the last day of the Safari we spotted a huge rhino in the bush; I was impressed by this animal for his snort and stamp of defiance for our proximity. There are parks and zoos of various calibers in the U.S., and thus a visit here brought a reality and appreciation of all who serve to preserve animal life on this continent. If you came out alive,[128] and like all guests, you will be given a certificate to validate your visit to Harry's Kamp.

The guide took us to the Skukuza Airport where we took transportation back to different places; I flew back to Johannesburg, and once again to the Holiday Inn where I retrieved my stored purchases. I had a day to organize everything before taking Swiss Air back to Zurich and then home. There is a Chinese proverb that states to know the road ahead, ask those coming back, and thus the reason I expect of why you're taking the timed in reading my account of this fascinating areas of the world.

---

128 Some humor here…of course you'll come out alive; that is, if the guide or agent hasn't surmised you're been an obnoxious guest.

Chapter Nineteen:

Asia—1992

I don't know what increased my interest to visit Asia. I know that when I read my brother's account about his visit to China shortly after Kissinger persuaded the Chinese government to open its doors to American travel, I would not want to travel as he did. His travel notes were exciting, and yet travel as he did meant a group tour as it is impossible to travel on your own. Reading *The Travels of Marco* Polo is such an enticing diary—Marco was there from 1275 to 1292 and found favor during the reign of Kublai Khan of the Yuan dynasty— that alone gave me the lingering

Panmen Gate, Suzhou on the Grand Canel

interest to see a part of Asia for myself. And by the way, my brother compared his short jaunt on the Grand Canal[129] with that of Marco's traversing the same canal, which would probably now make Marco turn

---

129   The Grand Canal flows from the Shanghai area, actually Hangchow, to Beijing, a distance of 1,200 miles.

in his grave for the amount of heavy pollution on the Grand Canal that exists there today.

In February 1992, I began my long flight across the Pacific. I flew to Honolulu where I spent a couple of days. I could not rent a car as I forgot my driver's license so I took a local bus tour. How could one not weep at the U.S.S. Arizona memorial, one of three warships out of 18 warships caught unprepared on that fateful day December 7, 1941? Waikiki with its entire splendid pacific beach is a concentration of high hotels with spectacular views. It's a splendid way to break up a long trek across the Pacific.

From Honolulu, I flew on Singapore Airlines to Taipei, where one might consider that you are under "house arrest" as I did not have a visa to enter this Chinese island nation, and I saw no more of Taipei than the airport. This happens to others who were in transit to another part of Asia as I. I was permitted to spend my American dollars in the Duty Free area. It all wasn't as bad as the airlines served me a lunch in the transit area.

Later in early afternoon aboard Singapore Airlines, I was winging my way to Hong Kong.[130] At this time Hong Kong is still a British Crown Colony, covering just 404 square miles. An aerial view of the harbor reveals a truly unique harbor skirted with tall buildings and reflecting a monstrous population for such a tiny area.

I took a taxi to my hotel, the Eaton located on Nathan Street. It was near the famous Peninsula Hotel, which, by the way, had a great deli on a lower floor. One doesn't come here to gawk at beaches or run out to the new territories for the scenery on a first class train, actually meaning seats with an overhead fan. Workers in the lower ranked cars sit on benches. Everyone comes to shop, eat at some of the very best restaurants or take a speed boat to Macau to gamble. Whatever you are looking for to purchase, it's here. I dropped in at Craig's Limited where the best of fine bone China, such as Royal Crown Darby, is available at much lower

---

130   Derived from Heung Kong, meaning Fragrant Harbor, and is a safe area for sailing ships to take-on fresh water.

costs than if one purchased it in London. The clerk actually let me handle and closely inspect the ware, but with my clumsy wrist and finger control it would be a misadventure to purchase such dinnerware. To say there are lots of shops surrounding the Eaton Hotel area is almost ridiculous. Anyone who has been here knows retailers are everywhere. Passengers off ships like the Queen Elizabeth 2 docked at a pier would not have to leave sight of the ship to do more than adequate shopping. It's exciting to have so many things readily available for purchase.

Taking the Star Ferry across to Hong Kong Island where one finds additional luxurious hotels, many restaurants, and shops is run by continuous ringing of bells with gates opening and closing with little or no waiting to board a ferry. On the island I caught the cable car to take a ride up to Victoria Peak where the view of the harbor is a photographer's delight.

The Eaton Hotel did not have an easy access to the lobby as you had to ride a steep escalator to the Hotel lobby, and then take an elevator to my room, which had a huge bed larger than king size, bath with shower, and a safe. I was pleased with the accommodations.

I had been to Hong Kong before so I did not feel the need to take any extra tours. And the best advice I can give my reader is not to order any kind of fish preparation as you cannot be sure they were not taken from the harbor, which waters may look clear and blue but fish taken from here have fed on many a polluted cesspool. Remember, no fish. The voice of experience has spoken.

Before leaving this shopper paradise, I did take a speed boat down to Macau to observe the government controlled gambling. If you want to go gambling, go to Las Vegas. This once Portuguese colony at one time has Fan Tan gambling where a basket floated up and down with bets of whether the stick comes out even or odd. On my first visit here I found this fascinating. On a return trip this gaming was eliminated. As I understand, the Chinese poor became too easily addicted.

On my last evening in Hong Kong, I did discover a marvelous Italian restaurant—can't think of the name now, but ask and I'm sure natives will convey the information to you. Walking in the vicinity of my hotel, I noticed food stalls selling chickens split lengthwise and cooked or uncooked and there was a special price on just the chicken's claws/feet; a sure sign that poverty had not been eradicated.

Thai Airlines flew me into Bangkok three hours later after departing from Hong Kong. After retrieving my luggage, I was bombarded by tour operators who were extremely aggressive to sell you tickets for tours. Before I managed to get a taxi, I did relent and bought one tour ticket. The taxi driver drove to the Classic Place Hotel where I had reserved a room. The hotel personnel were friendly and spoke English and served you pink punch while checking into the hotel. It was at this hotel that I first became aware of a new device using a card key; upon entering your room, you place the card key in a slot inside the room and the power is turned on and you immediately have lights and air conditioning. This room was quite suitable and included a refrigerator, saving me a trip down the hall looking for the ice machine. I was tired and went to bed, waking up quite early to unpack and organize things in my room.

The next morning I took the boat tour on one of the tributaries of the May Nam Ping, which diverts itself before emptying into the Gulf of Thailand. It is fascinating to travel through this floating market where women in small boats sell a variety of items to tourists on the tour boats. A thought twisting idea that rings true in

Market on May Nam Ping River

locations like these is that these sales ladies are ones who sell goods that won't come back to customers who will.

Later our group visited a Buddha temple; taking off your shoes before coming into the main part of the house has been a religious principle at our house. Entering the sacred areas of this temple was showing respect. No problem about that, but I did have a tinge of anxiety of someone stealing my shoes among some areas where poverty is so prevalent. There are so many Buddha temples/monasteries that reflect a calm and unstressed life. You can't help but be attracted to these places of worship. I think it is a fundamental concept that you must accept that first Buddha is not limited to any form—he can be male, female and child and in my understanding elements retained by animals. Buddha is a passageway to enlightenment. It can be a state of freedom or salvation. The Atman principle in Buddhism relates to the idea that there is no self or soul seeking rescue from the process of change and death. Think of it as no soul sitting inside the human

Buddhist Altar

body like the driver of a bus/taxi and gets out at the end of the journey. There is only the aggregation of components which is caused by the previous moment and causes the next. It's the Dalai Lama principle that there is no one person who is the Dalai Lama. He is rightly momentarily identified as this person now, but there is no one person who the Dali Lama always is. I like the symbolism of the

Buddhist site

Buddhist in the lotus blossom. We have our roots in muck, struggle through the water of life and blossom forth in the light that we all seek. I saw handsome Chinese chairs with the lotus blossoms carved on their back. I was tempted to purchase.

Thailand is the land of Rex Harrison and Irene Dunne's efforts to bring some 63 million people into 20th century. Literacy is high yet it's most crowded. Vendors are most aggressive to sell whatever they have and I am not myself when pressed into a bargaining situation like this, especially when Pidgin English is limited. I tried to avoid these circumstances. Food preparation and eating is more often than not, right on the sidewalks; more often than not, passageways.

A tuk tuk

I did little venturing out from my hotel and carried the hotel business card in the native language. Not knowing anything about public transportation, I'd hired a Tuk Tuk[131] taxi to take me back to my hotel. I used this taxi several times during my stay in Thailand.

Near my hotel there was a tailor shop, and I ordered slacks with more than two deep pockets because I felt insecure carrying a purse where it could be snatched off my shoulder during times that I found myself alone in various sections of cities; "alone" means no fellow travelers in my vicinity. An attempt had been made, and thus carrying only the necessities in pockets I felt safe from a street robber. Besides, after the horse injury on the ranch, it was difficult to for me to open and close a purse with safety on crowded streets. Wearing slacks with pockets allowed my hands to be free; I also wore a fanny pack to carry my camera.

While shopping I found a store that sold bronze figures. Prices were most reasonable and the price for this 18 X 22 inch fish was a marvel, and I knew it would be an ideal birthday/Christmas gift for my brother. All for just

A bronze fish

---

131   A Tuk Tuk is a covered cart pulled by a man peddling a bicycle.

$200, which included shipping; this was a steal. This was too heavy to take with me, so I had it shipped directly to my brother Jack, who I knew would create some charming feature of his backyard landscape.

The time in Bangkok passed quickly, and I was on another Singapore Airline flight to Singapore. There were ample taxis available to take me to the Amara Hotel, where I had my reservation. The fare was reasonable. My hotel room was attractive with a fine air conditioning,[132] and an above average bathroom facility. My room rent included a buffet breakfast every morning.

The Amara Hotel was within walking distance to Chinatown, which gave me the advantage in browsing at the items the shopkeepers sold in front of individual stores. They had quite a few items made from stainless steel that I could use in my own kitchen. Prices were most reasonable too.

Indonesia, at this time of the year, was extremely hot and humid; just walking across Singapore streets one felt the humidity so much that you hurried to get into a place with air conditioning. While shopping I found a place nearby where I could buy hangers. Often times the hangers in the room are not detachable. A wise word to travelers is that you need at least two hangers to be used hanging the nightly washed necessities.

I took a taxi from my hotel to go to the famous Raffles Hotel. I was amazed at the complex as the entire building was in a standout white color. I found this curious that people off the street are not welcomed to come into the hotel lobby and thus an arrangement for the lobby is up one floor from the street, and from there you catch an elevator to take you to your room. I suppose this keeps street people from entering and

Raffles Hotel

132   She's just making a point that air-conditioning is a necessity and she was glad hers was operating.

making use of the lobby facilities. The Raffles Hotel has a significant ambience of the Victorian Era of the Commonwealth of England. Grand chandeliers, Oriental rugs and solid furniture were the décor.

I am in a city where dropping your gum or spitting is an offense and you can be severely fined. The streets, at least where I went, were clean of such debris. It rained almost every day in Singapore; not a hard rain but it would still get you wet. One morning I took the bus to Orchard Street and what a difference; the area is beautifully landscaped with green lawns and trees. The shops on Orchard Street are more expensive than shops near the Amara Hotel and Chinatown as one would expect. It's a matter of shopping in elegance or shopping in areas for price.

| Singapore street scene | Causeway to Malaysia |

In front of the Singapore City Hall, people have their picture taken as this is where the Japanese surrendered to the allies after WW II. There was a mini van giving tours to Malaysia. Entering Malaysia was a little hectic and tedious. We passed over a causeway built in 1924. and destroyed during WWII and then rebuilt by the Japanese later. Johor Bahru is a town for tourists with all kinds of jewelry and watches for sale. I purchased a Rolex for $15. Of course, it was an imitation but appeared like an original. In Malaysia there were obvious signs of great poverty even though the country produces almost half the rubber the world uses. Malaysia is more Muslim than other religious denominations, and thus our tour bus drove to a the Sultan's home, which gives the appearance of being spacious and luxurious.

There are literally hundreds of small islands off Malaysia and Republic of Singapore. One was a tourist attraction for its free loop railroad that took you around the island. The place was called Sentosa and it would be a gorgeous place to live in serenity. After the tour and during the time to go back to the hotel, I saw a native with a huge snake circled around him as he was selling postcards; needless to say I avoided him and would find a more suitable place to buy my postcards of Singapore and Malaysia.

| Sentosa Hotel | Sentosa Hotel beach |

One incident while at the Amara Hotel was in using the elevator; it stuck between two floors. Being alone and claustrophobic, I became panicky and pushed the button several times yelling that I was stuck. Fifteen minutes later the maintenance people had the elevator released and me free from my entrapment. This was a lesson for me to get a room closer to the first floor and I try to rationalize my anxiety for confinement in small places as something that grew as my age advanced. The hotel management were apologetic and sent up a basket of fresh fruit; the looks of the fruit was deceiving as most of the items were not mature enough to eat. The gesture was appreciated.

Singapore flight to Seoul, Korea, was a two deck plane and full passenger capacity. Upon landing and retrieving my luggage I took a taxi to the President Hotel where I had a reservation. At the time of my visit there was much congestion and much pollution here in Seoul. My room was on the 26th floor was unattractive to say the least; the rug was dirty as well as the curtains. The room was very disappointing in comparison to my other reservations in other hotels. I asked for a different room and was assigned one on the 15th floor Finding the first six floors used as officer in a hotel building was a new experience for me in that you had much waiting as people were getting in and off before the elevator reached my floor.

Traveling from the latitude of the equator to 38 degrees north latitude is a change; much cooler here in Seoul and wearing a jacket was necessary. The Hotel was located within walking distance to a shopping area; it was difficult to shop in department stores as clerks were not versed in understanding or speaking English. This traveler had expected better results from the U.S. efforts in the "police actions" crisis which lasted from June 1950 until July 1953.[133] Our numbered dead numbered 33,741 and 92,134 wounded. There were 7,245 prisoners of war of which 2,847 who died in POW camps. These statistics do not include those of the twenty-one other nations in this endeavor that entered into the conflict with N. Korea, Soviet Union, and the Peoples Republic of China. Such sacrifices one would think English would be more prevalent than it was, and then again many countries favor our cinemas, news media, seeking new ideas pertaining to the self, health wise, and social advancement. C'est la vie.

As I have done elsewhere, I took a tour of the area. We stopped at an open market where I purchased another Rolex watch for $20; many of these vendors sell imitations of name products such as Rolex watches. Since I already had one, why another you may ask? I preferred the second over the first and would give the first one as a souvenir gift.

Being on your own is difficult to venture into a restaurant and try to order a meal from a menu I did not understand. A little old lady trying to point what others order in a society where men have tight hold over women is not circumstances that I'd care to engage. Seeing a McDonald sign solved my immediate problem of eating, regardless how much I

---

133   Statistics compiled by Ed Evanhoe on 4/17/01: www.korean-war.com.

despise the fast food agendas. To me, Seoul was the most disappointing place. It was terribly crowded and I felt intimidated even in trying to ask for services. I felt I was in a hostile situation, especially when trying to cross a street where drivers were not respectful to pedestrians and assumed the right-of-way even while in cross walks. So, if you visit this country, be sure you're with a respectable travel agency.

Money was running short; I had already gone beyond my travel budget and thought it was time for me to go home. From Seoul I took Japan Airlines to Tokyo and Singapore Airlines to L.A and then flew to Portland on American Airlines. See, I am a cosmopolitan traveler who will always have two bags packed full: one should be patience and another of money.

Chapter Twenty:

Switzerland, Liechtenstein & Bavaria

T hrough my travels into various areas of Asia, I learned something about myself. As much as far away places with strange sounding names intrigue me, I find that I enjoy travel best when communication takes place between me and whomever I meet. Approaching fellow travelers and sharing an exotic moment of viewing scenery, a cable car lift or teasingly telling a total stranger "I'm Marilyn Monroe and I'm traveling incognito. I have another name; would you like to hear it?" I'm sure that many a person went home and told her family of this nut she/he met on the street today.

Most people whom I meet are always surprised when they ask and learn that I am traveling alone. Even more surprised when they learn that I was driving a car by myself. The traveling bug (if there is such a thing) bit me intensively as Shakespeare would say in my "salad days." Being a school teacher helped me gallivant to places I otherwise would not have gone. Now in retirement I have the means to go when and where I like. I always preferred not to travel with a group tour, for too often some guide wants to take me to a museum and have you look closely to the item on the third shelf to the left; it is dated 34 BCE[134].

---

134   Before Christian Era

Besides, have you stamped your foot waiting in line to use the bathroom facility on group tours? Well, I have. I prefer my own schedule, which means considerable research of where and when I want to tour.

In the fall of 1992, I decided to return to Switzerland, Liechtenstein, and Bavaria. An agent of Capital Travel here in Salem was always eager to assist me in obtaining airline tickets and hotel reservations. AAA travel office generally furnished me with more than enough information about the area I wished to tour. There is more than one tour available in the large cities where driving would be foolish and parking is almost next to impossible for a stranger. The beginning of October became another one of twelve times I visited this area of Europe. I flew to Zurich, rented a car and drove to Basel. Three countries are joined here on the Rhine (France, German, and Switzerland), and it is the home of Hans Holbein, who did the portrait of Anne of Cleves[135] (1515-1570), who was daughter of John, Duke of Cleves, who was a leader of the Protestant movement of western Germany. She was selected by Thomas Cromwell to become the fourth wife of Henry VIII after the death of Jane Seymour. The Kunst Museum houses paintings by artists such as Holbein, Braque, Gris, Chagall and even Picasso. It is worth a visit.

Holbein's portrait of Anne

Next I headed for Garmisch, one of my favorite towns located in Bavaria, Germany. The road going east from Zurich to Garmisch passes through several tunnels. This is one way to save time even though the tunnels are a little frightening as some are quite long—remember now that I can become claustrophobic in tight places. During these times I

---

135   From all accounts, Holbein made Anne slimmer than she actually was. Although a marriage took place, it was never consummated. In the divorce Anne received a munitions plant as well as other benefits. She subsisted on such income quite content to reside in England. She was an excellent mathematician. Her journal reveals that she thought she lived better in England than she ever did in Germany.

play musical tapes to soothe any anxiety that I may have during the drive through the tunnels.

The first city I traveled through in Bavaria, southern Germany, was Mittenwald. I had to stop and take a photo of the sign as it was here in 1950 that I served as a camp-counselor to a group of girl scouts summering here in southern Germany. It was my first enthusiastic love for this section of Germany.

Entering Mittenwald

And yet remembering just north of nearby Munich is the ever lasting horror of Dachau. Here is an example to teach the meaning of the word about a conundrum. There is such beauty and such horrors of a Nazi camp existing in a same area.

Baby clothes on clothes line

Before entering into Bavaria, I went through Liechtenstein and visited my friend Erica Schneider and her mother. The few times I visited the area, I was always asked for dinner and learned so much about customs that are practiced by the Swiss, Liechtensteiners and Bavarians. Through their entertaining stories, I learned about a rather unusual custom pertaining to a new construction and newlyweds. In Garmish I viewed this custom for newlyweds to place clothes line hung from a house to their house across the street. On the line tiny clothes are hung to wish them many

Tree on apex of house

children. Another custom is that the builder in the construction of a house places a decorated tree when they complete the uttermost top of the building. Both are signs for friends and neighbors to celebrate an accomplishment. Hey, I'm ready to party.

Erika Schneider and her family were always helpful in finding my way about Switzerland. For instance near Meirengen is the Aare Gorge, which I visited on a previous 1990 tour, and then again on this visit. Its walkway/passageway lies between straight walls of granite and the walk is fascinating. They are called flumes; there a many such flumes in New England area. Erica was a great naturalist in that she enjoyed nature and would unabashedly hug a tree whether people looked or not. I took a photo and later sent her a portrait painted by William Pulley.[136] She was most appreciative for the painting.

Aare Gorge

Erica hugging a tree

Though my first visit to Garmisch was during the winter, it is just as appealing in the summer. Even in the summer when you visit the top of the Zugspitz, over 9,700 feet, you can feel the intense cold. The guard rails at this height have icicles. Adjacent to Garmisch-Partenkirchen is Berchtesgaden, a few miles from the Austrian border. Here Hitler kept a residence in a secluded high mountain area. I took the opportunity to visit the site and was amazed at the exceptional view. It's a gorgeous site. Unfortunately, my photos were

136   William Pulley, an amateur artist, won 1st prize at the California State Fair in 1982 for his portraits of birds.

not returned after the development by the film agency. There is no logical reason that I didn't at least have over-exposed or under-exposed negatives.[137] Years have passed since I was here last and the site is so majestic you cannot help but admire the builders' intent to invoke amazing thoughts pertaining to the appearance of space and beauty.

Zugspitz

It was on November 15th, 1938, that Neville Chamberlain, Prime Minister of Great Britain, came here to talk with Hitler, which resulted in the Munich Agreement.[138] Hitler's travel from Berchtesgaden beckoning to Dachau desecration was relatively short.

Many farms are on such steep slopes that I imagine farm machinery may not operate, and thus I watched a group of women and men working the fields and pitching hay in bunches to give the impression of giant birds.

Hillside farm lands   Hay stacked as if birds

---

137   If you can Google or search out MSN website, type in "Berchtesgaden." You will find an array of marvelous photos in this area and these photos are restricted, meaning certain museums and historical houses forbid the taking of pictures. I found this true while taking photos of the bog man presented in a private museum in Denmark.

138   Others in attendance were Edouard Daladier of France and Benito Mussolini of Italy. Agreement forced Czechoslovakia to give up the Sudetenland, a fifth of Czechoslovakia land. Neville declared that the agreement brought peace for our time. History declared it as one of the tragic blunders leading to WW11.

If one flew to Munich, you'd be able to rent a car and drive through some of the most sensational scenery in the world.

In the middle of the 1800's Bavaria was ruled by King Ludwig. During his reign, two castles were constructed: the Linderhof,[139] near the city of Oberammergau, and Neuschwanstein, near the city of Fussen. At the latter, King Ludwig was a great admirer of Wagner, who visited the castle. Journals read that Wagner would play the piano for hours there. The intimacy of man's experiences may not always be manifested in words. For instance King Ludwig could listen to Wagner[140] play the piano for hours as journals report. One man is playing and the other is listening and yet both communicating completely to each other through the music. Obviously the photo to the right is not taken by my camera, but I purchased a puzzle of the site, assembled it and photographed it. Neuschwaanstein Schloss/Castle serves as the model for the Walt Disney castle in Disneyland.

Neuschwaanstein

Entrance to Neuschwaanstein

Each time I go to Switzerland I do visit some of the same places. I usually drive to Ibach, a very small village noted for the Victorinox knives. I visited the factory and purchased serrated kitchen knives to give to all my friends. Those little, red

---

140   Richard Wagner (1813-1883) was an accomplished poet and composer. Some biographies suggest that his early association King Ludwig was most important for his rise in fame.

pocket knives with the Swiss cross etched on the side are popular gifts as well as an array of bread, carving, tomato and other knives. Everyone who has used them find them a valuable kitchen tool. I warned them about their use as they are extremely sharp and that I had cut myself more than once while using the knife. If you find yourself within the vicinity, do consider them as excellent souvenir gifts.

Victorinox shop	Victorinox Mfg at Ibach

Near Ibach, I stopped in Einsiedein, which is the home of a well-known Benedictine monastery, which contains the famous Black Madonna of Einsiedein. The Benedictines follow the dictates of Saint Benedict (about 480-543, C.E) and it was Benedict's plan that each monastery should be a separate organization. Followers were strong advocates of learning during the Middle Ages and no branch of art or learning was neglected. The Black Madonna is most likely a carry-over from followers known as the Black Monks. The abbey is huge and this visitor was enthralled by the beauty and magnificence of the interior, feeling akin to those I felt entering Notre Dame and Westminster Abbey.[141] Coming to places as this monastery or on entering St. Peter's in Rome is like renewing a faith in humanity. There are many rotten people in this world, and, as suggested by Emerson, humanity is an ocean, and as Gandhi phrased the idea that a few drops of the ocean are dirty doesn't make the ocean dirty.

---

141   An abbey is a building used by a religious order; i.e. Abbotsford, which later became the home of R.L. Stevenson's home in Scotland; a basilica is a building w/two rows of columns, dividing the interior into two sided aisles as the Basilica de San Francesco in Italy and burial spot of St. Francis; a cathedral is officially the seat of a bishop.

Swiss mountain passes

Each time I revisit Meiringen I drive across the Brunig Pass, which is another scenic drive. While staying at the Sherlock Holmes Hotel,[142] I had the opportunity to drive across three well known passes in one day: the Sustan, the Grimsel, and the Furka. These three passes have very high points where one gets breath-taking views; I noticed at times my leg shaking, making an unsteady flow of gas. When that occurs I realize I am driving at a risky elevation and sight-seeing must stay in the background so I can give full attention to my driving.

Life size

Bulle has a large market place dealing with Gruyere cheese, and it logically follows that there will be a cattle fair. Cows have been a love in my life. They provided me with an income when renting out my acreage would not even pay my taxes. My collection of photos or miniature cows methinks unusual. I've included some here. The cow to the left is in full

142   For photos see p. 179.

size; compare the background. The cow to the right is the size of a cream pitcher.

Cream pitcher size

Near Wildhaus lies the town of Altdorf; probably one of the most celebrated towns of all Switzerland because as history relates William Tell allegedly shot an arrow through an apple on his son's head, thus becoming the symbol of Swiss independence.

William Tell statue at Altdork

All towns have various town symbols. Bern, for instance, lies on the banks of the Aare River and received its name because Berthold V, Duke of Zahringen, named the place after the first animal he slew. And The Bear of Bern became this city's trademark. The photo is one of the many marvelous fountains one finds while traveling throughout the country. Bern is the place where you may catch daily tours of varying duration in this region. You may also catch a bus to the funicular railway stations.

Having toured Switzerland, Liechtenstein, and Bavaria at least twelve times, I can testify that I never tired driving over hill and dale. What? Hill?

The Bern fountain

Methinks there are hardly much of hill; it's more likely to be Mountains and dales, if you please. You betcha! You may conclude that I love the place. Unusual and grand views are common place. I cannot remember exactly the village, but it is one typical of the Tyrolean Alps. I do love to travel here. Travel here may be a childish delight in just being somewhere else. In Switzerland there is not only grand scenery, comfortable hotels, English is spoken and understood most everywhere but also there are clean restroom facilities. Such is a necessity for this aging woman.

Traveling through Tyrolean Alps

Chapter Twenty-One:

Australia

Australia is a continent with roughly 1,800,000 square miles of land. U.S. has 3,500,000 square miles of land, but this includes Alaska, which is not too far off 600,000 square miles of land. U.S. has a population of approximately 270,000,000 people. At the time of my visits we're talking about only 18,000,000 people. When you think of California with its 33,000,000 you may conclude that Australia is sparsely populated.[143] And then again you have 70 percent of its land space that is entirely arid. That great wide center of Australia can be basically described as a desert. I've made seven tours during this latter stage of my life. Too many days were spent with spacious and monotonous driving. I learned its better to fly to an area and enjoy your surroundings whatever that may be. Like areas of Europe, I found people most friendly and eager to discuss the affairs of the day and assist me in any way they can.

In February 1993 and through my brother's urging, I planned a South Pacific tour and flew to Cairns for a trip out to the Great Barrier Reef. Cairns is located in the Northern area of Queensland. I rented a

---

143   Accuracy has no point; my figures here are approximate and are only to suggest comparisons.

car and began a search for suitable accommodations; I finally settled on the Coral Towers, where I rented a very spacious, self-contained apartment. There were two bedrooms, a living room, dining room, bathroom with a tub and shower and an extra stainless sink if you wanted to wash clothes. There was also a washer and dryer for my personal use. The furniture consisted of 2 chairs, a couch, beds, a glass top dining table with chairs; the kitchen was furnished with every thing you would need to cook, bake and eat a meal. There were two sliding doors, one in each bedroom to allow me to walk out on balconies for a 360 degree view of the Bay and the nearby hills. The cost to rent this unit was very reasonable, especially when you translate it into US dollars. The cost of the unit was $65 Australian, which translated to $44.00 U.S. The location was convenient for parking the car, and easy to drive in either direction to other places in the area.

It was hot and humid in Cairns and one thing I noticed is that when you first get into the car with the windows having been left open, the number of bugs was a nuisance; but once you turn on the air conditioner, they suddenly disappear. From then on, I became conscious of parking in a cool place or under shade whenever possible. Shopping for everything was convenient; particularly at the store Woolworth, which are located most everywhere. Woolworth in Australia meant that you shopped there for not only groceries but you may find just about everything we imagine you could buy at the U.S. version of my childhood. Woolworth eventually went out of business and became K-Mart in the U.S.

While driving on the back roads I found a few produce stands where I bought the most delicious, fresh pineapple and watermelon. In this particular area peanuts are grown and they seemed to be larger than normal. From the first day I began placing all food items in the refrigerator away from any attempt by bugs to encroach on my food supply. In going thru small towns I had the impression that the buildings reminded me of the 1940s. In the out of the way places, some roads are quite narrow and an approaching car would have to ride on the shoulder to pass.

Most tourists who come for an experience on the Great Barrier Reef take advantage of visiting the rain forest park at Kuranda. You may take

a short tour on the Kuranda train, for it's better than a walk through a humid forest. Birds fly about and pathways are often well established wooden walks. There are many opportunities to experience rain forest parks and like the others, Kuranda is well planned/ developed for tourists. You may purchase anything and every-

Barron Falls

thing relating to products made here in Australia. Opal jewelry abounds. You may purchase the stones and bring them home without a duty tax and then have them placed in a setting designed by yourself or your favorite jeweler. There are a number of Djabugay, the local aboriginal people, who engage tourists into purchases or having your photograph taken with them. The train stops at the Barron Falls, which is spectacular, not for its great height but for the amount of unrestrained rush of water over the falls. Again thoughts of a dynamic nature gave this tourist a reflection of unrestrained energy. One of the stop-me-dead incidents was the time I noticed a snake on one of the branches above a river boat cruise on the Barron River. I firmly decided that I would not take that tour. No! There is no thrill of witnessing a python in his/ her environment.

I came here for an experience on the Great Barrier Reef. There are so many tours to accommodate thousands who come to Australia for just this prize of viewing animal life that abounds on reefs. I selected a short tour to Green Island, which was overrated when I compare the tourist brochure with what is actually there. Green Island has sandy beaches, but you have either to rent snorkel and fins and breathing tube and venture forth or hire a professional to guide you safely onto reefs. I was disappointed in the Green Island day, but others who took first class accommodations on Green Island have told me otherwise. My view is that it is a very small island and nothing to keep my attention.

On a second return to Cairns area in 1994, I drove up to Port Douglas, perhaps a smaller town than Cairns but the number of shops and cafes, bars, and obvious luxurious resort complexes run to full capacity, which tells me that a great number of people prefer Port Douglas over Cairns. Perhaps it is because of the sandy beaches and then perhaps it is because it is also the main departure point for Quicksilver, a major Great Barrier Reef. And it was Quicksilver that I chose for another venture into snorkeling. This was a luxurious ship which took tourists out to a reef area and anchored. There was a ledge on the side of the ship where you could dive into the water and explore the coral reefs. Seeing billions of hard shell life piled upon one another where sudden steep chasms reveal, in some instances, hundreds of fish of various sizes darting in and out among the caverns and from one another was a fascinating view. Other animal life belonging to the Porifera or sponge family enchanted my imagination. For a moment in the recesses of my mind, I made a wish that, if I came back reincarnated into another life, my second choice would be a one of these brilliantly colorful fish feasting on whatever energized their tastes.

Quicksilver Reef

The ship personnel loaned me a wet suit and even a life vest; I wasn't acquainted with using either, so did not do much in the way of snorkeling. I can swim and I swim regularly at home in the Courthouse exercise pool. But swimming over and about a reef when I am not familiar with currents and everything else that goes with swimming in an ocean that is not absolutely calm for this near 70-year old lady arouses problems of remaining calm. My venture with the Great Barrier Reef was short lived. By the way, I found getting out of a wet suit was more difficult than I could imagine. Personnel of the cruise ship also gave us tourist an opportunity to go on their submersible sub with ample windows to look closer at reefs.

On my return to Cairns from Port Douglas, I obtained accommodation at the Coral Towers, meaning a self contained unit for $65 Australian (equates with $48 U.S.). I didn't need all this room, but when I can afford it, why not live it up. And I did. My intent on this visit was to rent a car and drive from Cairns to Brisbane on the Bruce Highway, which is about 1800 kilometers or 1,100 miles. Cairns is in the northern part of Queensland while Brisbane is in the most southern part. This is a long drive for this old woman.

On my second day at Coral Towers, I drove to Atherton Tableland. The highest point of this area is about 3,000 feet above sea level. The combination of rainfall, cooler temperatures and fertile soil creates one of Australia's better farm areas. I was aware of a number of produce stands where you can buy fresh pineapple, watermelon and other mature fruits that have that delightful sweet taste. The town of Atherton itself reminded me of any U.S. town that still carries the characteristics of buildings in the 1930s. On driving down from the tableland back to my motel, I encountered unbelievable and magnificent views of the Cairns area and the waters indicative of the Great Barrier Reef coastline. This was not a heavily populated area and most tourists generally stay on the coast, so roads here were only a two lane highway; in fact, at times you had to ride the shoulder when cars were passing. I had to keep reminding myself, "Stay alert, girl."

It was on a Sunday when I arrived in Townsville. Here was one of the best beachfronts that I encountered in my drive. This area is quite popular with the Aussies because they can either hire boats to take them to individual Whitsunday Islands or join a flight to take you to some other islands in the Coral Sea Islands Territory. It's a beautiful spot and worth a visit. Townsville was founded about the time of our Civil War by Robert Towns, who initiated the practice of "blackbirding,"[144] which means kidnapping South Pacific islanders and bringing them to Australia for cheap labor. From an odd selection of reading, I came across this English novelist who wrote upon labor...

> Remember, you have to work. Whether you handle a pick or a pen, digging ditches or edition a paper, ringing an auction bell or writing funny things— you must work. If you look around, you will see the men who are the most able to live and are the ones later in life who can in the rest of their days without work are the men who work the hardest. Don't be afraid of killing yourself with overwork. It is beyond your power to do that on the sunny side of thirty. So find out what you want to be, and do, and take off your coat, and make a dust in the world.[145]

I still chuckle when I see his phrase "on the sunny side of thirty." Travel is a great educator and I advise everyone to do as much as he/ she can. I would never have known what "blackbirding" was unless I came to Townsville.

After driving 817 kilometers (about 507) miles, I found motel accommodations in Mackay. Beach front accommodations are not always easy to find, especially if you commence looking so late in the day. Everything was fine until, for some reason, I woke up early

---

144   Blackbirding practices haven't disappeared altogether; to attain cheap laborers, there were some CEOs, namely a famous shoe manufacturer who persuaded Asians to come work for them by saying they would be sent to the U.S. and then put them on Guam or one of the previously owned Trust Territory Islands.

145   Charles Reade (1814-1884); educated for the bar, but became successful writing plays and novelist, which depicted/exposed social abuses of his time. The better play and later a novel was *Masks and Faces* (1852).

and found my motel room had visitors; unwelcomed visitors. Ants! Hundreds! No, thousands of them. I didn't take the time to count. I just packed up and left at 4:30 in the morning.

I don't know why we have never taken the time to switch over to the metric system. Kilometers to miles means you multiply the kilometers by .62137 to get the miles. For guessing purposes on the road I'd just multiply them by .6 and put the decimal point in or, more often than not, dropped the last numbers; such was close enough for me.

After leaving MacKay, I noticed innumerable cattle in the fields. I did stop in the town of Rockhampton, which is called the cattle capital of Australia. I was a retired rancher and my interest has not faded with the passing of years, and I just had to take photos of

Rockhampton cow statues

the statues of steers signifying that cattle has a special recognition in this part of Australia. Rockhampton is also on the Tropic of Capricorn.

Driving south from Cairns all the way to Maryborough on the Bruce Highway may be called a secondary road as most places of the highway maintain a lane for each direction. Towns were rather far apart. I was pleased when I came to a town, so I could stop, have something to eat, or

Surfers' Paradise

just to get out of the car and walk around a bit; "pleased" sprang to "elated" when I found a Woolworth store to buy food or browse at a sundry of other goods. Traffic picked up at Maryborough.

The areas of Surfers' Paradise north and south of

Brisbane are apparently popular tourist areas even for the Aussies. North of Brisbane is the Sunshine Coast and south is the Gold Coast. Rather than staying in Brisbane, I preferred the water's edge and delighted in the breezes and view from my motel in Surfers' Paradise, where there were block after block of motel units and, again, an endless rush of waves rushing to plant wet kisses on a blonde beach.

On my second—or was it the fourth—I planned that trip to drive almost the entire length of Queensland to New South Wales near Murwillumbah. The coastal drive was scenic and the resort towns offered coastal accommodations within short distances to the beaches and intermittently accommodated many shops. I was paying roughly $15 a night, and as you can imagine these motels did not offer the best in accommodations. With a little more money the traveler can advance to the grand scale. Observing from a high rise motel window, room lights from the numerous sky high apartment buildings makes a dramatic setting. Time passed quickly and soon it was time for me to drive back to Brisbane and catch a flight to New Zealand for my remaining holiday (covered in chapter 17).

In the 1999 tour, I flew from Bisbane to Melbourne. I stayed there only a couple of days as my guide book called it the Garden City of Australia. My initial accommodations were terrible and this set the tone of my attitude about Melbourne. My room was very small and dark; you could only see the outside if you stood on a chair. I knew right away that I couldn't stay, so changed accommodations to the Park Royal Hotel, which was a block or so away. And even with the switch into better accommodations, Melbourne was too large a city for me to cope. My dissatisfaction of Melbourne was probably due to a lack of studying Victoria province before I arrived. So I changed my plans and flew to Hobart, Tasmania, an island south of Melbourne on the Bass Strait. The length and width of Tasmania is about a third the size of Oregon.

According to my guide book, this island was named after an early Dutch explorer named Abel Tasman (1642). As in other areas of Australia, Tasmania has a history of containing British convicts during the 1800s and continued on until the 1850s. Remains of the prison system can be seen at Port Arthur, located at the southern tip of the Tasmania Peninsula. There is a museum and theater where they show a film about how the prison was built and maintained. This silent film was made in 1927 on the same grounds where the prison was located; the film received historical recognition for its content. The museum provides a system where family names are recorded if one were interested in tracing a nefarious ancestor.

With a rented car and a week to explore, I started my reconnoitering of Tasmania. Tasmania is a scenic and hilly island, especially the coast. As I drove I was careful not to drive on unsealed roads as insurance only covered driving on sealed/paved roads. A third of the 26,000 square miles of island land is protected as a World Heritage area, which means that all four of the criteria to be eligible under World Heritage are met: geological period including the Ice Age are here, wide range of plants unique to the island, and is home of some of the oldest trees, and well represented of caves, some of which are the longest in the world.

My stop in Bicheno offered terrible accommodations but the great fish dinner at the waterfront made the stop worthwhile. Bicheno is a good vacation spot for anglers. It also includes the Douglas Apsley National Park, which has a dry sclerophyll forest.[146] There are also patches of rain forest as well as superb marriage views of land and water.

It was Valentine's Day and I will always carry fond memories of celebrating this day with my husband. When I stopped in a tearoom in Derby for refreshments, I had with me a package of See's chocolate heart candies. I went to every table wishing them a Happy Valentine's Day by giving one and all a specially wrapped chocolate heart. This little gesture was smilingly accepted, but I think some patrons were a little surprised that this old lady went around this tea cafe bringing an unexpected salutation on a day that evidently was not as important as it was to me and, for the most part, other Americans.

---

146   (ski lēr/ ∂ fil' ē) it's a rather unusual development of supportive and protective tissue in the leaves.

I stopped in Launceston as it was a larger city and had an attractive shopping area. Situated on the Tomar River, it has an ambience of older buildings and riverside walks. There are ample craft galleries. In Tasmania they had discount stores called Chicken Feed and Peanuts. They are much like our Dollar Store in the States.

I drove along the coast for the most part of my tour of Tasmania, and I found many places one can stop on the coastal area for pictures of absolutely magnificent scenery. Experiencing warmer temperatures here on this island, I started wearing shorts until I noticed that I had an unusual insect bite on my thigh, so I changed back to slacks.

On my second or third day of driving, I noticed a sign that indicated it was a scenic drive, and in the beginning it was scenic. Then the road became a terribly narrow, steep unsealed road so I decided to turn around and go back. This became a challenge as there was so little room, I had to inch by inch reverse and move forward until I finally got turned around and returned to the paved highway. My insurance coverage would have been invalid should I have encountered an accident. No sense in taking a chance of financial ruin.

I toured around the Island to see as much of Tasmania as possible since it offered so much in the way of scenery. I would check into a hotel and drive around a different local area each day. Many towns have a sign posted on the road indicating this was one of the Tidy Towns of Tasmania; they used the word "tidy" to emphasize that their town was very neat/clean.

While in Tasmania I had my first experience staying in a Caravan Park. And there at Wynyard, I rented a villa which was self-contained with two bedrooms, living room with a TV, and bath. I also had my own private washer and dryer. The cost was $45 Australian, which translated into $26 U.S. The last couple of days were spent in Hobart where I would be catching a flight to Christchurch on the South Island of New Zealand (covered in chapter 17).

Often in a lifetime, you visit a place and it becomes special in your memory. Switzerland is one example, and now it was Australia. I returned four more times because the Australians were special people—all derivatives of the English hospitality and friendliness that I found in my teaching career in England in the fall of 1954. There were other reasons, of course; i.e. the American dollar translated 25 percent discount on just about everything; this was a drop from 50 percent in 1992. Another was that the areas I wished to visit had a sparse population outside the larger cities and I could still drive a car.

In my 2000 visit I ran into complications that I didn't expect. My flight out of Portland was delayed and by the time I arrived in San Francisco, my flight to Australia had left. It was United Airlines fault and they had to find accommodations for me until the next flight. I was told by United that no rooms were available in San Francisco, and they would have to fly me to Los Angeles for accommodations and then fly me the next day to Australia. I did not expect this and my luggage was already checked in so they provided me with a utility bag having necessary items. I did not have clothes with me so I washed everything I wore and slept in my birthday suit at my accommodations at Wyndham Hotel near the airport in Los Angeles. I improvised by making slippers with the extra wash cloths; there are precautions to be considered by the older senior. I also used the hair dryer in the morning to remove all dampness left in the clothes I washed the night before.

That evening I was flown by United to Brisbane where I planned to spend a few days. I did not rent a car, as I planned to stay in the Brisbane area and a car would not be necessary. Brisbane is a delightful city; my hotel was in a very convenient location being a block from the center of town. I had a tremendous view of the city day or night from the window of my hotel room.

Brisbane is densely populated: third after Sydney and Melbourne with at least 1.5 million people situated on this east coast of Australia. It was the governor of New South Wales, Sir Thomas Brisbane, in 1823, who gave the city its name. In the same year, Sir Brisbane was searching for a more secure incarceration for British convicts. Names of streets for the salad days of Brisbane were unique: streets running north-south are named for queens and princesses; streets running east-west are named for kings and princes.

The Queen Street Mall was only two blocks away from my hotel, and this street is designated for pedestrians only. Restaurants are in the middle section with many different kinds of shops on both sides of this wide street. Victoria Bridge was only two blocks away in a different direction. There were two wide walkways on each side of the bridge with entirely different scenic views of Brisbane, and all the more scenic at night. At one end of the Brisbane Bridge was Queen's Mall, and on the other side was South Park, which had decorous walkways with the many flowers of the Botanical Gardens and fountains. The Brisbane River skirts the city on three sides. On weekends the area became an open market with numerous vendors selling attractive hand crafted items.

The Brisbane Ferry, called City Cat, operates along the Brisbane River and provides great views of Brisbane and the water front properties. The all day fare was $4, and a round trip takes about two hours, making frequent stops to allow passengers off and on. It was truly a great way to see parts of Brisbane and the waterfront properties.

During these late years of my life I wanted to do something most people wouldn't consider and that was to be able to swim in the buff. So, when I decided to return to Australia in 2002, I researched places where this might be possible. I saw an ad in a travel brochure that listed a hotel with private pools. It was built by the Versace family and was located in Main Beach near Surfers Paradise on the Gold Coast south of Brisbane.

I called the Versace Hotel from Salem to inquire if this was possible, and they assured me it was.

Now that I was in Brisbane, I thought I finally would have this fantasy come true. From Brisbane Airport I rented a car and

Versace Hotel

drove south to the Gold Coast. Their reception process at the Versace was different than most hotels; however, I had made a reservation for two days, and was readily checked in and led to my room. The room was furnished with quality furniture but not designed for comfort for my taste; it was difficult to open the closet, draw the drapes and even use the TV because the doors on the cabinet did not open wide enough to view the TV except from the bed. I was disappointed to learn that they did not offer the use of the pool by myself so I could swim in the buff as other residents would also be using the pool at the same time. I am still searching for the opportunity before I leave this world.

On my return to Brisbane, Adelaide was the next city to visit. It is the capital city for the Southern Australia state. My hotel was within walking distance to the city center, which is bordered by beautiful parks. When Adelaide was planned it was designed to have much open space and parks. It was founded and colonized on the premise solely by land sales. No convicts were transported here. Adelaide's economy is based on agriculture and mining as well as manufacturing cars and household appliances. A city tour included a short cruise on the Torrens River, a chocolate factory, Parliament buildings and a glimpse of some of the luxury homes. I noticed a porch or veranda on most homes, which is a way to reduce the cost of air conditioning.

Rundle is the main shopping area and within walking distance from my hotel. While browsing in Woolworth, I bought a second battery-operated toothbrush. The price was not obvious nor did the bar code reveal the price, so the manager asked me what I would pay for it. I said I would give him $5 dollars and he remarked, "Sold." Translated to US dollars would be about $2.50. This is one item I would recommend when traveling as a must and an easy way to brush one's teeth. Methinks enjoyment comes from a bargain toothbrush.

My tour to Lofty Mountain (2,385 ft in elevation) was disappointing as it was too hazy to see the scenery. Just below the peak, there is a park where you can meet some distinct natives to Australia: the emu, kangaroo, and the koala as well as a walk through an aviary. Hahndorf is a little village settled by people from Germany in 1839[147] who were escaping from religious persecution in their homeland. Captain Dirk Hahn was their leader. As you may surmise, architecture of town buildings and shops are typically in the German style. Tourists may hire a horse drawn carriage for a tour of the town.

Instead of taking any more city tours, I hired a car and driver to show me the sights around the outskirts of Adelaide. He drove down the coast as well as visiting the Wirra Wirra Winery, where I took photos of the very attractive entrance way. The countryside is a decorous green and scenic with the grapes on the vines everywhere. It's much like our wine country around Napa, Sonoma, Healdsburg and other excellent wine areas of northern California. I was told that there were more than 50 wineries in this Barossa and Eden valleys that produce excellent wines. Wine is the blood of grapes.[148] I am amused with Judah Al-Harizi's remarks that wine is an unreliable emissary.

I send it down to my stomach and it went to my head.[149]

Back in Adelaide and in the middle of Victoria Square, I rode a trolley to the seashore town of Gleneg, which has many tourist shops and a wonderful beach. The Fleurieu Peninsula is much exposed to southern ocean and contains long expanses of sand, areas of sheltered bays as well as stark cliffs. It's a place where a tourist can run out of film; that is, if you're using a camera using film. I switched much later in my life to the Olympus that used cartridges.

On Sundays the farmers come to an area near my hotel known as the Central Market, a picturesque river setting and farmers sell their home grown fruit and veggies. They start early and by noon or a little thereafter they start selling all they have left for less than half price; I

---

147   In 1939 Prussia initiated a law restricting child labor to only 10 hours per day.

148   Genesis 49:11

149   Al-Harizi (1165-1225) besides a rabbi, translator, poet and traveler was one of the last great personalities of the "Golden Age" of Jewish culture in Spain.

was able to purchase some fresh, sweet, seedless grapes at a price lower than that offered in stores.

My visit to Australia this tour was to include Alice Springs that is located just north of South Australia in the state of Northern Territories. Alice Springs was made popular through the sitcom dealing with the character and pride of its people amid the struggles arising in the background of WWII. It was an excellent BBC series. Anyway, up to now the weather was not hot in Adelaide—just comfortably warm. When I arrived in Alice Springs, there was a notable change in temperature. Hot, I tell you it was hot. Alice Springs reminded me of towns you would find in Eastern Oregon on any July or August day.

Fortunately for me, my hotel was within walking distance to city center. It was too hot to walk much and I didn't even think of walking up Anzac Hill; so I hired a taxi to take me. Anzac is a name that is used frequently in Australia, and it stands for Australia New Zealand Army Corp. They celebrate Anzac Day here like we do Veterans Day in the states. Anzac Hill is at the northern end of the town and has a fine view of the MacDonnell Range, where layers of rock, which, according to my guide book, are evidences of a mountain

MacDonnell Range

range that perhaps equaled the Himalayas, but now some 300 million years old. I find trying to grasp these vast time periods puzzling. What I'm trying to say is that taking the Biblical interpretation of creation is not the 24-hour period that I daily must live with. The fleeting of years expands my mind to another dimension of realizing that all this energy /exertions of my life will rightfully join Emerson's concept of his view of the Oversoul. Clarity is only momentarily there and dissipates into fuzziness.

With all my trips to Australia about the same time of year, I finally learned that there were three days for holidays in April and May: Easter, Anzac and Mother's day, which means many stores are closed, and became an inconvenience for a tourist like myself.

I was impressed when I read a story in the newspaper about the Clarke family during World War 11. A Mother had eleven sons that served in the military, and the government made a special brooch with eleven stars for this mother. This is the kind of story that Hollywood could pay attention to. Imagine having eleven sons serving during WW 11: four were in the RAF, four in the army, and three in the navy. The most significant outcome of this story is that all eleven sons survived the war.

I flew from Adelaide to Alice Springs and it was a 55 minute flight from Alice Springs to Ayers Rock. They do not use the name of Ayers Rock any-more as the Aborigines now have ownership, and it is called the Uluru-Kata Tjuta National Park. My photos here is just Uluru. Upon my arrival at the park, a private shuttle was provided to take me to a multi-million dollar complex, which had several different ac-commodations varying in prices. I had a reservation at the Lost Camel,

Uluru

which was in the medium price accommodations. My room was very modern and equipped with a tape deck, coffee maker and stainless steel cups and saucers.

Behind the Lost Camel was a common shopping complex, which all guests

Lost Camel

could use; it consisted of a photo shop, travel information, take-away fast food shop, a restaurant with a bar, several souvenirs shops, grocery store, and a post office.

The most recognizable symbol of Australia is to my view Sydney's Opera House, but Ayers Rock or, as Australians are insistent now to take the name those aborigines call it, Uluru. There are tourists who come here to make the climb of Uluru, but conditions are not the best because it's a mile chain/rope pathway 1.6 Kilometers. This is not for me. I'd rather wait for them to install a cable car as they have for Stone Mountain, a monolith just outside of Atlanta. The aborigines have posted signs not to climb the mountain as it is considered sacred to them. The 36 domes of Kata Tjuta are behind Uluru.

Kata Tjuta

And as I have previously stated, the whole area is sacred to the aborigines. My guide book stated that in 1985 the area was handed back to the indigenous owners, and now run jointly with the local Anangu people and the Australian government. Anyone can opt to take the sunset tour, which I did. The bus drove to the main section of the park and drove completely around the rock which is about 9 kilometers. Our guide told us that six kilometers of Ayers Rock is beneath the surface. Our tour group was parked in an area where we could watch the sun go down to view the changing colors of the Rock in the process. While waiting for changes in sunset, the bus driver and personnel had arranged for passengers to have a snack with champagne, wine or soda. The color ranged from deep red at sunrise to a deep coral during the day.

At sunset it changes to a red and in the night a tone of black, a shiny black, after a rain I'm told. There was no rain while I was here. The photograph of Kata Tjuta is not a good replica as I have tried to piece two photographed sections of the rock together.

Perth

My flight from Ayers Rock to Perth was a little longer than my previous flights. Perth is considered the most isolated city in the world. And I suppose it is when compared with the eastern coast of Australia. The Swan River cuts through the east and south sides of the city and facilitates parks or what I call green belts. In Perth, I rented a suite at the Gateway Hotel, which consisted of a bedroom, living room with a balcony, kitchen and bath. The location of the hotel was within walking distance to the town center and Swan River. I opted to take a wine cruise. The small boat seemed to have only one deck and designed with windows so you could have an unrestricted view of both sides of the Swan River. Since it was a wine cruise, wine in a carafe was set on each table for six passengers. We were served a delicious buffet dinner.

Up the river we made a stop at the Olive Farm Winery to taste the different kinds of wines they made. On the way back, the scenery seemed more beautiful; ah, yes, I'd say wine does make the world a little rosier. We were served a delicious dessert, and there was live music. Passengers were invited to dance. I had not been on the dance floor for years, but I was game to make a fool of myself with another passenger at our table who invited this now 78-year-old lady to dance. We tried our best to put on a good show, and evidently we did because we received a polite round of applause. Corry, my partner, was a good many years younger than I. This event became a memory that will not easily fade from whatever on-coming years I have left in life. It's the kind of memory that Mark Twain says will drag you away from your troubles—by the ears, heels or any other way you may manage. The retired couple, Joan and Corry Stenta, who live in Sydney area, became more than just fellow travelers; they were unique travel companions during this short wine cruise tour. They also invited me to visit them if and whenever I came to Sydney. And I did.

Joan & Corry Stenta

Freemantel is a lovely coastal town south of Perth; population is sparse and downtown section is small enough to walk around the city center. There are historic buildings and a huge market; one that is large enough to have about a hundred vendors selling fresh fruit and vegetables, and handmade items. One nice thing is that you can ride the bus around the city free. I took it to see a little more of the city other than the city center.

While touring Freemantle, I decided to take the Ferry to Rottnest Island, which is one of the most popular destinations for the Australians and tourists. When the ferry docked at the pier, I was surprised to see so many bicycles that passengers had brought with them. Rottnest is a biker's paradise as no cars are allowed on the island. I chose to take the Bayseeker Bus which completely encircles the island taking passengers with or without bikes and surfboards to various coves and locations to have a picnic or to hike near the beach.

The island gets its name from a mar-
supial called Quokka by the Aborigines.
Some say it has the appearance of a larger
cat. My guide book says that when Wil-
lem de Vlamingh[150] first visited the island
at the end of the 17th century (1696), he
noted the Quokka and thought it a species of the rat and concluded the island

Quokka

was a rat's nest. Thus, this island was named Rottnest Island.[151]

My flight from Perth to Darwin was a long flight. Darwin is the
capital of the Top End province/state of the Northern Territory. It is rather
sparsely populated compared to other capital cities in Australia. It is closer
to Singapore than it is to Sydney. In 1839, when the British captain John
Lort Stokes, commander of *HMS Beagle*, sailed into the tropical harbor
here, he named it after his friend Charles Darwin. And one of the reasons
for me to come here in the first place was to satisfy my curiosity of visiting
a place where Darwin explored and his theory was forthcoming into
fruition. Somewhere back in my mind I vividly recalled my Aunt Blanche
in confrontation with my grandfather about his collection of National
Geographic that lauded the Darwin theory of evolution versus a more
Baptist strict interpretation of the 6-day creation. Coming here then was
not to come to a far-away place with a familiar sounding name, but to
satisfy a curiosity that invoked thought.

Upon arriving, I instantly noticed a change in the weather, as it was
not only hot but humid. I had to walk outside from reception to get to
my room and even in this short distance I felt the heat intensely. And
walking distance to town center was short; however, it seemed long
when you felt the heat. In browsing the various stores, I appreciated the
air cooling systems that provided refuge from the oppressive heat.

---

150   De Vlamingh (1640-1698) was a Dutch sea captain who explored SE Australia. In
      1696, he commanded a rescue mission to the Australian west coast to look for survivors
      of the *Ruddershap* that vanished 2 years earlier.

151   The quokka photo is one by Hesperian and dtd 11/25/09. Obtainment of quokka file
      is licensed under the Creative Commons Attribution 3.0; permission CC-BY-3.0

Two tours took my interest while I was here in Darwin. The first one was to the Museum of Aboriginal Art, which included a maritime section displaying different size boats the natives used in the history of Darwin as well as the exhibit on carvings of aboriginal burial poles, which are used in place of tombstones. The bark paintings were unique and fascinating. My guide book stated the exhibition on regional aboriginal art and culture is considered to be the best in the world. This tour also included many of the harbor areas and one in particular was very attractive with sandy beaches, which, as our guide related to us that people do not use it because the crocodiles claim it as their own. At this particular shore, Australians hunt for the crocodiles once a year and catch over a hundred, and move them to a different location to thin out their prolific reproduction. And I shuddered at the reminder of having to meet here a descendent of "Sweetheart," the 16 ft stuffed crocodile exhibited in the museum.

The second tour was a sunset cruise on the Timor Sea, where we were taken far enough away to watch the sun go down over the city of Darwin. I was a little apprehensive on this boat tour just thinking about all those *sweetheart* crocodile descendents that must be swimming in these waters. Nothing really happened as you can tell that I survived my anxieties. Just north of Darwin are the Tiwi Islands of which the largest is named after Melville.[152]

The Tiwi people/aboriginals have maintained their culture intact and separate from the mainliner aboriginals. One example is the burial poles where the qualities of the deceased are inscribed. Melville in his various books[153] deals with a variety of experiences with these Melanesians, whom some may say do not possess the best qualities by Christian standards, but

---

152   In trying to relate Melville's history to his present honor of an island named after him by the Australians is a stretch of my imagination. In chapter 12 of *Moby Dick*, Queequeg (for which there is much symbolism imbedded with his characterization) states he's from Rokovoko Island, which is obviously fictional. Melville's tour as a whale man aboard the Acushet jumped ship on the island of Nukahiva, which is part of the Ills Wallis (a part of French Polynesia).

153   Those that deal with island people and experiences were in *Typee* and *Omoo, 1847.*

by examining Queequeg you have a definition of a fine fellow. Ishmael honors him much. In this Top End of Australia, one-third of the people are aboriginals and they own fifty percent of the land.

Darwin's history includes bombing and it was heavily damaged during the Second World War by the Japanese. In 1947, cyclone Tracy almost completely destroyed the city. Like all havoc reaped upon an area such as this, came forth a modern Darwin. It's definitely a place to visit.

The last big metropolis I visited was Sydney, which is probably the most visited city in Australia, and it is certainly its largest. Aside from the Aborigines,[154] the early settlers were convicts shipped from England. Perhaps not as many as in other locales of Australia, but nevertheless, Sydney has a share. Convicts were sent to Australia in the late 1700's, and they continued to come for another 100 years. Some of the Australians can trace their heritage back to these early settlers since we're talking about a relatively short history of a little over 200 years ago. I had a favorite hotel, the Radisson on Liverpool Street that was conveniently located within walking distance to city center and Chinatown. And I used this hotel in my return visits in 2003, 2004, and 2006. In checking in at the Radisson, I would inquire for a room on the lower floors since the episode in the Amada Hotel in Singapore where I got stuck in the elevator, weighed heavily on my mind. I shun renting those rooms that are above the 2nd floor.

My second floor room had a balcony and from there I could watch pedestrians and the Monorail which passed at eye level about every 15 minutes. There were facilities in the room to make coffee and you had use of a small refrigerator. The Radisson was most conveniently located. Across the street I could enter the Chinatown District. In another direction I was two short blocks from George Street and another two blocks to the city center.

Usually, when I visit a city for the first time, I try to book a structured day tour to get an overview, and then explore the city on my own. In

---

154   References suggest at least as much as 40,000 years ago.

Sydney, this tour included The Rocks, Circular Quay, Darling Harbor, Macquarie's Chair, Opera House, Harbor Bridge, government buildings and Bondi Beach.

If there is any large city of Australia that I had a great affinity for, it is Sydney. Not only because of the hotel conveniently placed for me— a stone's throw from Darling Harbor where restaurants and cafes abound—but also for the great convenience of using public transportation to get around the city and its surrounding satellite towns. Purchasing a city pass permits the tourist to use the subway or underground train service, street cars, buses and ferries. It did not include the above ground monorail train circling the main area of the city; this transportation was a separate service charge. So, with the next succeeding three visits, I had ample time to explore this tourist friendly city.

During this first tour of the city and surrounding area I wondered how the early settlers managed to get around with so much water everywhere, a city of harbors. But with such a fine harbor, smaller crafts were used in these earlier colonial days as they are used now. And then again there were not that many people to be concerned. Barracks, hospital, church, bastions of civic power were basically all located in the area of Mrs. Macquarie's garden/farm lands.

The Macquarie Chair was cut out of a rock cliff for Mrs. Macquarie to sit and view her garden and a wonderful view of Sydney Bay and particularly Farm Cove. Elizabeth Macquarie's rock is situated on the right point of Sydney's Botanical Gardens. She was the wife of the governor during the early part of the 19th century, and it was she who insisted that a road be built in her area in 1816. If she could sit there today when I visited her rock chair,

Macquarie's chair

she'd have one grand view of one of Australia's grandest symbols, the Sydney Opera House.

The Botanical Gardens is an area that basically surrounds Farm Cove; to the right of the cove, where Mrs. Macquarie's chair rests, is an

Banyon tree

area called the Domain, and this was acreage set aside for the first governor's private use. In the Domain area, there is a gorgeous banyan tree and on Macquarie Street were some of the oldest surviving public buildings; this street also is where the Art Gallery, New South Wales museum is located. Picasso's *Nude in a Rocking Chair* is housed here, but one must have permission from U.S. representative from the Picasso Administration, ARS (Artist Rights Service) before inclusion in this text. Anyway, I'm told its symbolism depicts the struggle between man and woman. I can't help but chuckle at this less than serious art. I'm revealing how naïve I am

Sydney's art museum   Les Demoiselles d'Avignon

about Picasso, but nevertheless, art that reflects just chunks of thought does not deserve the high price given for this man's art regardless whether his painting ranks among the highest ever paid. *Les Demoiselles d'Avignon* was completed in 1907. Les Demoiselles d'Avignon photo above indicate Picasso's African influences and the two ladies on the left suggest the beginning of his Cubism. A copy of *Les Demoiselles* first appeared in the May 1910 edition of the *Architectural Record*, a U.S. publication.[155] *Nude in Rocking* Chair was painted in 1956 and obtained by Art Gallery of New South Wales in 1981.[156] Picasso's most famous work is of the Spanish Civil War titled Guernica (1937), and the viewer can readily reflect on war thoughts of inhumanity, brutality and despair. Personally I prefer looking at the humanity expressed by Norman Rockwell than something by Picasso. Anyway, the garden here is well worth the walk. I have never seen so

Botanical Gardens bats   Botanical Gardens cockatoos

many bats hanging upside down among other tropical foliage and so many cockatoos outside a pet shop. There is also a café suitable for a cold plate lunch in one of the arms branching out to various sections of the garden.

The replica of Ill Porcellino

If you visit the inner courtyard of the historic hospital here, there is a fountain where *Ill Porcellino* (pig/hog) sits in the center and I swear it is a replica of the one in Florence at Mercato Nuovo.[157] The photo here is the one in Florence. Rub his

---

155   Picasso: 25 Oct. 1881—8 April 1973. The image is in the public domain in the U.S., meaning that this copy of a photo was first published prior to 1/1/1923. The original now resides at Museum of Modern Art, N.Y.

156   Go to www.artgallery.nsw.gov.au and you will find Nude in Rocking Chair and many other fine example paintings of gifted artist.

157   Research reflects that the original is a 17th century fountain that rests near the Mercato Duovo.

snout and good luck follows you; toss in a coin, you'll not only have good luck but also the coins support the hospital. In the nurse's wing

World War 1 Memorial fountain

there is a stained glass window which Florence Nightingale approved (1868). The World War I memorial fountain is also here. Sixty-four percent of the Australian 340,000 men were killed or wounded, and primarily this loss/ toll were mainly at the battle of Gallipoli.[158] Not far from this memorial fountain, a group of men (and I suppose women can play also) at this giant chess board with three foot chess pieces All interesting. If you continue your walk along the left side of Farm Cove, you'll eventually arrive at the back side of the Opera House.

Each day I walked downtown for necessary shopping where everything a traveler would need can be found within the vicinity of the Victoria Plaza. Queen Victoria's statue sits in front of a building named after her; within this building you may find a great many elegant, individual shops and places to eat. In the lower level of QVB there is a shop which sold a mass of household items for kitchen and dining. There always seemed to be a sale on the items displayed with a choice of patterns and designs in dishes and silverware. If you have the money, the Crown Darby china may be purchased here. There is a train station located in the basement of QVB; trains from suburbs are available as well as catching the circuit elevated train on the 2nd floor. There is a wishing well as well as a statue of Islay, the Queen's dog here.

---

158   Gallipoli is in Turkey and the battle took place 4/25/1915. The battle was an attempt to control the Dardanelles and Constantinople. It was a failure, but Australians gained a reputation of bravery and endurance.

QVB: interior and Crown Darby

On Several Sundays I was able to attend service at St. Andrew's Cathedral on George Street near the QVB. It was built in 1819. While waiting for the doors to open on one of my visits, I met a young man from Scotland who was attending a seminary in Sydney. We talked about some aspects of its history. The south wall includes stones from Westminster Abbey, and St. Paul Cathedral in London. There is evidently great pride in having even a stone from these famous buildings of London included in this cathedral. St. Paul is only second to the St. Peter's dome in Rome; crypts of the Duke of Wellington, Lord Nelson, Christopher Wren as well as untold others of British fame. Westminster Abbey has innumerable crypts and memorials among which stand out to my mind are the crypts of Queen Mary practically next to Elizabeth, who ordered her execution. Mary's son, James 1, was sure that his mother's sarcophagus outshined that of Elizabeth's. I always am touched by links of the present to a past; such evokes thoughts not only of admiration but also, and more often, a sadness of moments spent in error/folly.

Since Chinatown was only a few minutes away, I made several trips there and discovered a Chinese bakery that sold the most delicious pastries with prices that were unbelievable. I was often a visitor to this shop drooling over the fresh pastry I wished to purchase. A matter of a couple of blocks away was the large warehouse market with fascinating stalls offering unlimited types of merchandise for sale: jewelry, tools, luggage, umbrellas, tourist souvenirs, such as wool slippers, flags, and much, much more at very reasonable prices. Maybe it all came from China, but nevertheless it was a fascinating experience just to look.

If I walked out of my hotel door and turned right, I'd be a short distance to Cockle Bay; the further side was called Harborside and the nearer was Darling Wharf or Darling promenade. Every city should have

Fountains at Darling Wharf & promenade

such a delightful wharf. Wide walkways with almost continuous fountains were an ever delight. It's the reality of a dream what every wharf should look like. Site induced sight to sparkle gladness. How can I relay to you that the expense Australians spent on their wharfs

Corry and Joan are seated

changed the area into everyone's delight? Restaurants and cafes were numerous. On one occasion in 2006, I invited Corry and Joan Stenta to come to dinner here; my treat. We both enjoyed fish & chips and it was a grand reunion of reminders of our gala time touring Perth.

If you walk to the farther end of Harborside, you come to the Chinese Garden. I returned to these wharfs again and again in my several visits to Australia. I paraded many a wharf and found none can reach a comparison in what borders Cockle Bay.

Chinese Gardens

The Radisson Hotel was two short blocks to George Street where I caught a bus to Circular Quay area. Here one can catch a variety of ferries to various areas of Sydney Harbor. With a pass you may ride an indefinite number of times, and you'd want to because the views of Sydney Cove. Facing the harbor, The Opera House is on the left and the Sydney Harbor Bridge is on the right and both comprise a most dramatic view. I don't think anyone could ever tire of looking at such marvelous structures. Once you're at Circular Quay, you walk along the promenade passing stalls, shops, and restaurants until you reach the Opera House itself. The Opera House comprises a theatre, a concert hall, and a smaller theatre called The Playhouse. From the promenade point area, I was able to get photos of the Harbor Bridge and the surrounding areas, but the best photos of the Opera Plaza are taken from ferries.

Circular Quay, Opera House & Harbor Bridge and bridge with climbers

Once you leave the Circular Quay it's an easy walk through The Rock area and across the Harbor Bridge. This 1932 bridge has only one single span. Double lanes facilitate some 150,000 autos as well as trains crossing. Notes pertaining to the bridge length, height, and cost also included the colloquial name as the "Coathanger." There are lanes on each side of the bridge for pedestrians, who all become photographers shooting pictures of the harbor activities—ferries kicking up a wake as they carry passengers to their destination— Ft. Dennison is another subject to photograph. I learned that you can walk across on the top of Harbor Bridge for a fee around $100. In order to do this you have to make a reservation which will give the personnel time to check to see if you meet the physical and emotional standards; it's a matter of the superficial physical examination. This walk takes about three hours; you wear special coveralls so as not to distract the drivers below, and each person also wears a harness and a cable hooked up for safety reasons. As I walked across the street level of the bridge, I watched some of the progress of these daring people walking on the top of the bridge.

These dare devils had to climb up steep steps much like climbing a ladder to get into position to walk across the bridge. At the young age of 82, I declined to take the physical exam, although I was tempted.

You may also obtain good photos of Ft. Denison from Mrs. Macquarie Chair. As you can see you can hardly tell that the fort is built on a rock outcrop in Sydney harbor. It was a place to confine convicts and they named the place "Pinchgut," for the meager rations they received to sustain themselves. It was the middle of the 19th century that the rock/fort got its name from the presiding governor at that time.

Ft. Denison

Many times I took the bus to the Circular Quay area where I could catch the ferry to suburban places. The ferry ride to Manly Beach was short but a little rocky when crossing the bar and wash from the Tasman Sea. The town center had many shops on both sides of the street; it was interesting, and so utterly convenient to browse thru so many shops across from the ferry dock.

It's only a brief walk from my hotel to Centerpoint shopping area of Sydney where the AMP Tower is located. The AMP Tower has many elegant shops to peruse if you have the time. I took the escalator and then the elevator to rise to the observation floor; much like what one does to visit the Empire State Building in NYC. The AMP tower is the tallest public building in the southern hemisphere where there is this 360° stunning view of Sydney and her harbor.

APM tower view of Sydney

While in Sydney in 2004 and 2006, I had the opportunity to see Joan and her husband Corry, who live in the suburbs of Sydney in Arncliffe. They picked me up at the front of my hotel and drove me to scenic places I had not yet seen, such as Kings Cross district where there is a small square with the El Alamein fountain. It was built in 1961 and commemorates the Australians participation in the battles of Tobruk, Libya, and El Alamein in Egypt in WW11. I've seen the fountain in the night

Joan & Corry Stenta

and prefer viewing it then rather than during the day. The fountain is so ethereal, a gigantic maturing stage of a dandelion puff. It is gorgeous and worth a visit via a trolley or bus. There is an excellent fish market in the vicinity; I do enjoy a good piece of smoked fish.

Al Alamein Fountain

While visiting Joan and Corry the subject came up pertaining to real estate. I suppose I'm out of the realm of any real knowledge pertaining to prices of houses, but the first house that I ever purchased was on NE Going Street in Portland, and the price was $3,000. My monthly payment was $50—less than I was paying for an apartment—and the payment included property tax and insurance payments. Corry showed me a house in Artcliffe that recently sold for a little of over one million dollars. And it was unimpressive, telling me that prices here were as high and perhaps more than those priced in the L.A. or San Francisco area. Where will all this inflation come to a stop?

The icon of Australia

Anyway, I had a lovely B-B-Q dinner with the Stentas and part of their family. Their son Dominic and his wife were recently married and spent part of their honeymoon at the Versace Hotel. We reminisced about our different experiences and we agreed that the service was good, but not equated with the price we paid per room. We both thought that the Versace was living on an undeserved reputation. It was always a joy to see the Stentas. And it was they who encouraged me to join one of the tours that take you into The Blue Mountains where Kangaroos abounded and hopped about without a concern with tourist camera clicking away at their antics of play and grazing. The Blue Mountains are blue; my guess is that the intense blue skies nesting on a verdant, green, rain forest area casts a blue hue to the surroundings. What amazes me is that the Australians have so many dramatic view spots. I've been to our Grand Canyon—walked down and back up, gaining many blisters and I'll not do that again—and the Copper Canyon of Mexico, but the Australians beat them all because of the proximity the tourist can come to the edge of the precipices. I get a little nervous when I visit the observation floor of the Sears Building of Chicago. You will note that the floor does not exactly attach to the inside of the tower of glass. All perfectly safe, I'm sure, but I do stand back from the glass framing. What I'm trying to do is to relate my experience with a tour of Echo Canyon, one may take a tram over the cliff there and descent into the rain forest below. The height of the canyon wall was 737 meters,[159] which means about 2,700 feet.

Canyon train station & Canyon tram tracks

---

159   A meter is 39.37 inches

This is quite a drop; it's as if you're falling in slow motion, and it's quite a thrill. The canyon floor is dense with various, giant pteridophytes as well as giant termite hives.[160] It was an education to have explained the various valley floor plants as one walks through the rain forest floor.

Pteridophyte & Termite hive

After the walk, our group of seven was lifted back to the viewpoint area via a cable car to the vantage point of the Three Sisters crags and, perhaps, the most photographed cliffs in this area.

Looking back at canyon wall   Three Sisters crags

Other areas of viewpoints were Anvil Rock, the Wind Caves/Cavern, Govett's Leap and Pulpit Point, which was my favorite because of the sheer drop. It was here at the Wind Cavern that the wind gave us all too aggressive caresses. I think my photos can best describe my intense

160   While visiting the Cairns area, I saw many such hives but didn't know what they were.

Pulpit Point & two distant views

emotion while visiting The Blue Mountains. My visit may be somewhat strenuous for an old lady, but nevertheless our guide was most considerate and concerned for my safety, especially at the Wind Cavern.

On one of my several visits to Sydney, I ventured forth via the underground trains, a part of my daily pass, and rode to Bondi, where there is collective small town shopping area—there is no stress here. I

Wind Canyon

then took a bus to Bondi Beach. It is a quaint cove involving activities that encompass sand, sea and sun. There is a small incline bordering the cove where evidently it is not against beach regulations for a woman to bare her chest and create an all upper body exposure. The walk is charming and scenic.

Bondi Beach and promenade

One view is of the Rock Baths and a private lifesaving club. There are multiple cafes and full meal restaurants as well as a number of shops catering to the tourists to purchase coffee mugs, t-shirts, and baseball caps and more.

In my years of travel in and about Australia there are created feelings that are not the "Cinderella of our inner life, to be kept in her place among the cinders in the kitchen." [161] Emotions derived from some experiences separate in us in a way that our intellect cannot be. It's reviewing and quoting out of context the latter rather meaningless lines of Keats' "Ode on a Grecian Urn":

> Beauty is truth, truth beauty.

An attempt to analyze emotions in a scientific way does not lead to fruition. On my 2006 trip to Australia, I spent most of my time on the Sunshine coast and parked myself in Maroochydore, which I carry emotions that are most difficult to define and I discuss in a later chapter.

---

161   John MacMurray (1881-1960) was an American diplomat: minister to China, Estonia, Latvia, etc.

Chapter Twenty-Two:

Spain

Α ll travel is a delight, and what piqued my interest in Spain was the conversations I had with my brother and a friend James Pendleton pertaining to its history at certain periods and its art. The Prada Museum is incomparable. The history at certain periods is fascinating; for instance, the marriage of Isabella of Castile and Ferdinand 11 of Aragon in 1469. United in marriage they became powerful and leading monarchs of Europe who not only sponsored *Cristoforo Columbo's* (Italian), *Cristóbal Colón's* (Spanish),[162] explorations of the new world, but also were the monarchs who finally drove the Moors out of Europe. Actually Spain was the last Moorish stronghold. Isabella was quite intelligent,[163] for she was in constant communication with her daughter Catherine, first wife of Henry V111. Thru correspondence and journals, one learns that Isabella urged her daughter to sit tight and stay in England even though Henry's testosterone drive led him to the bed of Anne Boleyn.

---

162 Christopher Columbus's real name; why the Americanization of his name doesn't seem to have any valid reason of expediency, especially when we are constantly asked whether we want Spanish or English language spoken for phone assistance; I'm chuckling. Christopher was born in 1451 in or near Genoa, Italy.

163 Exception would be one of their appointees Torquemada, who directed the Jews to accept Christianity or leave the country.

She knew that eventually either she or Henry Vlll's daughter Mary must come to the throne. Isabella's encouragement proved correct, Mary became known as Bloody Mary for her ruthless edicts and treatment of Protestants during her short reign as Queen of England. Anyway, Spain is full of interesting history. And then there is the world renowned Prado Museum, in Madrid.

In November 1999, I enlisted in a structured tour of Spain. Joining a tour group is not my cup of tea because I prefer to travel alone, meet my own schedule, rent a car and choose what and when I wish to visit. On a tour you do see special places of interest, but while on your own you have an opportunity to stop and converse with people you chance to meet. You also can shop in unexpected places. On a tour you are often taken to shops and restaurant that give a kick-back to the tour guide. Not always, but it's my experience it's more often than not. Such is part of the good and bad on ways to travel.

My hotels on this structured tour to Spain ranged from poor to luxurious. When I arrived in Madrid, I stayed at the Santo Domingo Hotel. I chose a hotel within walking distance to the center of town. My first concern here at the hotel was to get acquainted with the Spanish centavos currency. One centavo was worth 6/10 of one U.S. penny; 100 centavos equaled 60¢. But this all disappeared when Spain changed to the Euro.

I arrived in Madrid early so I could do some things not included in the structured tour; such as a longer allocation of time in visiting the Prado Museum. The Museum building itself stems back to the 18th Century. It houses, perhaps, the most complete and valuable collections of paintings. My brother said to be sure that you write down artist's representations that you would like to see. You cannot possibly see them all; you just wouldn't have that much time. My list included Goya, El Greco, Rubens, Titian, and Van Dyck. The museum's catalogue/directions aren't that difficult to follow even though directions were in Spanish. What surprised me is that some giant paintings were hung in panels like you would find in a good carpet store. People were flipping though these panels as you'd find a sharp housewife flipping through plates in the bargain basement of Selfridges. Like the Louvre, there were student artists painting copies of the most prominent art, such as the Goya paintings of the Naked Naja and The Clothed Naja. Both paintings were made using the same lady model. I was told that a stamp was made using the Naked Naja which was outlawed to be used on any letter to the United States; now the stamp is priceless. Ruben's work included the portrait of The Three Graces; and these were only a small representation of some of the great artists of the world. I was also told by my brother to ask about a marvelous new iron forger/artist of statues. My brother wrote his name down as Higueruela, and this artist forged a statue of Don Quixote, whose face was a replacement of something painted by El Greco; the madness and determination were strongly evident. The Don Quixote statue was exhibited at the World's Fair in Madrid in 1947. But have you experienced trying to get a clerk to check the files for information? She rattled off a stream of Spanish phrases only with a clarity of "Impossible, Senora."

Just walking down the main thoroughfare of Calle de Alcalá on which the city square Puerta Del Sol is located is a marvelous street, which I thought better than Av. De Champ Élysées for its fountains. In my long walk back to the hotel, I took the opportunity to peruse the Puerto Del Sol shopping area. It's the largest department store in Spain in the El Corte Ingles, a mall. Here I purchased two brown leather purses referred by the Spaniards as handbags. The sheen on the leather is lustrous and pristine with multiple compartments for the traveler. With heavy enough contents, it could become an advantage weapon against a pick-pocket thief. And it was here in this shopping area with the wide street and a statue of a bear reaching for fruit, that an alleged thief seriously jostled me and ran off. I immediately checked my pockets of my slacks to see if all was accounted for, especially my passport and traveler's checks. Fortunately, it was an incidental happening to me, and I felt it was an unsuccessful attempt to rob this old woman.

On the following day I took a city day tour from Madrid to Segovia and its amazing history is implanted most everywhere. The Roman aqueduct built in the first century, CE[164], between the reigns of Trajan and Vespasian. It still functions delivering water to the upper hills of the city. The tour included the Alcazar Castle, original home of Queen Isabella; it sits prominently on a precipice. It's a beautiful cream colored castle and certainly a delight. Seems impregnable and originally built in the 13th Century, and since then, remodeled and many needed repairs had been made throughout the years. There wasn't much as far as furnishings, but still you can't help but capture the spirit that within this castle congregated some of the most prominent nobility of all Spain. Isabel was crowned here. The throne room, study, and main halls were ornate in design, and from the windows were fine views. Somewhat like a child exploring an unknown, I climbed parapets and turrets.

Alcazar Castle

Near Segovia is the walled city of Avila, which maintains its medieval appearance. It was a Roman outpost at one time, and later controlled by the Moors. For many years Avila was prominent in the Christian-Moor struggle. Its walls were built in 1090, which helped keep the town secure with its 2,526 meters (8,285 feet) in length and 10 meters (32 feet) high. Avila eventually became permanently in Christian control. It's also the birth place of St. Teresa,[165] and a convent has been built here in her honor. Once up on the wall, I viewed what at first glance looked like a desolate plain but actually it's a grain center. And frisky,

---

164   In case you have forgotten, CE means Christian Era and BCE means before Christian Era.
165   St. Teresa (1515-1582) founded reformed order of Carmelite nuns; noted for her mystical visions.

swifts soared over the city catching insects. I called out to them and encouraged them to eat all they can.

Tour making visits to medieval towns requires considerable amount of walking as we followed a flagged guide through a narrow, curvy and aged cobblestone pathway. I'm sure there is some military strategy to keep the streets narrow, but I suspect that it's more to the liking of keeping the streets in the shade and thus conveniently cooler than had they been exposed to the sun.

Two days later I checked in the Agumar Hotel as this was the commencing point of the tour I signed-up for back home. The room assigned to me was not nearly as nice as the one I had at the Santo Domingo. Eh! C'est la vie. Sadly the next morning one lady in our group reported to us that her purse had been taken. It contained her passport and money. The thief or thieves struck while we were eating breakfast. I knew how she felt as I can vividly recall my harrowing experience in Prague under Communist domination so many years ago. Luckily she was carrying various travel insurances and our tour director helped her regain a temporary visa for traveling in Spain and an ID for returning to the U.S. My suggestion to all travelers is to wear one of those money/valuable cloth envelopes under your blouse/shirt or skirt/pants. Cornelia Otis Skinner[166] wore one, so why not you?

This structured tour would include the cities of Toledo, Granada, Torremolinos, Gibraltar, Seville, Cordova, and Mijas. When we got on the tour bus, the guide explained the rotation process on seating, skipping one row each day and moving in a clockwise manner would permit travelers the opportunity of sitting in the front with the wide picture glass for better viewing. It seemed a fair process. Unfortunately, it was a cold/flu season and a number of travelers in our group seem to be manifesting these cold symptoms. Fortunately I had a prescription for antibiotics with me to help maintain the status quo from my catching a cold, hoping pills would arrest any exposure. I also made a decision that

---

166   Cornelia Otis Skinner (1901-1979): She was that marvelous actress and author previously mentioned book, Our Hearts Were Young and Gay.

I would not attempt to avail myself of the optional tours offered, but go to bed early to preserve my healthy status and not succumb to the viruses. I kept water with me and took a ration of pills each day.

Our first stop was Toledo, which is basically surrounded on three sides of the Tagus River, which suggested to me the city's own moat. Windmills are often seen and again suggest that we are in the country of Cervantes' La Mancha. The 14th C Cathedral[167] is one of Spanish Gothic structure, and my guide books says celebrated for it mudéjar decorations, wrought-iron works, and its some 700 stained glass windows.

Obviously one of our members on the tour, stated before we entered in the sanctum, "Oh, no, another ABC." I inquired what he meant, and he replied, "Another bloody cathedral."[168] Not only was he sacrilegious but indicated that he was of British citizenship. But no matter, I am always impressed with cathedrals. My favorite happens to be the cathedral at Salisbury.[169] I'm sure I was influenced by the Pittsburgh U. Men's Choir singing that afternoon that I was there. The acoustics were inspiring. I have heard the nuns sing their vespers in the Basilique du Sacré-Coeur in Paris; I've heard the men and boys choir during service in Westminster Abbey.[170] I'm sure someone will ascribe that Chartres Cathedral in France is one top cathedral next to St. Paul's (S. Paolo Fuori le Mura) in Rome. No matter; here I am admiring these marvelous columns that seem to go on just short of forever and then bursting in spider-like veins in support of its roof. To think that it took a group of men along with the congregation and church wealth for a couple hundred years to build it is in itself a testament to man's devotion to his

---

167   Toledo Cathedral: brochure stated the building began in 1226 and completed in the 1400s.

168   Bloody is a British cuss word.

169   Edward Rutherfurd wrote a marvelous fictional book about the building of this cathedral entitled *Sarum*.

170   An abbey is a building used by a religious order—thus you have Abbotsford (R.L. Stevenson's home in Scotland); a basilica is a building w/two rows of columns, dividing the interior into two sided aisles as the Basilica di San Francesco in Italy and burial spot of St. Francis; a cathedral is officially the seat of a bishop.

beliefs. Anyway, we are here not only to visit this marvelous Toledo church but also examine one of El Greco's more famous paintings, *The Burial of Count Graz*. Our local guide spoke English and I was impressed with his knowledge and explanations. This 16'X21' painting was done by El Greco maybe in 1586 or 1588; it was an extraordinary painting and the color and content were still very vivid. The top portion reveals the heavenly world, especially St. John welcoming the soul of the count into heaven, and the bottom of the painting reflects the mannerism of the count being

Burial of Count Graz

lowered in his sepulcher by church officiates. He is in full dress armor, so he is a man honored for the projection of the church and country. I

The Knight

find the splay of El Greco's painted fingers intriguing. It's more noticeable in his painting of *The Knight*.[171] I call it the double Vulcan sign where the index finger is aligned with the ring one (2nd and 3rd fingers of the hand) while the first and fourth serve as a break. It may be a symbol of the great conflict going-on with Catholicism versus Protestantism, and the Spanish church was a great supporter in the Counter Reformation movement. No matter; this is a magnificent painting and worth more than the short time I had an opportunity to gaze at it. El Greco lived in Toledo, and died there in 1614 A.D.[172]

We also visited El Greco's home and adjoining garden. It's always fascinating to see where distinctive men lived. This is no peasant hovel.

171   The Knight is located in Prado, Madrid.
172   El Greco was born on the island of Crete in 1541 and died here in his home in 1614.

He had his difficulties in life, and yet the later years of his life reflect a man who achieved a certain amount of success. Certainly not as much as some of our movie stars who rake in outrageous fortunes for one film, but nevertheless success. His adjoining garden is an asset to his life style.

El Greco's home in Toledo

Granada was our next site of historical interest. It was a favorite part of Spain for Isabella, and she and Ferdinand are buried in the Capilla Real (Royal Chapel), which is attached to the cathedral. It was erected between 1506 and 1517 as a mausoleum for this famous Spanish nobility. I was resting in a pew and contemplating the altar as well as the façade of the royal sepulcher resting in front of the altar. I was also contemplating that among Isabella's possessions shown in the small museum was a small painting by Peter (the elder) Brueghel (1520-1569). Isabella died sixteen years before Peter was born. I asked the guard at the display "Why?" but received no logical answer. His English was worse than my Spanish. Anyway, there was a clamor made by 20 or so tourists tramping across the front of the altar and turning to descend the steps to the space where the actual lead coffins rest. As this rather uninformed group passed me for the exit, I heard a man loudly shout to a companion, "Who in the hell is Ferdinand and Isabella."[173] I couldn't help but chuckle at this man's lack of education and respect. He should have stayed home and listened to the history TV channel.

---

173   Isabella was born in 1451 and died in 1504. Ferdinand 11 (1452-1516) came to the throne as Ferdinand V with his marriage to Isabella in 1469, uniting the house of Castile and Aragon and united drove out the Moors in Granada in 1492; they also expelled Jews in 1492 as well as outfitted Columbus with his exploration to the new world. And sadly they were also responsible for the organized Spanish Inquisition in 1480.

Anyway, the Alhambra is probably the most tourist visited site in all Spain. The intricate mosaic works seen everywhere were basically begun in 13th century by a Moorish ruler al-Ahmer even though the Alcazaba, the oldest part of Alhambra began in the 11th century. Rome wasn't built in a day and neither was the Alhambra. For the next hundred years or so, additions and remodeling were accomplished. For instance the Generalife is the former summer retreat of Moorish kings. It has a maze of terraces and fountains and reflection pools. As I walked down the steps into the garden the balustrade was actually a passageway for continued running cool water to cool your armpits. I couldn't help comment to this ingenious feature to have on such a hot summer/fall day. The chief

Court of Lions

feature of the Palacio Arabe itself was the Court of Lions[174]. In the center of the room is this fountain with the heads of lions spurting water that overflowed a basin and trickled into a myriad of trails across the floor. Oh, the room was refreshingly cool, and I was greatly impressed with Moorish artisan geniuses, and I can understand Isabella's like of this fortress. Some historian associate this fountain to the like built by King Solomon and described in II Chronicles. My interpretation of the Solomon account is that oxen were used instead of lions, but his dias did contain the twelve lions. From one of the balustrades we could see Sacromonte, gypsy caves carved out of the mountainside. I visited the quarters where Washington Irving lived while he wrote Conquest of Alhambra. Although the rooms were bare of furnishings I could readily understand why he was so amorous about Spain and its antiquities. There were just marvelous

174   Permission: photographer is Fernando Martin and dtd 4/1/05; file is licensed under the Creative Commons Attribution-Share Alike 2.0 Generic (http://creativecommons.org/ license/by-sa/2.0/deedd/em) license.

panoramic vistas of the city, superb gardens, gentle breezes—really quite high above that section of what seems a treeless city—and exquisite fountains. Truly this is a remarkable shrine.

In Seville I had seen gypsy dancers who sing ballads and who dressed in brightly colored skirts that flounced while their male counterpart stomped their feet calling for them with sensual come-hither looks—no excuses tolerated. The flamenco dancers stomped, yes, stomped, emotions of demand for fruition. Isn't "fruition" such a depictive word? Anyway, this is land where Don Juan romanced the ladies, where Figaro barbered, where Carmen and Don José's emotions exploded. Our guide stated that the most famous district of Seville was the Barrio de Santa Cruz. The novice that I am, I could easily get lost in the twisting narrow streets bordered with shops of all kinds. Small cafes abound. I wrote down the name of Calle de las Sierpes as my favorite street to stroll. If the number of churches listed of merit and the number I passed during my short stay, then, indeed, Sevillian residents are a most religious people on Earth.

I have forgotten the name of my hotel, but still I had another great room assignment; it was spacious and luxurious. The hotel had been built for Spain's Exp 1992; the rooms were built in three different parts in this circular building; the lobby was very attractive. When taking the elevator, one could view the unique roundness of the complex.

I was impressed with my crossing a most unusual bridge constructed for the 1992 Fair, which seemed to be held up by a string of wires giving the appearance of a harp-shape structure. There are other such bridges in the world, but this one deserved more attention for its aesthetics.

ABC...another church was on our list of tourist attraction. From what I recall we were more into the city center and entered the "Catedral."[175] Most impressive collection of art works I've seen outside of the Prado. In the south transept is the tomb of Cristóbal Colón', who is also claimed to be buried in Italy. And that may be because Isabella

---

175   Seville Cathedral was begun in 1402. This Gothic church is dedicated to Santa Maria de la Sede.

and Ferdinand turned against him in 1499. This sarcophagus is most impressive because it is raised on pillars of pall barriers. Again I was impressed with the forged iron screens that decorate parts of the interior. There are obvious forged iron art and as I have previously mentioned, my brother's admiration and enthusiasm for this relatively new Spanish artist Higueruela, who creates statues in this medium.

Don Quixote

Higueruela captured Don Quixote in the spirit of the El Greco's face of bordering madness with an indomitable spirit as I have previous stated in this chapter. Personally, I liked his creation of the Spanish Dancer. I'd recognized this artist anywhere for his treatment of the hands and fingers.

Spanish Dancer

Our stop in Gibraltar was an overrated tourist spot. Yes, it's fabled as the Pillars of Hercules and marked the limits of civilization at one time. The Moors had control until 1462 when Queen Isabella gained control and then Spain lost it to the British in 1704 during the War of the Spanish Succession. Anyway you can take a cable car up to the top of the Rock with a stop at the den of the apes; wild monkeys that have free reign and these thieves have protection from the law. The fable says that British rule will end when the apes are gone from the 1400-foot-high Rock. By roaming the top of the Rock,[176] you can obtain vistas of land and sea.

Our stay in the Costa del Sol was for two days. Our hotel was located in Torremolinos (hereafter referred to as T-town) on the coast. My room was the best so far. I had a balcony with an impressive view of the Mediterranean Sea. I thought that if I ever return to Spain, I would like to stay here the whole time.

---

176   No Prudential policy available here.

Free time was a time to shop or loll on the beach. One morning I went to visit a little town of Tijas, located in the hills. All the buildings were Christian white with red tile roofs. The consistency may be called quaint. In T-town if you wanted to go to the city center, all you had to do was walk to take an elevator to the first level, and walking to the city center was a challenge in that the pathway was totally cobblestone and semi-circular as one would have to walk zigzag through narrow streets where cars are forbidden. I became aware of the modern city mingling with the older Tijas village.[177] It is most quaint and charming cafes and bakeries line the street. What a pleasant way to spend time away from the museum rat-race. I had left my tooth brush in the last hotel; I was able to purchase six in a sealed package for 100 pesetas, which equates with 60¢ in U.S. currency—imagine 6 for 60¢.

On our return to Madrid was via Cordoba, where we stopped to view a historical and former Arab Mosque, which was truly overwhelming. It's called the Mezquia.[178] If it were still maintained as a Mosque, I would not be permitted to enter because I am a woman. Today it is a cathedral, but still has the mosque appearance. Some 850 arches and columns were impressed with onyx, jasper, marble and granite. I think the guide said that spaciousness permitted 30,000 to worship here at one time; methinks this an exaggeration. The patio here is huge; one-third of the structure is this courtyard of fountains, and I think orange trees surrounded the cloisters. It is a great place to visit.

At the end of this city tour we had the opportunity to walk across a bridge which foundation was erected by the Romans; it was the first bridge to cross the Guadalquivir River. A bridge that originated so far back into the past is always of interest.

This tour ended with our return to Madrid at the Orense Hotel. We were to meet and take a scheduled farewell visit of Madrid and wind up at a restaurant to finalize the tour with a celebration. The couple from

---

177   Tijas named as the Tijas Mountains as a backdrop of Torremolinos.
178   It became a Roman colony in 152 BCE, and two native sons were philosopher Seneca and the poet Lucan.

South Africa had to leave the tour as the husband was very ill. Several others had bad colds, and I decided to rest up. On the following day, I returned to the Santo Domingo Hotel for a two day stay before I'd catch my flight home.

While at the Santo Domingo, I took a bus to the open market called the "Thieves Market" or *El Rastro* and held only on Sundays. This particular Sunday it was very cold so the first item I bought was a knit hat for $l.20 and a green knit sweater for $3.00. There were many vendors and I was able to buy quite a few things including leather change purses and T-shirts at unbelievable prices.

Thieves Market

On the day of my return to the states, I hired a taxi, and the ride I shall never forget. I think the driver was a retired race car driver; each second I thought my hair was getting a little more grayish. At times, I just closed my eyes and hoped we would get to the airport in one piece and alive. FAST is only a word but feeling the speed was beyond description. It was 4:00 a.m. and streets were not crowded; nevertheless, I believe it was not necessary to drive at such an unbelievable breakneck and reckless speed. Maybe if Paul Newman were the driver, I might have had a different outlook.

I made a second (in November 2000) and a third (in October 2003) trip to Spain on my own. Both excursions were shortened considerably because of unexpected medical problems. On the November 2000 trip, the last leg of my journey took me directly to Malaga, which is just north of Torremolinos. My flight was uneventful, and upon arrival I took a taxi to the Melia Costa Hotel in T-Town. My room assignment was spacious and convenient on the second floor. This hotel, as I remembered, had a great location on the boardwalk, and I was expecting to have a memorable time revisiting this Mediterranean coast area.

I signed-up for the hotel short trip to Tijas. Here I stumbled on the cobblestone walk and I fell and injured myself; I took a taxi to the hospital in Marbella, where the x-ray on my arm revealed that the fall caused a serious injury to my right arm; the same arm that my horse, Minnie, stepped on my wrist in the early 1970s on the Ranch. I was told that I may have cracked my collar bone. I took a taxi back to the hotel. After several phone calls, final flight arrangements were made so I could return to Portland the next day. The Airline personnel were very accommodating, allowing me to sit in an aisle seat and accommodating an empty seat so my right arm would not get bumped.

Upon my returned to Salem, Oregon, new x-rays were taken and the surgeon indicated that the rotator cuff was broken; a cast was not needed but my arm was placed in a special restraint until healed. The injury was serious so that an MRI was taken as well; the specialist could not do anything. I learned later, upon visiting a different doctor who looked at my x-rays and told me that a piece of bone was preventing me from lifting my arm to a normal height. This doctor was retired and did not operate any more. Since I did not have any pain, I would accept the situation as long as I could feed and take care of myself; I will learn to live with the status quo.

In the year 2003, I was determined to return to Coastal de Sol area of Spain. Lufthansa Airlines now had a direct flight from Portland to Frankfort, and from there I could then have a direct flight to Malaga. Flying on Lufthansa meant that I could accumulate miles on my Mileage Plus Account with United Airlines. From Malaga Airport I took a taxi to T-Town where I had a reservation at a different hotel; this was a mistake as this hotel was too far from the City Center and required a lot of walking. Within two days I noticed that my big toe was black and blue and swelling. I was advised by others at the hotel to immediately have my foot checked since I was a diabetic. I took a taxi to Malaga Hospital where a Doctor examined my foot. Afterwards, he advised me to take penicillin every eight hours. He also indicated that I should return in five days to have it re-examined. In the meantime I was able to obtain another room at the Hotel Melia which was closer to the town center and the boardwalk.

There was a nearby shopping area where I purchased an umbrella as it was raining hard almost daily. There was a shoe store nearby where I was able to purchase a pair of toeless sandals. The store was offering other sales so I purchased two attractive pairs of leather boots as Christmas gifts. There was an open market in a different section of T-Town that I wanted to visit. I hired a taxi to avoid walking too much. I'm in shopper's heaven as the area is full of vendors and prices were most reasonable for this American woman bargain hunter. I bought a pant suit, socks, and leather change purses for gifts. I had collected so many items I had to purchase a cardboard suitcase to pack and carry home on the airlines as luggage. Service was obviously better in 2003 than it is today.

At the end of the week I returned to the hospital where the same doctor examined my foot; he did notice some healing but gave me another prescription for penicillin to take until my toe completely healed. He also stressed that I should stay off my feet as much as possible. Stay off my feet when there is so much to enjoy here on the Mediterranean coast means that I wasn't able to stroll about or see the sights or to shop among the many sidewalk stalls and bargain stores. Such a fate is not desired for one such as me.

Finally, my time to leave Spain arrived. When I arrived at Malaga Airport, I became aware of a service which allowed a machine to completely wrap each piece of luggage in plastic for a small fee. When I questioned whether security allowed this practice, they affirmed that it was as long as such packages were not carried on board the plane. I felt better now that the cheap luggage was secure from thievery.

Of my three adventures into Spain, I found the 2003 trip was my most expensive and least enjoyed trip to Spain. Spain was no longer on the peseta as on the other two trips. Inflation? Yes, but the spirit of the almighty dollar that infused most pioneers in the days of Washington Irving[179] has come to roost in Spain. The "almighty dollar" phrase is one of my favorite phrases Washington Irving implanted in his writing and it seems so applicable to CEOs today:

> ...the almighty dollar, that great object of universal devotion throughout our land, seems to have no genuine devotees in these peculiar villages; and unless some of its missionaries penetrate there, and erect banking houses and other pious shrines, there is no knowing how long the inhabitants may remain in their present state...[180]

---

179   Washington Irving was on the U.S. embassy staff to Spain from 1822 to1825 and then he became U.S. minister to Spain from 1842 to 1846.

180   Washington Irving's *Wolfert's Roost* and *Other Papers*, was first published in 1837.

Chapter Twenty-Three:

Greece—2006

I f you are making choices for travel then there are two main reasons to include Greece on your itinerary; one is the obvious beauty of skirting in and out among crags with panoramic views of land-and sea and the other, perhaps just as important, is the association with historical events accomplished by extraordinary men.

Although my method of travel leans more to enjoying the day in scenic backgrounds rather than tramping ruins to tell the folks back home, "Been there and done that." There is no doubt through the urging of my brother Jack that said if I didn't do anything but board a ship and take a trek through the Cycladic Island and anywhere else your tour ship will take you, go! And this I did.

In the fall of 2006, I planned a trip to Greece with a cruise to visit a sundry of Greek islands.[181] I'm 82 years old now, so it's expected that I will not drive in a country where the traffic directional signs are not so easily recognized. Besides, renting a car at my age is not always an easy process. Insurances can be priced at a prohibited level for "wee," older folks. And then again, Athens is heavily populated, and it's been

---

181   Greece has the Aegean Sea on the right, Ionian Sea on the left and the Sea of Crete to
       the south. Inevitably there are grandeur scenes that stimulate thoughts of other times
       and other places.

my practice not to drive in large cities; all of Greece has maybe 10.5 million population, and it's no bigger than the state of Idaho.

My Lufthansa Flight was uneventful, and I arrived early in Athens a couple of days before the cruise. I checked in at the Royal Olympic Hotel, which was located in the older part of Athens and yet walking distance to the Acropolis and the Plaka. The room in the hotel was suitable except for the bathroom; I had to walk in sideways to use the toilet, and when I did, my chin and face were touching the marble sink. I took a picture of the bathroom and told the hotel personnel that my friends would not believe the poor design of the bathroom. I also asked if I could have a different room when I returned from the cruise.

Olympic Hotel bathroom

It was about this time my medical problems got my attention. A sciatica pain in my left leg prevented me from walking extensively; the streets and sidewalks of older city centers were not extensively paved as in some other countries. I have always been a fast-stepping, old woman and my experience in Spain was a forewarning to be careful where and how I walk. Maybe I'm repeating myself, but once you leave your hotel (as I read in various travel books), never stand and gawk at maps or books in deciding which way/direction you're going. Make up your mind in the hotel and follow through. Such hesitations reveal that you are a slow-minded tourist and may become a candidate for some pick-pocket thief or for a scam.

My first tour in Athens[182] was to visit the Acropolis. When I'm talking about the Acropolis, I'm talking about the time when this

---

182   In the mythological founding of this city, Athena and Poseidon entered into a contest. The story goes that Poseidon offered the people a beast, the horse and Athena thought along the lines of the economy and offered the olive. The Goddess of Wisdom, Athena won and thus the city was so-named.

outcropping was primarily the religious center of this city-state. There is an array of some of the very best intellectuals who lived during an amazing time of Greek history. The list of teachers includes people like Socrates (470-399 BCE), whose method is honored through the inquiry method. Regrettably he was charged with corruption of Athenian youth and chose to take a cup of hemlock than another type of punishment. One of Socrates pupils was Plato (427-347 BCE) and that teacher/pupil relationship came to an end with Socrates' death in 399 BCE. Plato traveled a great deal after this event and later returned to Athens and established the Academy, which meant he established the first university ever. And yet here is an amazing man who developed thoughts along the line that all things include a primary and secondary substance. The primary matter is the idea of whatever we're talking about. For a tree it's the treeness; the energy that carries out such things as photosynthesis or osmosis. And the secondary matter is the physical substance of the tree. Plato is better known for his writings dealing with government entitled *Republic*. One of Plato's students was Aristotle. (384-322 BCE), and he in turn was the instructor of Alexander the Great (342-335 BCE). It was also a time with artists who created reality sculptures that would be difficult to surpass. People like Phidias (5th C BCE) made his ascendancy at the time of Pericles.[183] He pictured Pericles and himself on the shield of the goddess Athena, who was the main statue in the Parthenon. He also created the Olympian Zeus at Elis. There was also Praxiteles (4th C. BCE), who is best known for his sculptures of Hermes (messenger), Dionysus (wine), Aphrodite (love), and Apollo (sun). Those leading minds in literature were Aeschylus (525-456 BCE), who wrote better known plays such as *Agamemnon, Prometheus Bound*; Sophocles (496-406 BCE), who wrote better known plays such as *Oedipus Rex, Antigone*, and *Electra*; Euripides (5th C. BCE, and lived in Athens in (408 BCE), and wrote *Mad Heracles* and the *Trojan Women*; Aristophanes

---

183   Pericles was a statesman and basically had control over this democracy state
      by 460; died 429 BCE. He participated in the Peloponnesian War (431 BCE)
      and died of the plague.

(448-380 BCE), who wrote what I think is the better play coming out of this era, *Lysistrata*.[184]

The Erecthelon, which is part of the Acropolis, is a temple ded-

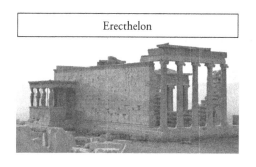

Erecthelon

icated to Athena and Poseidon; it was completed about the same time after the death of Pericles. The portico is supported by six caryatids, stone columns in the form of women that represent the maidens who carried offerings to Athena during specific celebrations glorifying the goddess.

The Parthenon[185] as all have read is the perfect proportional building and one of the greatest architectural treasures. It was erected between 447-432 BCE. So while I was here I know that I was treading where others have cast their shadows even beyond where they have been. A Cicero[186] quote: "If you aspire to the highest place, it is no disgrace to stop at the second, or even the third, place." The quote has changed somewhat by other poets, but it is best summarized as in trying to accomplish

Parthenon

---

184   *Lysistrata*, like *Trojan Women*, are both anti-war plays; while Aristophanes' is a comedy (denying sex to men), Euripides seeks to shock and horrify the audience.

185   Pericles ordered the building to be built; Ictinus & Callicrates designed the building and Phidias created the sculptures and supervised the building of it. Do visit Nashville, TN, which has a marvelous and only reproduction of this temple honoring Athena Parthenos.

186   Cicero (106-43 BCE) was a great Roman orator and statesman; rose to consul (63), sided with Pompey in the Civil War but reconciled to Caesar. After the assassination of Caesar, he attacked Anthony in orations, and then later outlawed by Second Triumvirate and slain in 43 BCE near his home at Tusculum.

something, you have success. Robert Browning says it best in "Rabbi Ben Ezra"[187]:

> For thence, —a paradox
> Which comforts while it mocks,—
> Shall life succeed in that it seems to fail;
> What I aspired to be,
> And was not, comforts me: A brute I might have been...

I was much affected by my visit to this ancient site. Anyway, when I took off my shoes back at the hotel, I noticed a rock the size of a jawbreaker embedded in the heel; I could not get it out and thought it just as well that I couldn't as the sole of shoe was separating from the main parts of the shoe. My point here is that comfortable walking shoes are a necessity. Spend wisely on them.

I visited the Plaka and the Agora, a flea market with various stalls and shops merged within the ancient trading ruins used for conducting businesses and leisure politics. A guide used the term "leisure politics," and I wondered whether any political discussions can be described as "leisure." From my experience, all too often they turn into heated debates.

Two days after my arrival in Athens, I joined my tour group and we were driven to Piraeus, where we boarded the Sea Diamond cruise ship. When I saw the room assigned to me, I made a quick trip to the purser's office to get it changed. This second room was on the 8th deck with easy accessibility to the outside deck area for fresh air and to see the views as we cut through the surface waves. The bathroom was almost an exact replica of a bathroom in an RV; a small sink, toilet, and shower next to the toilet with only a curtain wrapped around from the wall. After using the shower, you would have to use a mop or a squeegee to mop the water into a drain hole in the middle of the bathroom floor. I

---

187   The Ben Ezra Synagogue is located in an older part of Cairo; the rabbi had bargained with the Patriarch Alexander the LVI for this ancient site where Jeremiah and Moses had worshipped; cost was 20,000 dinars in gold. The area is worth a visit.

used the shower once and that was enough for me. Other ships, like the Q. Mary and even the USS Ben Hodges, had facilities with a separate stall or enclosure for the shower.

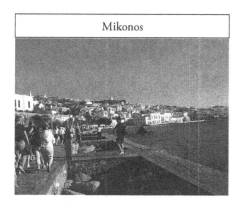

Mikonos

With a calm blue sea, a bright sun, a pleasant breeze, we arrived at our first stop Mikonos; we had to take a bus from the pier to the city center. The homes I saw in the city and on the hill reminded me of the kind of houses I saw in Spain, snow white with reddish tile roofs. Mikonos is a picturesque village where I purchased a small foot-long Cycladic statue of soapstone. It was much like ancient Egyptian art that was flat and one-dimensional. It reminded me of our Academy Award Oscar. Mikonos has narrow lanes bordered by small shops, and there are picturesque windmills seen from the quay where many fishing boats were moored. There are many, many cafes that are popular with the natives as well as other visiting tourists.

Cycladic version of Oscar

Patmos

On the second day we stopped in Patmos; I was told that this is where the Apostle John wrote the book of Revelation. He supposedly lived in a grotto about a mile and a quarter south of the port of Skala. In the town of Patmos is St. John Theoloogo towers and monastery, which resembles a medieval fortress. Our guide stated that thirty-three pages of the Gospel of St. Mark inscribed on 5th Century purple vellum are housed there.

The ship usually traveled at night and days were spent sight-seeing. The third day of our cruise we were docked at Rhodes. There is a great deal of rose colored rock and the name Island of Roses stuck. Some guide books state Rhodes was named after the Phoenician word "erod," meaning snake as the island was once infested with these creatures from the underworld.

Rhodes fort

I was suffering leg pains, so I hired a taxi driver to take me into the city for what I thought was a greedy price of $40 Euro dollars per hour. But, so be it. What's visible from the dock is the well-kept fortress of St. John. From the 10th through the 15th centuries the Knights of St. John, the Knights of Rhodes and later Knights of Malta were originally "hospitalers," an organization to care for the wounded, the poor and the sick in Jerusalem. Eventually they were driven out of Jerusalem and retired to Cyprus, and then to Rhodes and eventually to Malta. This long history of violence was due to political and religious differences under the auspices and direction of God—and you can well add the ego of countless men of position. Anyway, Rhodes is a marvelous place to visit, for shops abound with sensible souvenirs and sensible products for birthdays and Christmas giving. Children would love tramping through the fort itself, for it is in marvelous condition. It's a money maker and no lack of tourists who will spend enough to maintain /stabilize the island economy.

The next stop was on the coast of Turkey. Though the pain in my leg was getting worse and hindered my walking, I still got off the ship and visited Kusadasi, and an excursion to the Ancient ruins of Ephesus. The ruins are in pretty good shape. The façade of the library is still in admirable

Ruins of Ephesus

state. At one time, this was one of the leading libraries of the world. There is the story that St. John, Protestant version, came here with Mary, his mother, to live out the remaining days of her life. The house where she lived up in the hills away from the busy bustle of Ephesus was called Meryemana (about 5 miles from the city). There is a tiny chapel there and officiated by a monk. One Catholic tourist companion spoke quite loudly, "But where is her grave?" This brought a chuckle to this Protestant woman who knew that Mary was taken bodily into heaven; there was no death.

Since walking for me now was almost impossible, I again hired a cyclist pulling a hooded cart to take me around the city center. The storekeepers and vendors were very aggressive in attempting to sell their wares. But if you want to shop, there are bargains galore, especially in Oriental rugs. The harbor has an amazing number of private launches, ships, ocean-sailing vessels. Some people are quite wealthy as the harbor is virtually a vault of expensive ships. During the trip I was able to meet many passengers during the meals; their comments made me take note that many of them were not only seeing Greece with their eyes, but also very much with their hearts, especially at Ephesus. The ruins here are so evident of what was. The library was on this corner, the public toilet on another, and even the red-light district[188] evident.

On the 4th day we stopped at the largest Greek island Crete. El Greco was born here and a certain amount of the Byzantine influence is reflected in his art. From a distance you are able to see a Venetian fortress from the harbor, and once up closer, it has an iron gate embel-

---

188   Red-light district is a term to indicate a prostitute is available by a candle/oil lamp that cast a red light through a small aperture/window.

lished with the Lion of St. Mark. There are all kinds of ferry service coming to Crete, and I suppose to visit Knossos, which is a little more than three miles out of Heraklion. Again, I hired a taxi to take me to see points of interest. The photo here comes from the post card collection of Arthur Evans' reconstruction efforts to reflect the archaeological data here at Knossos during the period 1500-1480 BCE was a center of international power in European history[189]. The palace or residence is much restored and gives you much insight into the living arrangement. Many Minoan artifacts are kept in the museum. Anyway, here resided the legendary Theseus, who slew the Minotaur, and King Minos presided over his court; the throne room is tastefully/artfully restored.

Restored ruins of Knossos

With our arrival off the pier of Santorini or Thira[190] island, passengers were taken to the dock in small boats. You then took a cable car to the top of a hill overlooking the town center. Once on top you have a marvelous view of whiter-than-snow-white houses/ shops and a contrasting blue sea. I'd have no objections to living here; like all aged ladies leaning toward a rocking-chair life-style has its affinity, especially for one who is suffering much leg pains.

Santorini

Early the following day our ship docked in Piraeus and we transported back to our individual hotels in Athens. Arriving back at the Royal Olympic, I was greatly relieved when I walked into my assigned

189   Some authorities state Knossos dominated the Mediterranean area between 3000-1500 BCE.
190   Some guides books say that here is the lost Atlantis.

room with the adjoining bath—a night and day difference in the design of my first bathroom at this ho-tel. It pays to complain. My room overlooked the outside pool and garden area. I was much pleased with this assigned room.

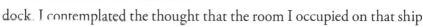
Royal Olympic Hotel

Years later, I learned that the Sea Diamond cruise ship sank off the shore near the Santorini dock. I contemplated the thought that the room I occupied on that ship was now at the bottom of the sea. I'm sure it will not be missed by more than one previous passenger.

Sea Diamond

I have been in many churches of various dominations with the exception of the Muslim faith, and that is because a woman, especially a foreigner, may not enter. It's a man's society; woman may appear on the balcony or behind a screen but not in the main sanctuary itself. I have stood in the doorway of mosques and noted the fine chandeliers there. It is also noted that the Greek Orthodox Church here in Athens houses some of the finer glass chandeliers that I have ever seen. There is no cheating on expenses here.

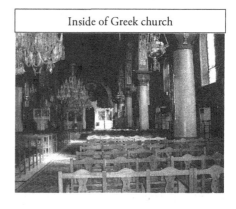
Inside of Greek church

My hotel was not too far from the Parliament building and here is also the memorial for the Unknown Soldier. It's inevitable that one feels sad to be standing here when so many Greeks who died during the turmoil of its history. And I'm not sure why the Greek army persists in the soldiers' dress guarding government building and palaces; perhaps more for attraction by tourist photography enthusiasts than practicality. We certainly know that the Spartans' stand at Thermopylae— roughly in 480 BCE— were in different costumes. But what do I know. Here I am just about to turn eighty-three, realizing that my health was changing as well as my attitude. I would not make another trip like this one as I ventured forth in Greece. There was so much that I missed: running off to Epidaurus, the Grecian medical center. If you remember the medical staff is entwined by snakes. From a fellow traveler, James Pendleton, who explained that the many labyrinth passages there were passages for snakes, who came from the under world to be interpreted any number of made-up prognosis for many a pilgrim. Thus Aesculapius' logo has for me a logical explanation.

Greek memorial for Unknown Soldier

And neither did I make an attempt to travel to Delphi (elevation is about 2,000 feet), where, through priestess (one named Pythia), Apollo spoke to rulers, generals and commoners who came and asked for heavenly direction/guidance.

At this time of my life, my hand prevented me not only from knocking on doors but also from shaking hands, for I would find pain in my fingers and at times in the wrist. No one likes to be a complainer; so, I have told many a stranger I can't shake hands, but I can give you a hug. Sometimes, and only in certain situations, I would tell the person that he'd have to be careful as I wasn't wearing a bra.

With concluding my travel in Greece, I have come to realize I have arrived at the stage in my life of having purchased much more than I could possibly use. Wisdom, then, is convincing myself to begin selling or giving away all the extras, and avoid an estate sale at which others would have to assume that responsibility.

> Surely there comes a time when counting the cost and paying the price aren't things to think about any more. All that matters is value—the ultimate value of what one does.[191]

191   James Hilton (1900-1954): English novelist; author of *Lost Horizon, Goodbye, Mr. Chips*; *Random Harvest* and others.

Chapter Twenty-Four:

Maroochydore

My incentive to come here was through the guidance of travel agents, who stated that I'd like the Sunshine Coast, and so I decided to see for myself for the first time in the year 2000. If I were asked which part of Australia I enjoyed most, I'd tell you that it is The Sunshine Coast with a prolonged stay in Maroochydore. The area is not as crowded as the Gold Coast; besides having various activities and many fine restaurants, there are nearby areas of gorgeous setting. So, I have returned here after four previous visits to renew this feeling of contentment and dispel some if not all, of my anxieties. Guide books have also included statements as "save the best for last." And this is how I feel about Maroochydore.

Chateau Royale

In 2000, on the day I drove north from Brisbane to the Sunshine Coast, it was raining so hard that my windshield wipers had difficult keeping the window clear enough for minimum vision. I left the Bruce Highway as soon as I saw an exit sign for a town to Maroochydore. Because of the rain and driving on the left side of the road I lost my sense of direction and found myself driving south along the ocean coast until I saw a huge building called the Chateau Royale. I parked under the overhead entry way to keep out of the rain. The lady at the reception was very friendly and showed me the vacancies available which were on different floors. The one that attracted me the most was the sub-penthouse. I told her that it was the nicest unit, but I wasn't sure I could afford such a beautiful condo.

She inquired as how much could I spend, and when I said $600 (Australian dollars). She accepted this bid as a weekly rental bid, meaning that this unit cost me $45 per day. Since this time the exchange rate changed drastically. Anyway, I decided that I could afford this unit and why not live it up. This was living.

Truly, the condo was beyond anyone's expectations; it was magnificent. The Chateau Royale has a great location with a narrow parkway that separated the hotel from the sandy shore of the South Pacific. To describe the unit, words would fail to characterize the overwhelming essence of the spaciousness and luxury. Obviously I thought this the best and most wonderful place I have ever stayed. The unit included three bedrooms, two bathrooms, living room, dining room, kitchen, and in a space between hallway and second bathroom with a walk-in laundry room equipped with my own private washer and dryer. The master bedroom had a king size bed, a glass enclosed shower, mirrored sliding door closets on two sides of the room; one could enter the balcony thru a sliding door to view the all impressive surroundings: the ocean and the merging of the Maroochy River and Pacific Ocean. The windows were from floor to ceiling enabling me to view the outside world with a sense of luxuriating comfort, even from lying in bed. The dining area included a huge glass top table and six padded chairs and a second sliding door to enter onto the balcony; an attractive set of patio furniture available to sit, view scenery while having breakfast or having an early cocktail hour with hors d'oeuvres. The other two bedrooms each had twin beds, and more than ample closet spaces with sliding door mirrors. The living room and dining room were designed in an oval fashion with windows from floor to ceiling, making it possible to have an 180 degree view of the coastal area where water rushes continually to plant kisses on a sandy shore. There were three sofas in the living room plus a TV with remote, a VCR, CD player, and a small library/desk table with two chairs by one of the front windows, providing a closer view of the outside. Oh, yes, so necessary when the wind or rain confined you to the interior of this palatial space. In front of the sofas was a gigantic coffee table which I used for constantly organizing information to plan my daily itinerary. The kitchen was fully equipped, and I mean fully equipped with pots and pans, microwave, automatic dish washer, garbage disposal, electric stove, electric coffee pot, an oversize refrigerator-freezer, and many cupboards that contained every kind of dish, glass, and cooking utensils you could ever want or use including several counter places to prepare the food. In measuring the distance from the entry door to the drapes in the living room I discovered that it was around 75 feet; thus, indicating the awesome space allowed for this beautiful condo. Actually this condo was more complete than my own home in Oregon.

As I have stated, the scenery was utterly magnificent. I could see a great distance: the Maroochy River looking north. Looking south, I could see as far as Mooloolaba and the Point Cartwright Lighthouse. On the opposite side of one kitchen counter four high stools were provided for eating at the counter. It would be ridiculous to look at a kitchen wall or cupboards when other space with view was provided.

Maroochy River view   Ocean view

Although I continue to take my exercise by swimming at the Court House gym in Salem, I am leery about venturing into the ocean to claim "you-Tarzan, me-Jane" swim. So, I waded, and the first time I waded in the warm water here at Maroochydore, I became aware of how much power the receding waves made upon my legs; it took strength to stay upright. For serious swimming, I prefer a confined pool.

I was assigned my own parking space in the underground garage. The Chateau had its own Jacuzzi and swimming pool in an outside area near the main entrance and it was enclosed. You had a key so you could enter near the pool to use a faucet to wash sand off when returning from the beach, a short walk from the condo. Across the street is a wide attractive sidewalk that parallels the beach; and if you have the energy, you can walk from Maroochydore to Mooloolaba, which is a distance of seven kilometers. I took this walk along the ocean almost every day as I never tired of this marriage of land and sea. Of course, I did not walk the whole seven kilometers all the time, but at least twice. I thought I did well for an old lady.

Mooloolaba Espanade

Across the street was a block long shopping area with stores on each side of the wide street, and parking was allocated in the divided middle section. There was a post office, two bakeries, grocery store, meat markets, a newsstand, several restaurants, barber shop, candy store, liquor store and a clothing store. So, I was well located to replenish my needs. I noticed that there didn't seem to be home delivery of newspapers; instead, an inside newsstand sold various printed materials, like a mini bookstore. At the Fish Market you could choose your kind of fish, and they would cook it for you to take it back to your condo. Ah, yes, this was for me. I enjoy cooked fish, and preparation for one is a nuisance. For the vacationer, there was also an internet business; for a small fee, you could be in touch with your loved ones. This method of communication is certainly cheaper than sending a post card, and besides you're going to have the opportunity to bore one and all with your collection of travel photos. And yet so many people carry their own laptop and thus save even more. Dining here al fresco is popular; it is so with my wishes.

I concluded that Australians are very water oriented because I see so many on surfboards sliding on waves both in the mornings and early evenings. Most of my travels have been done during the beginning of the so-called off season. Here in Australia I had roughly twelve hours of daylight and not a day passed by that I didn't watch from my windows views of so many interesting activities. One day I noticed school children with an instructor giving physical education classes. Having been a teacher, I could easily tell which child was slinky at his chore. Shore fishing was a common sight. Another sport that young Australians seem to enjoy is riding the waves by holding a small sail attached to an enlarged surfboard, seemingly a confrontation between some new Aegaeon[192] and Aeolus[193]. This sport is also most popular in the Columbia Gorge near Hood River in Oregon. Around the corner of my building was an area that was designed for lawn bowling. Not necessarily all Italian protégées but Australian teams of both men and women wearing entirely white clothing and bowling with a small black ball on a designed, grassy area. It was something that appealed to me for exercise in my later old age.

Surf riders

---

192   A Homeric epithet; Aegaeon is represented as a son of Poseidon, a marine deity of the Aegean Sea.

193   Aeolus, in mythology, is a son of Poseidon and given dominion over the winds.

Transportation to and from the Chateau Royale was very convenient. The city bus stop is less than a block away. The RSL (Retired Serviceman League) Club will gladly pick you up at the entrance of the condo complex if you make an appointment in advance; they will also give you a return ride. The bus shuttle to the Brisbane Airport stops within a block of the condo complex; there is also shuttle transport to the Sunshine Coast Airport which is a few kilometers north of Maroochydore.

After the first two times I visited Maroochydore, and renting a car at the Brisbane Airport and driving myself to the Chateau Royale, I learned that a car rental agency was here in Maroochydore. Thereafter, I opted to take shuttle from the Brisbane airport and rent a car in Maroochydore that was conveniently delivered to my condo.

Everyone likes to shop at an open market, and Aussies are no different for such are well patronized. On Sunday morning they close off the street where the Chateau Royale sits and create a temporary mall by setting up tables and portable stalls with vendors selling their wares until noon. Of all the malls that I have visited/ shopped at, my favorite is the Sunshine Plaza Mall, a short drive from my condo. Basically it's a two story complex with over 200 specialty stores; its uniqueness is that it is surrounded by water, and in some places entry means crossing a short foot bridge. Such a beautiful setting encourages spending; it certainly did for me. On Sundays, there is also a larger open market on Fisherman Road.

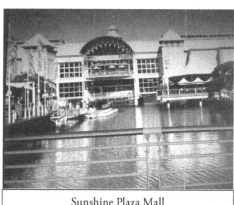

Sunshine Plaza Mall

Coles is a grocery store in the mall and offers a wide selection of quality food items. In the adjacent area is a food court where you may purchase fresh meat and fish as well as fresh fruit and vegetables. There is a choice of several bakeries as well as having both new and second-hand miscellaneous items for sale as they do in gigantic garage sales. On Wednesdays and Saturdays the markets opens on Memorial Drive in the little town of Eumundi. This is a must for tourists, for Aussies, also come from miles around to shop in this open market. My guide book says that the name probably stems from a local aborigine who came to the rescue of an expedition led by Lieutenant Offer (1836), and it is Mrs. Fraser's mispronunciation of a tribe named Ngumundi. Bulcock Street in the town of Colundra is another place for tourists to shop; it certainly was for the Australians. Kawana Waters has another large shopping area all on one floor. I noticed on the day the seniors receive their government checks, the stores are crowded; parking is difficult at this time of the month. I think it's in James Beard's cookbook that he says something about not buying the specials without checking the quality. He seems to think that some fruits like apples in a bag are marked down because they are bruised. He also advises not to purchase more than you immediately need; stocked up foods will lose some of their flavor. Anyway, all in all, truly the Sunshine Coast has so much more to offer than the Gold Coast; maybe it is because the Sunshine area is more sedate, quiet, less crowded, and more scenic in my view. The more I traveled on the Sunshine Coast, the more attractive it became to me.

I made the drive several times to encircle a large area on highway 23, which included several interesting towns: 1) Nambour you may have an interest in a red-flowered tea from which the town is named. 2 & 3) Mapleton and Flaxton are a part of a rainforest resort area. I found both areas most interesting. 4) Montville is in the Blackall Range, which by the way has stunning scenery. You can find marvelous galleries and hand-made Black Forest cuckoo clocks there. Montville stands out more than the other little villages with its many unique shops and interesting places to eat. Returning to Maroochydore, I passed through Landsborough before leaving Highway 23 for the coast. This is a beautiful drive that I never tired of revisiting. If you come to Maroochydore, do take this splendid drive. Isn't it odd—at least to me—that I now recall something that Winston Churchill (and I think it was to the Prince of Wales) stated as I seem to recall that it went something like this...

> If you have an important point to make, don't try to be subtle or clever. Use a pile drive. Hit the point once and then whack it again...and again.[194]

Why does the line come to mind while I'm talking about points of interest of the Maroochydore area? I don't think I'll ever know, but stranger thoughts have pranced into my head without consciousness of their coming. Funny.

While in Maroochydore and out of curiosity, I took time to visit the local senior center and talked with the director. The senior center is subsidized by the local government; they pay for the rent of the building, and the salary of the director. As with most centers, seniors volunteer to organize and to supervise activities. I explained to the director about

SSS complex

the South Salem Senior center that I belong to in Salem. A small group of seniors got together in 1989 and started their own individual center; initially, they bought two modular units and rented space to place them. Land rental included water, sewer and garbage services. The influx of new members made these two modulars obsolete. The board, elected by its members and after much thought and appraisal, decided that they were financially able to build a 12,000 square foot building for their use. It would include a gift shop, a travel office, computer room, and a large kitchen with adjoining dining room, classrooms, huge lobby and a library where videos and audio books as well as popular novels would be available for its members. Membership would be $15 per year

---

194 This Churchill axiom I wrote down from one of those internet lists of clever thoughts; I think it was www.toonz-Russ.com.

and a small monthly fee if one wanted to use the computer station with internet service. All very reasonable, but such fees alone would not pay for the mortgage payments. Other income is derived from semi-annual rummage sale, yearly style shows called Rummahge Boutique and recycling newspapers dropped off at boxes on the south side of Salem. The South Salem Seniors do not receive any monetary assistance from the city of Salem. There is a fine group of ladies who knit/ crochet hats, knee caps for veteran amputees, lap robes, etc., which help bring forth monies for the operation of the center. This is just one of its philanthropic endeavors. It's an amazing group of seniors, for the mortgage in a matter of a few years is now below $200,000. Through determination and perseverance of people like Nina Novak, one of the initial founders of SSS, they have brought about what I feel is a grand and admirable organization. It's an organization with seniors helping seniors that much can be accomplished along the lines of philanthropic and social activities. Besides, to have good health, you must be active as much as you can. John Dryden[195] phrased it…

> *Better to hunt infields for health unbought*
> *Than fee the doctor for a nauseous draught.*

The reception desk at the Chateau Royale kept clients oriented to what entertainment was available in the area as well as travel tours nearby and yet outside Maroochydore. More than once I hired a motor boat at the Boat Hire on Bradman Avenue and scooted up the Maroochy River. I also quenched my desire to Jet Ski. The reception agent here made an appointment for me and someone from the ski jet business picked me up at my condo and drove me to where he had a small motor boat to transport me to a place on Goat Island. I was given some instructions how to operate a Jet Ski, and then allowed to Jet Ski on the Maroochy River. Once I became accomplished operating the thing on the river, I was

---

195   John Dryden (1631-1701) was an English poet; from quote is from Epistle to John Dryden of Chesterton, line 92.

permitted to jet ski on the South Pacific Ocean under supervision of the jet ski business agent in Mooloolaba. Jet skiing on the Ocean is a challenge. I was not only in deep water, but also I was over my head in keeping balance with wave action. Perhaps seeing just land on one side of my activity meant that I required a little more nerve and grit. Of course I wore a safety jacket and a line so that I would not be separated far from the contraption should

An 80-year-old jet skier

I fall off; still my apprehension increased being in such deep water. Here I am, an 80 year old lady at the time, and the operator was surprised that a gal my age would attempt such a sport to jet ski on the ocean.

One item that I felt worth shopping for was reading materials. I found books in malls, and open markets; initially I could buy books three for five Australian dollars, but by 2006, the costs have doubled. Most of these cheaper books were paperbacks and generally had contents of cheap romances. I guess I was no different than my grandmother, because I know she stuffed *True Romance* under the sofa cushions at times. It doesn't matter what anyone reads as long as they read. I think what J.K. Rowling has done for encouraging children to read with her Harry Potter series is just marvelous. We're all over-whelmed with her inspiring/encouraging children to read. Some religious right congregations have damned the book as instilling into children's mind of evil; no matter the citations. Ridiculous. What's the Milton line?

> As good almost kill a man as kill a good book; who kills a man
> kills a reasonable creature, God's image; but he who destroys a
> good book kills reason itself.[196]

196 John Milton (1608-1675), English poet; "Areopagitica."

If you are not smiling at Milton's quotation/his logic, then you need to read his divorce tracks; that will make you smile. Milton also suggested the idea that nothing related to sin/foul language can defile you/your body; it is that what leaves your body that is injurious to good character. Books are good things; no matter what you read, even that foul thing, *A Million Little Pieces* by James Frey is an example of Milton's philosophy. Anyway, should you come to Maroochydore, check out books at Crazy Clark's and The Warehouse. If you're lucky, you may encounter a Maroochydore city library sale on used books. Once I read them, I sell them in a garage sale or more often donate to South Salem Senior organization.

In my advanced age, I often need a sleeping aid/pill. I prefer Stillnox as I do not awake with a headache. At home I need a prescription to make the purchase. If I try to purchase that medication here, I first must make an appointment with a doctor even though I am not ill—$35 dollars, please—and then spend $32 for a 30 pill-prescription filled and I pay even a few dollars more at home. While in Spain, the same medication would cost me $5 U.S. dollars. I could purchase this medication via mail in Canada until Bush's/ Congress' new Medicare Medication law came into effect, which forbids such transactions. What I'm trying to say is pharmaceutical companies certainly enrich their pockets beyond a fair profit.

> In points of honor to be try'd
> All passions must be laid aside;
> Ask no advice, but think alone;
> Suppose the question not your own,
> How shall I act? Is not the case;
> But how would Brutus in my place?
> In such a case would Cato bleed?
> And how would Socrates proceed?[197]

---

197   Jonathan Swift (1667-1745), English poet and author; I believe the quote is from Polite Conversation of which there are three dialogues.

My point here is to look for the humor. How do you address abuses of a government administration or acts of Congress that are obviously not in principle the primary benefit of its citizens. In prescription of drugs, it's the CEOs who are the primary recipients. I have criticized governmental farm policies toward the small farmer as Willie Nelson and others have done, and then again against nuclear power plants. I'm sure my editorial comments went nowhere, but at least I tried. Yes, how would Socrates proceed?

On one visit, I took a tour available to Fraser Island. It is listed as the largest *sand* island in the world. It is also noted as one of the last remaining *subtropical* rainforests. From the Maryborough area the ferry docked at Hook Point, the southern point of the island. Once seated in our vehicle, our driver drove along a sandy beach for about 50 kilometers. The driver was careful in trying to avoid hitting the ebbing waves. Our first stop was to view an old ship wreck, the *Mabeno*, which was beached in 1974, now rusted and embedded in the sand. As we left this area with the tide coming in, our guide, in trying to avoid the waves, drove more inland and got stuck in a small sand ridge. Everyone except me got off the bus—I offered to leave,

Frazer Island Getaway Bus

but the driver insisted I stay seated—to push the bus out of the sand; the driver let air out of the tires to get more traction while the passengers exerted their energies pushing the bus forward then backward to escape the natural clutching of the sand. The ride to the inland was on a terribly rough and unpaved narrow road. Road? I should say pathway. And here the bus proceeded very slowly with its 4-wheel drive transmission. I would call this adventure one of the bumpiest rides I ever had. I wear a 38-B bra but after this ride I could contemplate wearing a 44-G. Truly I did enjoy riding along the scenic beach on such a clear and enjoyable day. The final destination of this tour on the island was Eurong Resort, close to the shores of Lake McKenzie. The lake has beautiful blue hue and skirted by white sand and then black butt trees. What a pleasant place to have our lunch. Time was allocated for some passengers who wanted to swim in the lake. What I thought was excellent guidance was the fact that the driver provided smokers with a bucket of wet sand to deposit their butts when we stopped for scenic viewing, which reflected a concern of preserving the environment free from debris. Amen to that. Our return trip to the ferry dock was as enjoyable as our going.

In April of 2006, I ventured forth on my sixth trip to Australia; this time I did not make the trip alone. My brother, Jack, helped pay my way through college, and I wanted to do something special for him while I could, thus he and his friend William Pulley joined me to tour primarily parts of the eastern shore of Australia. We all arrived in Sydney and had rooms at the Radisson. It was understood that they would do their thing and I would do mine. After a couple of days becoming acquainted with Sydney, they flew to Cairns and the surrounding areas that I discussed in chapter 20. Afterwards they flew down to Brisbane and rented a car and drove to the Sunshine Coast. We met at the Chateau Royale. I had prearranged for an ocean view, three bedroom condo. They had heard me speak so highly many times about the Chateau Royale, and now they understood why I enjoyed my condo here in Maroochydore. I still vividly remember their comments when they arrived and saw the unit. They both were extremely impressed with the 180 degree view and the spaciousness of this rental. Jack said he felt like Donald Trump on a holiday with such a sumptuous apartment. Bill Pulley was equally impressed and stated he felt like he was in paradise. For that evening we had gone to one of those fish markets that prepared your choice of fish and returned to the condo to complete cooking other condiments and chips and salad for our dinner. No restaurant could have such a magnificent view.

It was fun sharing with others what I think is a most impressive area in Australia. On their second day, I had arranged for the three of us to jet ski on the Maroochy River. We took a motor boat to Goat Island where the jet ski operator stored his jet skis. Kicking up a fantail four or five feet high indicated the machine was operating at full speed. There was no need to worry as the river was clear and we wore life jackets. Should the event of falling off the apparatus, our line to whatever kept the Jet Ski operating would cancel the propelling and come to a stand still. To end the day, we had

Jet skiing on Maroochy River

drinks at the condo before going for a scallop dinner in Mooloolaba, where we had been scouting for a restaurant the previous day.

Mooloolaba promenade fountain   Mooloolaba coast view

The next day we drove to Noosa Heads and rented a catamaran, and we toured the Noosa River and on Lake Cooroibah inlet, viewing not only the scenery, but the fine, luxury homes and condos alongside the river. It was here years before that I had been motoring and like a dummy forgot my warning to stay on one side the buoy. I got stuck on a sand bar and

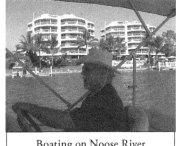

Boating on Noose River

had to be pulled off by the river police who were very kind in giving new instructions about the river signals/buoys. Anyway, the water passageways were skirted by million dollar homes and moored boats at their own piers. Somebody has money in Australia.

Afterwards, we drove to Hawkins Street in Noosa Head, where there are endless shops selling t-shirts, prized souvenir cups, insignia caps as well as restaurants skirting a cove with sandy beaches. Beautiful. Driving along the ocean back to Maroochydore, we stopped at Peregian Beach where there are shops selling Australian wool slippers and opals. I didn't purchase anything because you can purchase such in Sydney cheaper if you know where to shop. At Coolum we stopped for a late lunch of chicken shish-kabob salad. Methinks it was poor quality.

Noosa Head beach

There was enough time for Jack and Bill to take a swim in the ocean; they noted that at this time of the afternoon there was a terrific undertow and didn't venture too far into the water over their waists. We had plans that evening to eat at a place called Ebb's at DuPorth Esplanade. A wedding was taking place and thus had to change our plans and decided to try LA Vigo, which was recommended by a brochure near the elevator at Chateau Royale. We all had grilled scallops, grilled red and green peppers and Verde salads with water cress and a fine bottle of Chardonnay: costs $106 Australian dollars. This tab is just a touch over expensive, but what the heck.

View from Buderim Mts.

On Bill and Jack's last day in Maroochydore, Bill drove his rental over the route 23 that I had driven several times on previous visits. And on our way, we passed through the Buderim

Mountains—I hesitate to say "mountains," as what we call mountains in Oregon is not exactly "mountains" here on the Sunshine Coast. It's more like our coastal range. Regardless, do purchase at least a jar of Buderim Ginger (lemon and lime) Marmalade; it's great on breakfast muffins.[198] Our first stop was in Nambour, where I wanted to purchase more plastic envelopes that I find so handy for inserting things and which keep security agents from handling my personal objects. I'm just touchy about men—or anyone—fussing with my undies. I asked the clerk if they take cash as a matter of being friendly. Her eyes widen and rejoined something to the effect as along as it is Australian money and not Monopoly kind. I presented my Australian dollars and said, "I'm really Marilyn Monroe, but I'm traveling incognito. I have another name; do you wish to know it?" She gave a burst of laughter, and said, "Please to meet you, Miss Monroe and that is enough for me, thank you." So another magic moment of table conversation was created.

In exchanging American Express traveler's checks for Australian dollars at the A-Z Bank here I was charged $14. This is all rather an unnecessary expense, because most shops or businesses will cash such without a fee; besides it is just as easy to use a credit card than going through the inconvenience of standing in line and paying bank fees. Either way you feel financially secure is just fine.

Mapleton is a town with a variety of shops for purchasing unusual birthday and other holiday gifts. At or near Flaxton there are sites in the Kondalilla Nat'l Park where you can actually see the coast. At Montville there are boulders with carved faces for $19 Australian dollars. These I know would be charmers in my garden, but—always "a but"—how would I get them home? Far too heavy to carry; and if I were able to carry, these faces would probably smash everything and anything in the suitcase. C'est la vie. Some things in life are just not

198 Ginger comes originally from China and India; some say 5,000 years ago. It has culinary and medicinal purposes. Ginger is a natural food that is good for the lung illnesses; arthritis in a poultice form; in form of a tea: digestive aid, for flatulence, motion sickness, and morning sickness—that will be the day. But do consult your doctor for advisement of ginger medicinal cures.

that important to possess. Montville is a charming and lovely town. Everyone goes there.

| Montville shop area | Montville waterwheel |

After having our 5 o'clock cocktail hour with appetizers, we drove to Maroochydore RSL club for dinner; the dinner ordered was buffet and a casino. The lamb I had was very good; it's something I would not cook at home. I'm not a gambler, but what can one lose at the penny slots. I walked away with $2. My motto is to quit while ahead. We returned to the condo and had coffee and a marvelous pastry we had previously purchased. The Maroochydore sunset symbolized a capital day we had.

The following day Jack left for Brisbane and I stayed on at the Chateau Royale. I have fond memories of Maroochydore packed away in a thousand and one cells of my brain. I cannot forget this lovely spot. And two weeks later, the night before departure, and while listening to the radio—Muller was conducting a musical opus invoking this Miltonic "Il'Penserose" mood or perhaps more akin to Keats...

> My heart aches and a drowsy numbness pains my sense, as though of hemlock I had drunk.[199]

How do I explain this mood that was invoked by looking out of my window and seeing and grasping Coleridge's thought that nature is a term

---

199   John Keats (1795-1821) wrote these lines from "Ode to a Nightingale" in May 1819.

in which we comprehend all things that are representable in the form of time and space, and subjected to the relations of cause and effect.

The sun's rim dips, the stars rush out;
At one stride comes the dark;...

So lonely 'twas , that God himself
Scarce seemed there to be...[200]

It's a time one that doesn't want to stab into reflections around a jabbering table of people and to watch the memories spill into the chaste or unblessed mind. Look, what I had to await— an elongated, irritating, and anti-climatically, 17-hour flight home.

---

200 Samuel Taylor Coleridge (1772-1834) wrote "The Rime of the Ancient Mariner" in 1797-98. The lines quoted here come from stanzas 13 (part III) and 22 (part VII).

Chapter Twenty-Five:

Been There, Done That

This chapter is a conglomeration of various places that I have visited/ toured, and I think worth the reading if my reader has also created his bucket list. My previous chapters have not dealt with United States, not that it doesn't have important and fascinatingly scenic places to visit, but because most Americans have made their jaunts to the most popular national parks. So, my inclusion here will do with what I have encountered that was particularly unusual or I have some comment, hopefully of merit.

In 2000 I had a 2 day stopover in London before flying to Malaga, Spain, providing enough time to browse through the shops and revisit some London historical spots of interest to me. For instance, Oscar Wilde was not represented in Poets Corner because of his life style. But now there is a memorial glass window all in a blue hue. It was a distant relative that commented that the window is appropriate in that his memorial is not entirely in and not entirely out of Westminster Abbey.[201]

---

201   Oscar Wilde (1856-1900), noted for his witty sayings and paradoxes in his brilliant plays of satire. Wilde's downfall came when he brought suit against the Marquis of Queensberry's attack on his character. In the first trial, Wilde was prosecuting and enough evidence was brought out so that Wilde became the defendant in the next two succeeding court cases and found guilty and sentenced to two year in the Old Bailey and Reading Goal for homosexual acts through what critics suggest as bribed evidence by Lord Alfred Douglas' father.

Although Wilde was not ever so-to-speak in the closet—S.F. vernacular to hide his homosexuality—he detested being called names in print by the Marquis of Queensbury.

In the late 60s, I was not afraid to be out at night. I wanted to be on Westminster Bridge at sunrise to align myself with the Wordsworth thoughts about London. So, in the 60s—yeah, my salad days—I was enthusiastic about Wordsworth and wanted to unite my imaginary impressions with reality: to compare Wordsworthian thoughts about London and my enthusiastic endeavors for anything British; thus, walk across Westminster Bridge at what I now term an ungodly early morning hour.

> Earth has not anything to show more fair;
> Dull would he be of soul who could pass by
> A sight so touching in its majesty:
> This City now doth, like a garment, wear
> The beauty of the morning: silent, bare,
> Ships, towers, domes, theatres, and temples lie
> Open unto the fields and to the sky;
> All bright and glittering in the smokeless air....[202]

The result of my attempt to focus on the Wordsworthian spirit of looking up and down the Thames River didn't match what I imagined that of Wordsworth's. Near Westminster Abbey, I was stopped by a bobby and told that it wasn't safe to be wandering about on the Victorian Embankment, where there was an Underground station. I agreed and returned to the safety of my hotel.

I always believed in the Wordsworth principle that we are a part of all that we behold. Pantheism, if you extend the meaning to all nature as he did. I know that I'm getting over my head when I abbreviate

---

202 William Wordsworth (1770-1850); sonnet composed upon Westminster Bridge on 9/3/1802. He was 32 and I am now a little older, and as one bobby at one end of the bridge patrolling the Victorian Embankment stated that I should not be out at this ungodly hour. But when you have a bucket list, this item had to be fulfilled.

pantheism, but earlier philosophers designate a pantheist as one who holds that everything there is constitutes a unity and that unity is divine. Not separating "the divine" between God and creatures would not be ethical to my up-bringing. Nevertheless, Plato, Emerson (the Oversoul) and Brahman (in Hinduism) align themselves to Spinoza's doctrine that there is only one substance. What a mouthful of words I spew forth here when I am no authority on anything, but if my reader has an interest in such ideas, I can recommend The Oxford Companion to Philosophy, edited by Ted Honderich. It's quite a compendium of abridged philosophical thoughts.

There are so many charming and beautiful places to visit in England and I found it intensely interesting to talk to others who have gone where I have been. One, near Charring Cross is Foyles Book Store. It is a fascinating place to shop for new and used books. The first time I was in there in 1954, I found an 1894 edition of Shakespeare Concordance in usable condition for 2 £. If you have an interest, another place to find books here in the states—which didn't exist in the 50s—is on the internet: Amazon.com. This website is impossible to fail to find your book to order.

Here it is 2000, and I find myself seeking out Selfridges or Mark and Spencer's basement food sections with prices much lower than Harrods'. Oh, the fresh fruit, bakery, pick-me-up kinds of foods, I always found tempting and ones that I could afford. Such shopping is an effort to save the money for a complete dinner at the evening meal while traveling. And, of course, lunch is always good at the many pubs throughout the British cities. Anyway, on my walk I encountered a store named Surprise. I have a teacher friend

Shopping in London and finding "Surprise"

in Spokane whose last name is Surprise; I took a photo of the store with the sign of her last name. There is also a town in Arizona call Surprise. Norman Rockwell painted a picture of a teacher standing in front of her class with the word Surprise on the blackboard. My friend was a first grade teacher and she enjoyed telling me how her first graders responded to her name, especially when she later talked to parents and how surprised they themselves were when their youngsters told them their teacher's name was Surprise. "Good Morning, Mrs. Surprise" was a name they would have to get used to. Seeing the sign "Surprise" is a memory unexpectedly jumping forward into my present.

It was in 1963 that I drove over the Allegheny Mountain passes to tour Gettysburg battlefields. Brinkley's journal stated this is a highly visited historical battlefield and accommodations are not all that easy to find and somewhat unreasonable. At the time, I found out that he was so right! Churchill wrote that the Civil War must, upon the whole, be considered the noblest and least

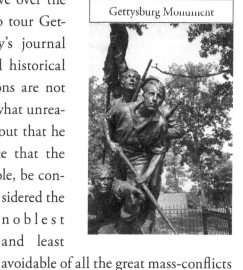

Gettysburg Monument

avoidable of all the great mass-conflicts the world had yet experienced. The number of men lost at Gettysburg is more than four times as great as the whole of the Revolutionary campaign. I search out the Willie House where Lincoln stayed and made the finishing touches to his Gettysburg address and then where he delivered it. His fourteen sentence message invoked blasphemy from school children's memorization

N.Y. 42nd Infantry monument

assignment. I walked and walked with my map of the campaign, searching out some 1400 monuments scattered over these memorable

Pennsylvania monument - In memory of sons who on the field found for the preservation of the union

meandering eighteen miles of roads. Too late did I realize that I could have rented a bicycle and thus saved the time of running back to the car and driving onto another section of the battlefield. I was most impressed with the Gettysburg Cemetery, Eternal Light Peace Memorial, scene of the first day clash, and the Gettysburg Cyclorama, a memorial painting of Pickett's charge (353 feet in circumference and 30 feet high), which is very aptly housed in a special tower-like structure with the most effective lighting. This is not to be missed.

It would be folly to think that one could cover this whole area well in only in the two-day, self-devised tour. I did overhear one lady comment that she did in fact spend all of 2 hours covering everything. She probably has no more comprehension of what took place here than when she arrived. Methinks her comment, "Oh, I've been there!" is about her conclusion of such a devastating battle field that changed a world of political policies. I noted markers "Unknown, Corporal Unknown, Unknown." A marker indicating rank drew my atten-

Unknown, Unknown Corporal, Unknown

tion and I wondered about this young man and his life taken so young from life's ever beautiful and inspiring days of cheer. Sadness envelopes one in what was not to be. And again what pops into one's head is what this marker unites me with him in the quote, "Life itself is the proper binge."[203]

Other cemeteries that impressed me as much as Gettysburg were our National Arlington Cemetery and the National Memorial Cemetery of the Pacific or Punchbowl Cemetery. The Arlington Cemetery has the Tomb of the Unknown Memorial along with those who gave their lives, their youth, not only in the preservation of the Union, but also the Revolutionary War and thereafter others who served our government. Originally the land belonged to Robert E. Lee and it was confiscated in 1864 as retribution for his part as general for the South in the Civil War.

The Punchbowl Cemetery on Oahu opened recently (1949) and contains the graves of approximately 40,000 arranged in concentric circles on the floor of an extinct volcano. Ernie Pyle is buried here. It has such a beautiful command of the city and ocean, you can't help be affected by the number of dead, especially of those who participated in the WW11 struggle.

| Amish country | Barn with cantilevered flooring |

In the same year of 1963, I visited York and Lancaster, which are notable centers of Amish, Mennonite or Dunkard religious sects as they are called. They are probably more alike than different, but there are differences. I decided to traverse some of the back roads off the freeway.

203   A Julie Child's quote; (1912-2004); she served as an OSS during WW11; later launched
       a love affair with American cooks in her televised cooking classes on Boston's WGBH
       that commenced in 1962.

Some farms have signs of welcome, but the one I picked did not. I drove up to the barn and met an Amish fellow, young and bearded and attending to his milking chores. I knew something about farming since knowing Emil and from my childhood experience of spending summers on my father's cousin's farm. With such a friendly fellow, I kept asking questions which probably disguised my ignorance. I was intrigued with some of his expressions as he requested, maybe to his son, "Throw the cow over the rail some hay." I don't know much about languages, but I am familiar with the uniqueness of crowding subject and object first in delivering the thought. Here you have an imperative sentence in which the direct object is basically the subject of the thought and the position of where the hay is to be placed precedes the object.

Amish stems from the middle of the 17th C. with Jacob Amman, Swiss minister, and found sanity from absurd Christian practices of the day; thus, the group separated themselves from the societies around them, retaining dress (beards and broad-brimmed hats for men, bonnets and aprons for women), no electricity in homes, no motor transport, refuse military service, have their own schools, declined SS benefits as well as no missionary activity. Marriages are formed within the Amish community. Mennonites stem back to the middle of the 16th century with a Dutch Roman Catholic priest, Menno Simons, who was most critical of the sinful religious practices by the church. His teachings include church discipline, pacifisms and non-participation of Christians in the magistracy and other practices of separation. The congregational then is autonomous. There is no common doctrinal basis for their united life, which I suspect parallels/assimilates the Dunkard sect: that religious life originates as a response to experiences of society. Certainly the Australian aboriginals found/ believed that it is the group that ultimately forms people's minds and controls their behavior. Nothing new here in this statement, but perhaps just another way of understanding primitive and our own social mores; the differences that we teach behavior for boys and girls for instance. I found that it's not true that Amish have remained unchanged for the latter 300 years.

Although, this farmer did use horses and not a tractor, he did have diesel milking machines. My short visit was interesting and I thanked him profusely for rendering his kindness to me.

Before arriving at Philadelphia, I pulled off the road and tried to memorize some the main arteries of this 4th largest city of U.S at this time. It proved helpful, for I had almost no trouble finding my picked auto court where I was going to stay for the next two days. How to squeeze in so much: Betsy Ross's home, Ben Franklin's grave, Independence Hall, Christ Church, Valley Forge, etc. I wasted no time setting out to see what I had outlined in my itinerant. I had a little difficulty in finding Poe's home, which is in a bad section of Philly. Got mixed up and had to cross the Ben Franklin toll bridge into Camden, N.J. and come back on the other side. Poe lived longer in Philadelphia than he lived in any other location. Here he wrote "The Raven, "The Tell Tale Heart," "The Gold Bug," etc. He paid $100 rent for a year, and this was the only time he rented a whole house, which I thought was in a very poor state. The housekeeper stated that funds have been sought and promised for a restoration.

In talking about homes, I found that there are several that interested me especially. So, on a tour of New England, I visited the home of Henry Wadsworth Longfellow (1807-1882) there in Cambridge, MA. His second wife Fanny Appleton wrote a marvelous journal of her tour of Europe. She agreed with Voltaire's criticisms of the Dutch and wrote this delightful sentence full of alliterations: "Ducks, dabbling in ditches, dribbling dams and dikes, dank dirty domiciles, dusty dams, disgusting dreary dullness and dolefully drowsy droughty drinking dolts of Dutchmen!" The Longfellow's home is kept immaculately. And in my mind I could visualize Fanny's screams as her flimsy, summer dress caught fire while using a sealing wax (self-sticking envelopes were not in use then). She ran up the back stairs calling Henry while he was running down the stairs in the front of the house. It must have been ghastly for Henry and in putting out the flames consuming Fanny, he obtained severe degree burns on hands and body so that he was confined to his bedroom and could not attend Fanny's funeral. Makes you weep reading of this tragedy.[204]

There are magnificent homes along the Hudson River. Another home for me to visit was the home of Eleanor Roosevelt (1884-1962). She had the

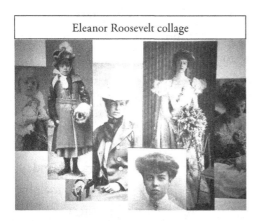

Eleanor Roosevelt collage

admiration of my Great Aunt Martha, whom I have already discussed in chapter one. I'm sure some of her admiration rubbed off on me. Maybe my reader may not know that she was the niece of Theodore Roosevelt and thus was well within the family realms for Franklin to marry his fifth cousin Eleanor in 1905. Some biographies claims Franklin as the politician while she as an agitator. The thing that I know was that she was the most outspoken First Lady as she served with Franklin during the years 1933 through1945. I can recall news reels with her descending down into one of John Lewis's mines and coming back and declaring she had never experienced such depressing and dangerous working conditions. And

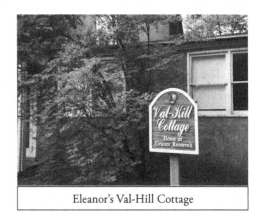

Eleanor's Val-Hill Cottage

then there was the incident of the DAR forbidding Marian Anderson from singing in a Washington auditorium and Eleanor reprimanded the group and resigned her membership and arranged for Marian to sing in front of the Lincoln Memorial. Eleanor was a much admired woman.

---

204   Mrs. Longfellow (*Selected Letters & Journals*), Ed, E. Wagenknecht, Longmans, Green, 1956.

In the near vicinity of Hyde Park is the Vanderbilt Mansion. Opulence unfolds as you parade these kinds of houses. Besides the homes on Fifth Avenue, there are two homes in Newport, Rhode Island. One was Marble Hall and built in 1892 for William Vanderbilt. It is referred to as one of "the cottages," among other impressive homes. If you go to Newport during the yuletide season, homes are decorated for the season, which of course match cost to the extravagant interior. Another Newport home was The Breakers, built in 1895 for Cornelius Vanderbilt.[205] The Hyde Park Mansion on the Hudson was purchased by Frederick Vanderbilt, who was the grandson of Cornelius. And we mustn't forget the Vanderbilt home in Ashville, North Carolina, built by George Vanderbilt, which has one of the most lavish formal gardens you will ever see. I admire people who have brains and suc-

Hyde Park mansion on the banks of the Hudson River

Marble House at Newport

ceed in this world. Brains and ambition makes a mighty force, but when such people have bribed legislators to insure their successes then something is remiss. Cornelius was an avid stock market speculator and

The library at Breakers, Newport, R.I.

---

205   Both photographs (Marble House & library at Breakers) are from the Wikipedia file. Marble House was photographed by Daderot in 8/05 and Breaker library is by upstate NYer (own work). Permission is licensed under the Creative Commons Attribution-Share Alike 3.0 (http://creativecommons.org/licenses/by-sa/3.0/deed.en).

often used the market to break his competitors financially. At the end
of his life he was valued at over 100 million, which was left for the most
part to his son William. There
is good in the Vanderbilts, especially in steamship and rail
transportation systems; later
many charities, yet all this does
not excuse what he paid in exchange for labor. Workers' compensation health benefits were
missing and the laborer barely
eked out a living for a family;

Vanderbilt home in Ashville

happening across America this treatment of labor mires a benevolent
exchange of labor for pay. The William Randolph Hearst's San Simeon
Castle, San Simeon, California, and the John Deering estate in Miami
area have opulence galore. They,
too, had brains, but when their
accumulated wealth was made
off the backs/expounded energies of the common worker
without adequate pay to support the family, then this wealth
has become greed. I can readily
remember all those strikes
where men have locked themselves in the factories of Wauke-

Millet's painting, S.F. Museum

gan to demand better pay. Every high school student during my day has
read the poem "The Man with the Hoe,"[206] which instructs and stimu-
lates thoughts of labor, labor strikes and the excesses of CEOs:

...

---

206 Edwin Markham (1852-1940) poem was written while/after viewing Jean
     François Millet (1814-1875) painting with the same title and which now hangs
     in the S.F. Museum of Art.

Is this the thing the Lord God made and gave
To have dominion over sea and land;
To trace the stars and search the heavens for power;
To feel the passion of eternity?
...
Through this dread shape humanity betrayed,
Plundered, profaned, and disinherited,
Cries protest to the Powers that made the world,
A protest that is also prophecy.
...
Give back the upward looking and the light;
Rebuild in it the music and the dream;
Make right the immemorial infamies,
Perfidious wrongs, immedicable woes?

Millet's painting is a glimps into the artist interpretation of a reality at some point of time whether it be El Greco's religious insight revealed in his *Burial of Count Graz* housed in the Prado Museum (see chapter 22) or some wild shocking thought of reality expressed in Picasso's *Nude in a Rocking Chair* housed in Sydney's Art Museum (chapter 21). My whole point in citing Markham's poetry is to renew a timeless thought that there are some men of position and power who care not about their laborers' welfare to the extent that they not only missed the boat, they didn't even know where the pier was located.

Yosemite has to be one of the most popular National parks in America. Methinks that at times the whole of California is visiting there at any one particular day. It's small in comparing where you may drive in Banff, Yellowstone, etc. Once up at Glacier Point, the view of the valley floor is awesome. So much majesty, so beautiful,

Glacier Point in Yosemite

so invoking time and the past forces of nature that created this park and so losing control of your bladder when approaching and not expecting the sheer drop just on the other side of the three/four ft. fence. When I told my brother Jack that I had never been to Yosemite even though having spent considerable time in graduate school at Berkeley U., he said, "We go!" In 1991, arrangements were made. We stayed at the Hotel and had reservations for dinner in the dining room. It was a lovely setting and we were so fortunate to have a prize table with a view of the Yosemite Falls. I was much impressed with this scenic park. There are so many areas where one can walk and I did choose one that was noted as a lesser walk

A Yosemite view

to the falls. As I remember, I sat down on a log next to the stream and immediately noted this pugilist little bird that braced himself against a submerged rock and dipping himself under water gaining whatever prize was there. He'd pop up and then plunged himself down again. I kept thinking how can this tiny animal sustain himself against such a fierce current? Here I go again sounding like Thoreau obtaining a lesson of life through the suggestion of this determined bird.[207] Don't we all have these adversaries while we struggle during life? And yet somehow we gain dominance and obtain what is significantly important: life. C'est la vie. Yes, that's it!

There are great museums; i.e., the Getty Museum in LA area. Their exhibits are so marvelous and so well displayed that nowadays you have to have an appointment to enter. So be it. Everyone should go at least once. But the museum that touched me greatly is the Norman Rockwell Museum at Stockbridge, Massachusetts. As a kid, I peddled magazines,

---

207   The text The Audubon Society: *Field Guide to North American Birds, Western Region* suggests that I had observed what the British call the Water Ouzel that feeds on insect life of streams; they're listed as item #492 and called Dippers.

along with my grandfather's vegetables from his garden in the summer. You got the Saturday Evening Post which always had one of Norman

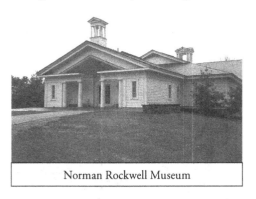

Norman Rockwell Museum

Rockwell's paintings on its cover. Price was a Nickel. I collected past covers of this magazine along with those used in calendars put out with contributions to the American Vets foundation. I was enraged that in the 50s this artist was accused as being a communist. Humbug! Attending the museum (1966) is as museum brochure proclaims "Step into Norman Rockwell's World," with its capturing of American life in all of its eccentricities. It's worth a visit. One painting titled *Village* depicts main street of a small town that Kincaid never can. My favorite Rockwell work is *Surprise* and primarily because my friend Mrs. Surpise taught first grade in Spokane school system. The tribute to all dedicated American first grade teachers was the cover of *The Saturday Evening Post* on March 17, 1956.

I can't help but include a paragraph about my travels in Kentucky: it is the birth place of Daniel Boone, who ventured through the gap which lead to the settlement of this Bluegrass country; Abraham Lincoln's birth house in Hodgenville in 1809; Stephen Foster penned "My Old Kentucky Home" here in 1853; and more important to me at this time in my life is the history of the Kentucky Derby in Louisville that began in 1875. As a young girl, I thought just about everyone talked about the legendary race horse *Man of War*. The news reels showed a

Churchill Downs

magnificent horse that copped honors beyond any horse expectations. So if you're on I-264 take the 3rd Street exit or Southern Parkway and you'll arrive at the museum annexing Churchill Downs. There is a horse there named Rapid Gray that holds Churchill Downs track record for 7 furlongs (7/8 of a mile) since 1985: 1:21:1 and made earnings of over $400,000. What all this means besides my interest invoked by headlines in American newspapers through many years is to cover the grounds where the very best of the horses raced for untold gamblers to place, win, or show. I have

Phenomenal horse Rapid Grey

come to understand—to change my view—that it is not just a sport for the very rich, but for the many average/poor folk who looked for a possible change of luck and live the lifestyle they never had. Very few come to an end as that of National Velvet[208]

In 1996, I took a tour on the Mississippi River. Met a gentleman who introduced me to Jamison Scotch; liquor I could drink straight without mixes and over rocks, was a pleasant before dinner drink. The gentleman was exceptionally nice. He and I had cattle backgrounds in common. I knew something about Hereford and we were well acquainted about the success or failure pertaining to such and the like. We had dinner together more than once during the brief tour. There was never any affection beyond just a friendship. What surprised me is how much I enjoyed Mississippi. My brother urged me to drive to the university there at Oxford. A quaint town that honors William Faulkner, for his bronze statue of him sitting on a bench is planted there at the town square. The

---

208 *National Velvet*, 1940: starred Elizabeth Taylor, Mickey Rooney, Arthur Treacher, Anne Revere (received best-supporting actress Academy Award) Angela Lansbury and many other notables.

university owns his residence, and I agree with my brother who was most critical about its up-keep. It needed some tender loving care. My brother is an admirer of Faulkner, who summarized race relations in his novels. Symbolism abound. If you care to read his novella *The Bear*, there are pages and pages where Faulkner does not punctuation or capitalize letters. So, if and when you come upon it, let yourself go into this stream of consciousness. It's a good read. From my brother, I learned that it is true of Faulkner's book that the past is never dead and it really never passes. It's always there; not as it was in the beginning, but still it's there.

One of the surprising travel highways in the U.S. is the Natchez Trace Parkway. It runs from Cherokee, Alabama, to Natchez, Mississippi. It's a

Natchez Parkway, MS

two lane highway, with the exception of entering and leaving Jacksonville. It's at Jacksonville that I turned off onto this parkway. If you would like to step into the past, you do it here. There are no billboard signs, no stop signs, no traffic lights. If a highway crosses the parkway, it either goes above the road or a tunnel is built under the parkway, and such are built in a way that is completely in harmony of the original road. There is also a speed limit; if you tire of it, there are arms where you may either turn off for gas or restroom facilities or to join a faster and perhaps more convenient method/way to arrive at your destination. It is a highway in which you can listen to sounds of nature and let the world rush on to its duties, but to this traveler it was inspiring that "this" exists at all. While here in Mississippi I did stop at a cemetery. I have often done this, visiting cemeteries. I've been to Lake District and stood by William Wordsworth's grave; been to Sleepy Hollow Cemetery for Thoreau and Ralph Waldo Emerson's and of course I just mentioned Eleanor and Franklin's site.

Here in the well-kept cemetery was a monument for the Confederate soldiers. There is always a sadness to note the expenditure of life by the young. And if they had the chance, would they have enjoyed their older age as I have?

If there is any amusement park where there is dollar value, then it is at Dollywood, Pigeon Forge, Tennessee. It's more than an amusement park and in some respects much like Disney World, Disneyland. It has features that the former doesn't: camping sites, rides for adults and adult entertainments and shops galore and some with regional crafts such as glass blowing,

In Memory of County Confederate Dead

basket weaving and other Appalachian chores. I think Dolly Parton is a fabulous woman who writes and sings her songs with panache. I'm not particularly a fan of western music, but I am when the artist is Dolly Parton and her ability to belt out lyrics that are understandable and at times as touching/emotional as Leontyne Price singing the aria from Butterfly: "Un Bel Di"—one fine day I shall see the smoke rising from the ship stacks… I still think that Plato's thoughts dealing with primary and secondary substance is best explained in the medium of music: notes carry the secondary matter to the essence of the primary.

Dollywood

There are so many other delightful places that I have had the opportunity to visit, but time and, perhaps, my reader has arrived at a feeling of ennui. So let me close with an expression of feeling close to God in some unusual churches. There is a chapel just outside Ephesus, where John took Mary after the crucifixion. It's a small chapel attended by a monk who keeps people in line in case of irreverence. It's unique and worth the side trip should you visit this area of Turkey. But I have already related this experience in chapter 23. At Constantinople is the Blue Mosque, which has the second or third largest dome in the world. Women are not permitted entrance to the main sanctuary, but you may gaze in and see the magnificent chandeliers and a sea of green carpeting; green, as I understand from my readings, is a sacred color in the Moslem faith. St. Paul's in London,[209] I believe, ranks second among churches with the larger domes (360 feet high). Christopher Wren's plan of restoration/rebuilding of the church in 1672 were not enthusiastically approved by church officials as it is by most everyone of today. Wren is buried here among other English notables such as Lord Nelson, and John Donne. The mosaics on the ceiling are impressive, as well as the superb wrought iron work presented as screens in the choir aisles. Vaulted ceiling with such intricate geometric designs calls for reverence, besides so much history is wrapped in various niches; I guess I was impressed with who is who; nevertheless, those who have gone before have cast their shadow where they thought it never had gone.

The church that overwhelms people like me is St. Peter's in Rome. It was

St. Peter's

the emperor Constantine[210] who erected a basilica to honor the Apostle
Peter. This project was being done in 324 C.E. and eventually fell into
ruin, especially during the period of some seventy-three years that the
Popes abided in Avignon. It was Julius 11 (1503-1513) who took on the
reconstruction of the basilica that tourists see today. It was Michelangelo's genius that designed the dome with its tint of silver-blue color.
The colonnade of two large wings in a half embrace of humanity is by
Bernini. The monolith/obelisk is by Fontana and raised onto the square
in 1586, and the two fountains, one by Maderno in 1613, and one by
Bernini in 1675. The bronze door was designed by Filarete and in imi-
tation of those in Florence by Ghiberti. Be sure to take a closer look at
these doors both in Florence and here in Rome. The Papal Altar stands
over the tomb of St. Peter. The four spiral columns support a canopy
by Bernini and the angels are bronzes, which I first thought were made
of wood but actually came from the Pantheon. The first time I visited
St. Peter's you could approach the Pieta, probably Michelangelo's more
famous sculpture. But since it was attacked by some coot in 1972 it is
now protected by glass, roped barricade and with a guard. I don't need
to tell anyone that it's a religious experience just visiting this world outstanding church, regardless of the sins committed by various popes.

The Salem Calvary Baptist Church on Liberty Street here in Salem
has its fine sanctuary, basically in a fine oak finish. It's beautiful in its own
individual way. Religion, as I see it, involves hard work. Put your back to it;
stick adversity out; work hard to live life. That's output. But the body, primary
substance, needs connection/receptivity to the Oversoul.[211] Some would say

---

210   Which Constantine initiated the basilica leads the novice into confusion. My deduction
      concludes that the son of Constantious, known as Flavius Valerius Constantous (surnamed
      Chlorus) ruled during the years 306-337. The basilica was being built in 324.
211   You cannot talk about "Oversoul" without transcendentalism. It's the truths
      gained without the world of senses, and that these "truths" are the only truly
      real things (ideas of Plato). Emerson, (studied Eastern religions at Cambridge).
      Carlyle, Boehme, Eastern religions & others stressed the spiritual unity of the
      world; thus interpreting God in non-transcendental, and pantheistic way. Re:
      Emerson's essay "The Over-Soul," revise in 1847: "We see the world piece by
      piece, as the sun, the moon, the animal, the tree; but the whole of which these
      are the shining parts, is the soul"

that this may be attained via Transcendentalism.[212] It's like running into an experience that you can't handle simply by trying hard. My husband's death is an instance for me. You need— what I needed was sustenance beyond yourself. And that takes a wide spectrum of things—it could be an aria, it could be a gaze at Half Dome in Yosemite, or it could be a showing of a loving friendship from strangers as I received from the Stentas, when I first met them in Perth. What I'm talking about are "truths" known to the spiritual heart (see chapter 26 on "brain," "mind," and "spiritual heart"). Although I follow my Christian direction, I also believe there is much solace in believing what 19 & 20 C philosophers profess/instruct.

I'm a great one in collecting axioms; I write them down from my readings, or from a TV/film script. My reader will find the index by classifications helpful because in a "backward glance," hindsight without foresight is an empty thought. For instance, Martha Washington's (1731-1802) quote reveals a woman much in control of her life and made pleasant because of her viewpoint, especially during those many trying years she lived in colonial America. She wrote...

> ...the greater part of our happiness or misery depends on our dispositions and not on our circumstances.[213]

I always like dining; you never just eat at my brother's house, you dine. Anyway, Elsa Schiaparelli, an Italian fashion designer (1907-1973), wrote, A good cook is alike a sorceress who dispenses happiness. Or take this one from Agatha Christie (1890-1976):

> I like living. I have sometimes been wildly, despairingly, acutely miserable, racked with sorrow, but through it all I still know quite certainly that just to be alive is a grand thing."

And I agree.

---

212 Transcendentalist believed in removing "wrongs" ...mockery of the divine/the will of nature/of God; such were child labor laws, suffrages, theological superstitions, unjust wars, economic practices that denied labor its fair share of the goods of life, etc.

213 An inference by use of the quote suggests that Martha read Milton thoroughly and abbreviated Milton's thought more succinctly: Paradise Lost, Bk I, l. 254; "The mind is its own ..."

Chapter Twenty-Six:

Lessons Learned in Life

In 2006, I have walked in this life for 82 years; my **DNA**, physical body, heart, mind, brain, accumulative experiences, responses to life's tests, and my spiritual essence are all tied into a single package that reflects the *idea density* of my life. To elucidate a finite *idea density* of my life is a difficult task, but perhaps my reader may follow my logic by switching the emphasis on the first noun—actually the noun adjunct. Plato tried to teach his students that the idea of anything is the primary substance and the only real form. All physical matter changes whether it's a chair burning in rapid oxidation or whether we're thinking of a cloud. The idea of anything is the permanence of it. Let me elucidate further.

Millions of implicit and explicit stimuli are passing thru my five senses constantly interacting with each other creating my own unique "idea density" of my life. I can not take credit that I was able to see and do so much in my life because it was God's gift to me. I'm sure other faiths would use other names as Shiva/Śiva[214] in Hinduism or primary

---

214   Shiva, as being a part of the Hindu trinity: Visnu, Brahmā, Shiva. Shiva representation has a multifaceted nature of creator, destroyer and preserver. If Shiva's hand is in the upright position, it indicates protection and with downward-pointiung hand indicating liberation for all who trust in him. The spirit of Shiva is also associated the Ganges River: bathed at the time of death means reincarnation desists.

substance in ancient Greece. I prefer here to use the pronoun "He" and He gave me the gift of determination. Determination is not a *DNA* trait. A prime example was that I was determined to live on a twenty dollar a day budget except when traveling in foreign countries. It took a positive mind set to travel to foreign countries, rent a car, drive, and sight-see all on my own determination. Determination was there when I jumped from a plane and made my solo flights, etc. Through these years I have also explored and searched some aspects of knowledge as it affects my own distinct *idea density* in living.

Words are composed from 26 letters of the alphabet. The *meaning* of the word is not inherent in the word; *meaning* is brought to the word and the onset in creating *idea density*. Idea density launches an infinite onset of other words and ideas, which interact with each other, increasing the idea density immeasurably. The act of *reading* is the process of human awakening by bringing meaning to the word. Each word has its idea density—a flood of other words and ideas interacting and bringing a deeper, extensive, enrichment of meaning to the word. Education enhances *idea density* through the acquisition of knowledge/information processed through five senses (hear-see-touch-smell-taste) and *learning behaviors*. *Idea Density* includes tactile perception. I designed a technique where color, shape, and size are manipulated and interact with each other in the same moment. *Learning behaviors* are the tactics in how you learn; some examples are defining, describing, comparing, contrasting, separating, combining, qualifying, quantifying, recalling, remembering, creating, pronouncing, evaluating, inferring, etc. These tactics are invaluable in enhancing *idea density*. Teaching does not mean teaching answers, but the ability to lead and guide the learner to discover the answer with his own mind.

The *brain* is a physical organ composed of cellular matter; it is the center of the nervous system; its energy relays and interacts with stimuli from the five senses. It is used in operating the mental abilities and storing information; it provides the energy to use learning behaviors and millions of pathways for incoming and outgoing knowledge.

The *mind* is not the same as the brain, as it is not a physical organ; it exists in a physical body. The OED (Oxford English Dictionary) has endless references to its meaning, but primarily found in the trite expression "mind over matter." Jane Austin used the phrase "the elegance of mind and sweetness of character." I like to define it as found in the Platonic thought/primary substance. The *mind* is composed of a reservoir of information gathered and organized from the five senses through **learning behaviors** relayed to the brain. The **mind** is used to process this reservoir of information and becomes the stance for any present and future behavior.

The **DNA** identifies oneself through cell structure and gives the individual its own essence; the **DNA** is not used to identify the individual *spiritual essence*. We have a *physical heart*—as I have stated earlier is the secondary matter which composes a very important muscle. A *spiritual heart*—and here I mean the primary substance composed of an energy that takes on the feelings and thoughts that are visible in our actions. When the *physical heart* stops beating, death occurs, but the *spiritual heart* survives a physical death as it crosses time and space. This last sentence almost reads like *Nirvana*—the attainment of "enlightenment" and, to my thinking, aligns itself to Emerson's *"Oversoul."*[215] The Oversoul has its beginning in **Hinduism** and the Hindu would look upon the Christians and conclude that they have limited their concept of God to a trinity of the Father, the Son and the Holy Ghost when the devout should take into consideration the entire whole of the universe. In keeping an appointment with the doctor, the patient knows him as a source for the betterment of his health, but the patient never has knowledge of the doctor's other attributes: as a father, a husband, as a philatelist, a golfer, etc. Via NASA and Hubble photographs we may see the Andromeda Universe, which happens to be 2.9 million light-years away and it has a diameter of 250,000 light-years. Remember, light travels at the speed of 186,000 miles per second; thus, one

---

215   "We live in succession…in particles. Meantime within man is the soul of the whole; the wise silence; the universal beauty, to which every part and particle is equally related; the eternal One… We see the world piece by piece, as the sun, the moon, the animal, the tree; but the whole of which these are the shining parts, is the soul." The Over-Soul, lines 20-27. (Go see Avitar for a visual picture of the concept.)

light year = 5.878 trillion X 10_{12} = miles, which my computer/calculator cannot compute nor can my brain contemplate that many zeroes. Brahman is the creator; the **Supreme Being** from which all creation exists. The Hindus strive to reach true contact with their spiritual selves—the Atman (the inmost soul in every creature, which is divine). Although **Brahma** is not definitive as the Christian God, **Brahman** believers would embrace the Biblical quote that "God is Love." We all posses this attribute: Love. As it abides in the **Supreme Being**, it also abides in us, his creation—the abstract cause of all. Plato would name the **Hindu** concept of **Brahman** as the primary substance. One reason Buddhism rose/accepted/flourish is its protest of Hinduism with its belief in the class system: 1) **Brahmins** (intellectual/leaders); 2) **Kshartriyas** (administrators/orchestrating people); 3) **Vaisyas** (farmers, artisans, creating things on which life depends); 4) **Sudras** (the untouchables, the followers, servants, the unskilled laborers). Didn't the depression years reflect an enmity between factory management and laborers with all the strikes for a decent wage reflect a Hindu class society with **Sudras** being the factory workers and the Blacks and such—the untouchables? Buddhism and Hinduism, I think now, has valid points. If all religions live on this house Earth, then surely God cannot be in any just one room. But I must go back to my main point of the *Spiritual Heart* aligning it with Emerson's *Oversoul* and Plato's thoughts. Perhaps, Plato asked if we can see the fire burning. Would you know when the fire has gone out?[216] Obviously, the reply to both questions is "Yes." Then the question to follow is where did the fire go? North" South? East? West? Can there be an answer? Just because it is not there for you to see, doesn't mean non-existence.[217]

The Australian Aborigines look upon Ayers Rock as sacred. They would look upon this aspect of their environment as "something" that provides a spiritual communication to their being, perhaps, providing a physical means of just existing, or sustaining themselves from the harsh surroundings. It

---

216   Emerson: "The things that are seen, are temporal; the things that are unseen, are eternal." *Nature*, vi (Idealism).
217   Ralph Waldo Emerson, *Nature,* (1836) vii (spirit)

is just as my husband looked upon Lake Louise in Banff, or just as I look upon Glacier Point in Yosemite, etc. It's not what I see is "God," but seeing a representation of his handiwork. The Australian aborigines see various aspects of nature as a part of the Great Spirit. As with some early American Indians their reasoning is that "the one God" is not in their oral or written history is because the "Supreme Being" is unknowable. Things/objects/aspects of nature/Ayers Rock are worshiped for such things/matters are His creation, for He is everything in His creation.

In my readings of primal religions, I came across a study of the Algonquians; the point:

> It is often difficult for those who look on the tradition of the Red Man from the outside or through the 'educated' mind to understand that no object is what it appears to be, but it is simply the pale shadow of a Reality. It is for this reason that every created object is waken, holy, and has a power according to the loftiness of the spiritual reality that it reflects. The Indian humbles himself before the whole of creation because all visible things were created before him and, being older than he, deserve respect.[218]

The *spiritual heart* is a term that is a nebulous thought that exists or doesn't exist according to the dictates of the mind. Again to my thinking, the Buddhist would want to know which the better part of the human self is: the head or the heart. To stay away from Bible verses, I'd like to reflect on the split of Buddhism just as Christianity has split into sects: *Theravada Buddhism* and *Mahayana Buddhism*. *Theravada Buddhism* means humanity is on its own in the universe; there is no God to help us over the "slings and arrows of misfortune in life." You depend upon yourselves and from this realization flow loving kindness, compassion, equanimity and joy in the happiness and well-being of others. Mahayana Buddhism embraces the thought of grace; compassion cannot be counted on to be an automatic

---

218   From a letter written by Joseph Epes Brown, quoted in Schuon, *The Feathered Sun* (p.47) and in Huston Smith's *The World's Religions*, p.379.

fruition. With the emphasis on compassion over wisdom, a Mahayana Buddhist winds up with something like the "Sermon on the Mount."[219]

> May I be a balm to the sick, their healer and servitor until
> sickness came never again;
> May I quench with rains of food and drink the anguish of
> hunger and thirst;
> May I be in the famine of the age's end their drink and meat;
> with manifold things for their need.
> My own being and my pleasures, all my righteousness in the
> past, present and future, I surrender indifferently,
> That all creatures may win through to their end.[220]

In celebrating Valentine's Day we have the candy heart, symbolizing the sweetness of life and behind the giving carries the emotional inference of love. Each of us has a *physical* heart and an *emotional/spiritual heart*. The *physical heart* is easier to maintain through diet and exercise, whereas the *emotional / spiritual heart* needs love and can sustain itself by Proverbs 4:23.[221] The *spiritual heart* interacts with life; it lives beyond a physical death. May I note that I interpret the word "heart" in the Bible verses as the "spiritual heart"; it's Platonic primary substance, it's the oversoul, the Braham/Atman as found in all creations.

Education is bringing knowledge to the mind. *Wisdom* is learning how to use that knowledge; wisdom also knows the difference between things you can change and the things you can not change. The most vital trait all government officials need in exercising their required duties is Wisdom. *Knowledge* is necessary but *wisdom* supersedes *knowledge*. Learning to disagree agreeably is *wisdom.* In our American government system, the basic premise is to represent the people and not the corporate

---

219   Matthew, Ch 5 & 6; Luke 6:20-49
220   Thomas A Kempis (German) 1380-1471; famed as reputed author of religious classics Bodheckavatara of Shantideva and herewith quoted from Huston Smith's World's Religions, Harpers, S.F., 1958, p. 123.
221   Proverbs 4:23—"Keep thy heart with all diligence; for out of it are the issues of life." Proverbs is basically not concerned with prophetic and legalistic Judaism, but with wisdom distilled from life. Chapters 1:7 to chapter 9 are in praise of wisdom.

world and/or private interests. In representing the people, many of our politicians (as I have said before) are not only missing the boat but also they don't even know where the pier is.

Each one of us has a unique *idea density* of our mind, emotional/ spiritual heart, and learning behaviors. *Time* is an essence in life that is measured daily in minutes, hours, days, and years. Often in our "salad days," time passes slowly and then much faster when you are 82 years of age. I am absolutely astounded that it has gone by so fast. I keep asking myself where the 82 years went! *Time* is something you cannot buy, but you can give it away; and when you do, it becomes priceless. Judging the best use of *time* involves *wisdom*.

Love is a word too significant to define; the *idea density* is best when *love* is described. John 3:16[222] epitomizes the greatest act of *love*. The mother nourishes the physical heart as baby develops a beginning of an emotional heart-to-heart communication in *love*. A wondrous *love* exists between mother and child; a new born baby hopefully brings overwhelming joy and love to both mother and father. Love is expressed between spouses. *Love* is expressed in different ways through parent and child, family members, relatives, and friends. "God is love."[223] This Bible verse suggests that a part of God's essence is in the primary energy of love. If there is no love within your being—pretty hard to even begin to imagine that—then there is no spirit of God within. God loves me and He wants the best for me and from me. My attention of *idea density* is centered on the form, me. God's love is an infinite gift and it exists in all.

The *idea density* centers on the 82 years of my life where I have committed acts of commission and omission often lacking the expression of love. The idea density of love can be described in such songs as "Tenderly," "To Each His Own," "I Apologize," "I Should Care," " There I said It Again," are just a few songs that involve the *idea density*

---

222 John 3:16 For God so loved the world, that he gave his only begotten Son that whosoever believeth in him should not perish, but have everlasting life.

223 First Epistle of John 4:8, 16 He that love not, know not God; for God is love; and in verse 16, God is love is repeated; and he that dwell in love, dwell in God, and God in him.

of *love*. I do think that through music one can understand truly what Plato talks about when he tries to teach the difference between the primary and secondary status of anything. Here you have words and notes transcribed in an arrangement to reveal, in this instance, *love*.

Twice in my life I have felt an absolutely strong feeling that I should beware of "that car" and "that truck." There were none of the 5 senses giving the warning, yet my consciousness signaled a warning. Both times I was the victim of bad driving. Thus, sometimes, in mundane and insignificant circumstances, I felt a strong positive anticipation and yet the incident ended in unexpected negative results. For example, you make a medical appointment for a specific time, and upon arrival, you learn you will have to wait unnecessarily since your appointment time was given to someone else. Just the opposite can occur. You are facing circumstances when you expect the negative, but surprisingly, the unexpected positive happens.

In life we are confronted with situations like these:

approach—approach
approach—avoidance
avoidance—avoidance

These approaches define situations where a decision is expected to be made, which has both positive and negative choices. The longer it takes to make the choice, the higher the frustration level. An over simplification, for instance, is when you have two approach choices: to leave by an exit in a store, you start for one but end up taking another. This choice can be made in a fraction of a second, and at other times, it will take much more time to decide. The *approach-approach* describes a situation where a decision has to be made when two attractive choices are present. The *approach-avoidance* describes a situation where a decision has to be made between attractive choices which are in conflict with the negative choice. The *avoidance-avoidance* describes a situation in which both options are less than ideal; one may decide to pick the lesser of the two negative choices.

In our contemporary society we encounter **WMD**, which we learned that it stands for weapons of mass destruction: referring to nuclear bombs, chemical destruction, etc. For me, **WMD** also has an idea density just as dangerous: **WMD** as **Words of Much Destruction**. Such operates in the spiritual heart and mind; examples of such are anger, dishonesty, untruthfulness, greed, hatred, and self-centeredness. The **WMD** can be extremely destructive since they are dealing with the spiritual heart and involve negative behaviors. **WMD**, as we all know, are probably even more destructive in affairs to family life as well as to a society.

Conversely, **Learning Behaviors**, which enhance and enrich and nourish the spiritual heart, include love, kindness, patience, gentleness, and self discipline, less of self, faithfulness, keeping a promise, and always telling the truth. Cancer in the spiritual heart is ignoring one's conscience. One's conscience acts as a life-long **test**. When one's conscience bothers oneself in instances where you haven't done the right thing, you can **change**! The real trouble is when your conscience doesn't bother you; you are not only in trouble, but have failed one of the life-long tests. The most important things in life are not for sale.

Truth is the basis of **moral authority**, and yet Truth has been falsely claimed in words invoked by circumstance, and thus **Truth** is the most abused, misused, maligned word in our courts of law. The **idea density** must reflect true honesty and actual essence, not made up of untruths and lies. Marcus Aurelius made the statement "Truth is one name of nature. The first cause of all things true" (applies to Keats' meaning, see p. 271).

Laughter is another word that has significant **idea density**. Its effects are enormous. Variance in application and response will reflect individual tastes, temperament, etc. In the last year while shopping, I developed a tactic which I hoped would prompt/evoke a smile from the cashier. Before paying the bill, I would ask the cashier, "Do you accept cash? I was told that you always accept cash on Saturdays." I get a smile every time, however, recently a smart and different cashier replied: "Of course we take cash, but we do not give change on Saturdays." We both shared communicating to one another our friendship even if it was only a moment in time. Perhaps she went home and told her husband, friend, mother about this incident and thus creating another smile and a mutual feeling of laughter. What I do know is that we both had a good laugh. I understand people can be annoying because of the behaviors they sometimes exhibit; *idea density* understands to dislike the behavior, and not the person.

Greed exists when a want supersedes a need. A *need* is necessary to exist; a *want* is more than what is necessary to live. The seed of *greed* starts somewhere, in the heart, or mind or both. Yes, a profit is necessary and acceptable in conducting business; but when a profit becomes obscene, and then it is *greed*. To me a vivid example in our contemporary society is the cost of a gallon of gas. When a CEO receives a billion dollars for doing a job, then to me that is ridiculously absurd. When a CEO receives salaries in excess of more than millions of dollars, it vividly emulates the epitome that *want* supersedes **need** unless he/she is giving ninety percent to charity.

The world lauds Oprah Winfrey[224] loud and long enough for her stance on improving the lower economic families of Africa. By enlisting young girl from the poorer economic families and educating them in both mind and body cannot but help the world to become a better place. Through Oprah's generosity, this education that she is sponsoring will give each girl a chance to explore the deeper meanings of words and individual's *idea density* because the student's mind cannot help but flourishes, thrives, and blossoms. These girls will have the opportunity to help create a succeeding society where women can compete and achieve equally and by using her God given gifts to learn and make a serious impact on the male dominated society.

As I previously stated, the *meaning* of the word is not in the word; the meaning is brought to the word. If you ask a child what is love, I am sure his/her meaning is limited in comparison to that of a newly married couple.

---

224   There is no one who has done more to erase the racial prejudices than Oprah Winfrey. Through her hosting one of the more spectacular TV talk shows, she has taught the Americans—no, the world —how we should be in our behavior to one another. It was she who made it possible for Americans to vote resoundingly for an African-American President-elect Barak Obama.

Meaning is thusly contained and incurred in these differences. These few words epitomize one of the greatest life-shaking practices of *wisdom*. This *idea density* should not be taken lightly; its consequential effects and relevancies are enormous. The seeds of understanding evolve and mature in the honest heart-to-heart communications. The *idea density* in these few words—*the essence of a relationship unfolds in the quality of their communications*—are adaptable in any set of circumstances, and relationships between spouses, parent and child, sibling to sibling, relatives, friends, clerks, cashiers, mailman, teacher, gasoline attendant, and the most significant communication with God, and in the Calvary Baptist religious meaning, the Father through His Son.

Idea density is not limited to the printed word as it is discovered in signs, pictures and other non-verbal communication. Christians may call upon the Holy Spirit for sustaining his/her faith founded on biblical passages or *Primary Substance* as Plato might have named *it*. The word nourishment has an *idea density*; I acknowledge and try to follow advice that tells me how to maintain a physical/healthy body/secondary substance through diet and exercise. Nourishment to my emotional/ spiritual life on earth lies in the *idea density* of these Biblical verses.

Teach us to make the most of our time
so we can grow in wisdom.225

Wisdom is the principal thing;
therefore get wisdom and with all thy getting
get understanding.[226]

I have disagreed agreeably with my brother Jack on many occasions. Most of these happenings are cause by our usages and meanings of specific words. Any promise not to negate a positive is not necessarily a fulfillment of aforesaid statements, for as in all situations with friends and family these brief confrontations are C'est la vie. Voila.

225   Psalms 90:12
226   Proverbs 4:7

Willette Helen Sheldon Kotan

2 August 1924 - 24 August 2007

Epilogue

W illette died today. It was a short illness that circumstances lead to her being taken to the Salem Hospital where her life ended. She had been placed on life supports as soon as she became a patient. Thorough exams...x-rays, MRI, blood tests, etc., cause of death was determined as a severe stroke...over 80 percent of her brain suffered lesions. If she did awaken from her comatose state, it was doubtful that she would ever gain control over her bodily functions, speech and rational thought to enjoy simple pleasure of life; i.e. reading... Thanksgiving dinners...birthday celebrations...give view to today's sunrise...and everything that too often we all take for granted.

It was just before her 83rd birthday, that she first thought she had strained a back muscle. Her family doctor arranged a specialist for her examination with special tests. Conclusion was that the severe pain was a result from stones in the gall bladder and removal of such would ease her intense pain. On the date of scheduled surgery, her physician refused to operate because he thought her tests were not intelligible...more tests would have to be rescheduled. This surgeon detected an unstable heart and other recorded bodily ailments were not consistent for this surgical remedy. In the following weeks, her pain subsided to where she was persistent in doing exercises such as walking and swimming in the Courthouse pool and spending some time in a Jacuzzi

With my morning visit on the 22nd, I asked her to come home with me so that I could attend her eating habits. She was slowly losing energy and appetite. Foods that I brought over were not being consumed for the most part. She rejected that idea of coming home with me for attendance care, preferring to be independent and sporadically working on her biographical notes, reading, TV watching. On the following day, she had not responded to a phone call—she had an appointment with her family doctor at 9:45. I arrived about 8:30 and found her sitting in her chair dressed only in her nightie. I could not arouse her and immediately called 911. Before the medical staff took off with her, she was attached to pulmonary artificial heart support. Multiple tests confirmed by her cardiologist and pulmonary specialist as well as neurologist specialist that she was brain dead. The hospital chaplain assisted me in contacting her minister of the Calvary Baptist Church. She died within minutes after taking her off all life supports.

Measurement of our farewell tears are a measurement of our happiness of having her in our lives. Tennyson's "In Memoriam" wrote it well in verse. There was not much that she missed in life. And one conclusion of Faulkner's writing is that the past is never dead and it never passes. . The pain of parting life is with those surviving and it is we who must remember the thrills ...the excitements...the happy moments...that will refresh our minds and hearts. One of God's gifts, which constantly maintain a status of positive goodness, is having known Willette Helen Sheldon Kotan.

Appendix A

"Critical Thinking"

What is this phenomenon that we call critical thinking?
Can it be taught…and if so…is it being taught?
This critical thinking is "good stuff,"
but how does the classroom teacher begin
to develop this cognitive style of thinking and learning,
it is influenced by the personality of the individual,
it will reflect the backing of his experiences
as well as the anticipation of what he will perceive
the ingredients…
the classroom teacher
the thinker
the thinking
the thought
getting something started that
will continue to be in motion
teachers sometimes place constraints on the thinker
by not giving adequate material to assimilate,
insufficient concrete facts,
presenting ideas at a low conceptual level,
talking…talking…talking
talking after her own thinking has stopped,
for talking does not enhance or further understanding.
It is like …"over teaching"….
Teacher ask eight to ten times
more questions than youngsters
children need to be participants
rather than spectators
for such an important process…
the thought may not be unique to the world
but can be original to the thinker.

Children are members of our culture
 and not candidates,
     the needs are too important,
       too necessary to overlook
                  They say teach our youth a sport
                   that they can use in the adult life,
                  but what about intellectual power
             for the adult life
 A cognitive style of thinking
     to fit his personality
                     Need a new generation of something beyond
                   surface thinkers coming up with the quick
                   and easy answers which seem to be right
               at the tip of our tongues
             the easy ones to reach
                          having knowledge does not guarantee good thinking
                          but a good thinker does need good knowledge
 defining what academic freedom can be more simple
     than trying to explain why it is necessary
       with all of its ramifications....
                    the answer will take much more
                       than what we find on the surface....
 it is open-endness
     not to be ensnared by deal-end logic....
                 it is the capacity for finding the answers,
                   to sift out the sense and facts
                      from a jungle of claims....
 it is fortifying self against hazy notions,
     keeping in mind that there is no ready-made formula....
       it is the quest of preciseness...clarity...depth...
          understanding...dynamic...
             as much as the nature of man itself.

A reprint from *Arithmetic Teacher*,   WILLETTE H. SHELDON, *Graduate Student*
Volume 12, Oct. 1965, p. 501   *University of California, Berkeley, California*

Appendix B

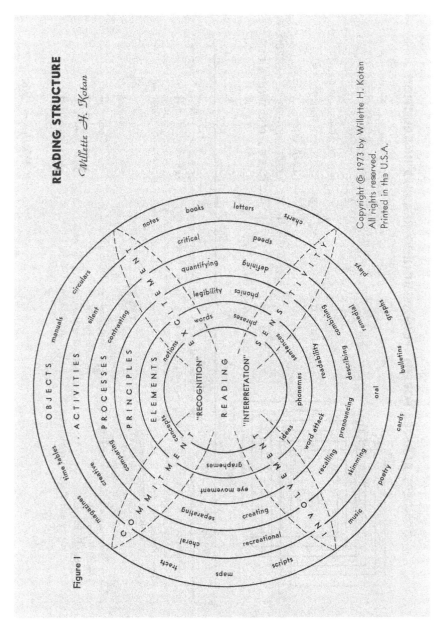

Figure I

*One critic in reviewing CISE stated she had forgotten to include the newspaper.

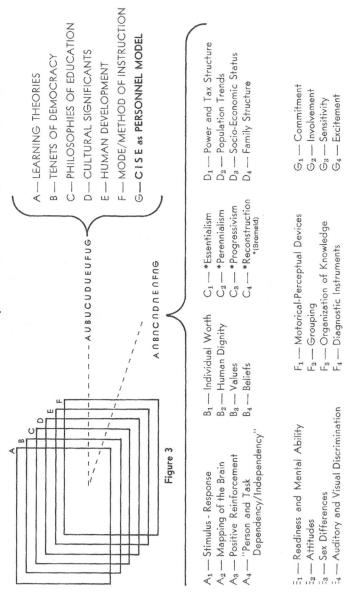

CONCEPT CLUSTER FOR SHAPING/DESIGNING READING INSTRUCTION

A U B U C U D U E U F U G

A B C D E F G

A — LEARNING THEORIES
B — TENETS OF DEMOCRACY
C — PHILOSOPHIES OF EDUCATION
D — CULTURAL SIGNIFICANTS
E — HUMAN DEVELOPMENT
F — MODE/METHOD OF INSTRUCTION
G — C I S E as PERSONNEL MODEL

A_1 — Stimulus - Response
A_2 — Mapping of the Brain
A_3 — Positive Reinforcement
A_4 — "Person and Task
        Dependency/Independency"

B_1 — Individual Worth
B_2 — Human Dignity
B_3 — Values
B_4 — Beliefs

C_1 — *Essentialism
C_2 — *Perennialism
C_3 — *Progressivism
C_4 — *Reconstruction
        *(Brameld)

D_1 — Power and Tax Structure
D_2 — Population Trends
D_3 — Socio-Economic Status
D_4 — Family Structure

E_1 — Readiness and Mental Ability
E_2 — Attitudes
E_3 — Sex Differences
E_4 — Auditory and Visual Discrimination

F_1 — Motorical-Perceptual Devices
F_2 — Grouping
F_3 — Organization of Knowledge
F_4 — Diagnostic Instruments

G_1 — Commitment
G_2 — Involvement
G_3 — Sensitivity
G_4 — Excitement

Figure 3

Willette H. Kotan

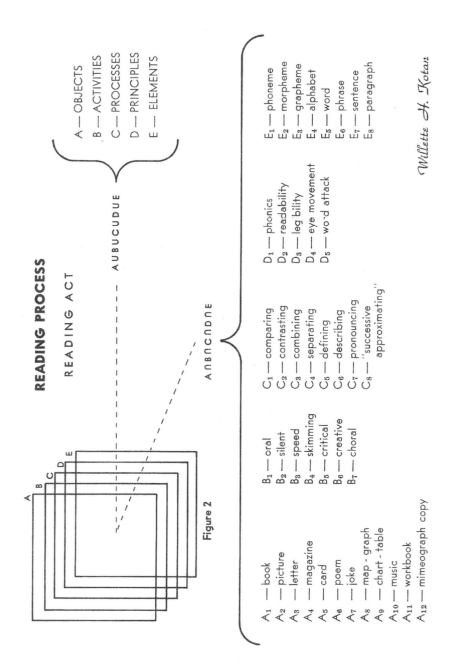

READING PROCESS

READING ACT

AUBUCUDUE

- - - - - - -

AUBUCUDUE

Figure 2

A — OBJECTS
B — ACTIVITIES
C — PROCESSES
D — PRINCIPLES
E — ELEMENTS

A₁ — book
A₂ — picture
A₃ — letter
A₄ — magazine
A₅ — card
A₆ — poem
A₇ — joke
A₈ — map - graph
A₉ — chart - table
A₁₀ — music
A₁₁ — workbook
A₁₂ — mimeograph copy

B₁ — oral
B₂ — silent
B₃ — speed
B₄ — skimming
B₅ — critical
B₆ — creative
B₇ — choral

C₁ — comparing
C₂ — contrasting
C₃ — combining
C₄ — separating
C₅ — defining
C₆ — describing
C₇ — pronouncing
C₈ — "successive approximating"

D₁ — phonics
D₂ — readability
D₃ — leg bility
D₄ — eye movement
D₅ — wo·d attack

E₁ — phoneme
E₂ — morpheme
E₃ — grapheme
E₄ — alphabet
E₅ — word
E₆ — phrase
E₇ — sentence
E₈ — paragraph

Willette H. Kotan

C

Commitment is giving the very best one has to offer
a stick-to-it-ness guided by a conscience
and self-discipline which will
ultimately emulate
distinctively
good character . . . . . .

I

Involvement is shaped and molded
in one's participation
in a belief . . . a cause . . . a code . . . a tenet
with their roots tagged to
indestructible and incorruptible
principles . . . values . . . ideals . . .
undying integrity . . . . . .

S

Sensitivity communicates the implicit behaviors
that embrace wisdom and clothe the personality
with an insight for which there
is no other substitute . . . . . .

E

Excitement is the "rare" dimension for it is as
scarce as the "Jefferson" half dollar . . . . . .
originating from the soul
the spirit ejects
deep tingling
heartfelt emotions . . . . . .

CISE® PUBLICATIONS

Box 149
Scio, Oregon 97374

Additional Copies $1.50 (each)

(20% Discount on orders of 10 or more)

AUTHOR'S COMMENTS

The four-page copyright READING SCHEMA was designed as a Reference Aid in Teacher Education and In-Service Education; the following comments are presented to aid reader in understanding and translating the copyright material.

A cursory examination may appear somewhat esoteric since a milieu of data was considered; however, an analytical approach will reveal congruity, valid relationships and distinctive logic.

FIGURE 1 projects a STRUCTURE OF READING into clear identifiable concomitants:

*OBJECTS   —what one reads tagging books, poems, maps, charts, etc.

ACTIVITIES   —kinds/ways of reading tagging oral, speed, silent, choral, etc.

PROCESSES   —what one does "mentally" when one reads tagging specific behaviors as separating, defining, pronouncing, etc.

PRINCIPLES—fundamentals governing reading act tagging phonics, eye movement, readability, legibility, etc.

ELEMENTS   —ingredients of reading act tagging phonemes, ideas, words, sentences, etc.

Thus, a STRUCTURE is conceived as a conceptual framework projecting the essence and general nature of the reading act. It does NOT, however, provide a panacea in qualifying all answers NOR touch all bases which embrace the reading act; it DOES, however, become a highly PROLIFIC RESOURCE to the essential and general phenomena of the reading act.

Secondly, FIGURE 2 further explores the STRUCTURE OF READING by manifesting varied and multi-relationships implementing the concepts of "subset", "union", and "intersection".

---

* A_{13}—newspapers
A_{14}—road signs

SET is used to refer to the READING ACT as the collection of concepts (SUBSETS) which will shape a body of knowledge that will characterize the general nature of the READING ACT.

SET = READING ACT				
SUBSET A	SUBSET B	SUBSET C	SUBSET D	SUBSET E
OBJECTS	ACTIVITIES	PROCESSES	PRINCIPLES	ELEMENTS

Within the READING ACT, an interdependence and relationship are illustrated by UNION (U) and INTERSECTION (∩). UNION is a state or condition whereby all SUBSETS are combined or united into a whole/entity. INTERSECTION illustrates a state or condition whereby a relationship exists between ONLY some of the SUBSETS.

ANALOGY

SET = [a collection of letters]

SUBSET A = [a, e, i, o, u] (vowels)
SUBSET B = [b, c, d, f, g, h, j, k, l, m, n, p, q, r, s, t, v, w, x, y, z] (consonants)
AUB = [abcdefghijklmnopqrstuvwxyz] (alphabet)
A∩B = [b, e,] [o, n,] (Almost all the words in the dictionary are made by intersecting/partial membership of Subset A and Subset B.)

Finite members in each SUBSET are denoted numerically: A_1—book, A_{10}—music, B_3—speed, B_7—choral, C_5—defining, D_2—readability, E_5—word, etc.

Examination of FIGURE 2 will reveal:

$C_4 \cap E_4$ = separating alphabet into vowels, consonants, etc.

$B_4 \cap E_8$ = skimming a paragraph

$C_6 \cap B_4$ = describing the act of skimming

$C_7 \cap E_5 \cap E_1 \cap B_1$ = pronouncing a word into phonemes orally

$B_1 \cap C_8 \cap E_5 \cap C_7$ = pronouncing a word orally until correct pronunciation is achieved

An extension of identifying finite members within each SUBSET can be almost infinite:

A_1 = Caldecott Award Winners, Newbery Award Winners, Claremont Recognition of Merit Award Winners, etc.

A_1 = A Tree Is Nice, Call It Courage, My Side of the Mountain, Cinderella, Julie of the Wolves, The Funny Little Woman, Durango Street, Island of the Blue Dolphins, The Little House, etc.

A_1 = Durant's Story of Civilization, Let's Keep Christmas, Sapir's Language, Russell's Children's Thinking, Gibran's The Prophet, Phenix's Realms of Meaning, Ruesch and Kees' Nonverbal Communication, etc.

A_1 = Buros' Mental Measurements Yearbooks, Gage's Handbook of Research on Teaching, Monroe/Harris/ Ebel edited editions of Encyclopedia of Educational Research, etc.

A_1 = Harvard Educational Review, Reading Teacher, Reviews of Educational Research, AACTE Yearbook, IRA Conference Proceedings. Claremont Reading Conference Yearbook. etc.

Thirdly, FIGURE 3 has woven the FABRIC for a multi-dimensional approach to reading instruction; it crystallizes enormous "idea density" which is unequivocal. Each SUBSET as well as the finite members of each SUBSET identify/tag/pinpoint significant substance that should be considered in designing/composing/organizing a program with **end** resulting in teaching the individual to read.

A_2 = mapping of the brain

A_2 = Singer and Holmes' Substrata Factor Analysis, Hebb's cell assembly and phase sequence, Lashley's theory of equipotentiality, Nielsen's cortical localization, Penfield and Roberts' Speech and Brain Mechanisms, Mountcastle's Interhemispheric Relations and Cerebral Dominance, etc.

E_2 = Auditory and Visual Discrimination

E_2 = neural and conductive hearing loss, refractive errors, otitis media, mastoiditis, fusion, telebinocular, Snellen chart, audiometer, sight versus vision, auditory acuity versus auditory discrimination, tacting, etc.

FIGURE 3 was initially conceived to be applicable for teaching reading, however, it does have immense validity and relevance in other areas of Elementary and Secondary Curriculum Courses.

One final and important comment, application and interpretation of each SUBSET (LEARNING THEORIES, TENETS OF DEMOCRACY, PHILOSOPHIES OF EDUCATION, CULTURAL SIGNIFICANTS, HUMAN DEVELOPMENT, MODE/METHOD OF INSTRUCTION, CISE AS A PERSONNEL MODEL) will largely depend upon reader and his/her "tools of inquiry" as the reader "brings meaning" to the schema.

"a set of inquiry tools" = [comparing, contrasting, combining, separating, defining, describing, inferring, classifying, identifying, diagnosing, creating, reproducing, recalling, qualifying, quantifying, evaluating.]

Willette H. Kotan

ıṣ℮® PUBLICATIONS

P. O. BOX 149

SCIO, OREGON 97374

C I S E   B E H A V I O R S

A thinking activity using CONCEPT CLUSTERS from

READING IS HUMAN AWAKENING by Willette H. Sheldon.

Tear all cards into segments so the learner and a second person (teacher
instructor - another learner) will each have a complete set of small cards
A symbol on the back of each card will indicate which ones are to be
used for each behavior activity.

 CONCEPT   Subset of concept cluster (minor unit of
                                    thought; e.g. penny, nickel, dime, quarter)

 CONCEPT CLUSTER   Concept clustered around major
                                            unit of thought. (e.g. MONEY)

 LEARNING BEHAVIOR   (learning strategies / tactics)

BEHAVIOR #1

        Pick up tool. . . . pick up time. . . . pick up animal. . .
put down time. . . . pick up clothes. . . . put down tool. . . .
. . pick up shape . . . . put down animal. . . . put down shape
. . . . pick up food . . . . etc.

BEHAVIOR #2   (Oral exercise to be related to printed
                   concepts in Behavior #5)

        Pick up round . . . . pick up dollar. . . . pick up blue. .
. . put dime down. . . . pick up shoe . . . . put down square
. . . . put green down . . . . pick up typist. . . . put down
dentist. . . . pick up heavy . . . . etc.

BEHAVIOR #3

Pick up the word with the letter L in the middle . . . . . pick
up all words beginning with the letter F . . . . . pick up
words beginning with the letter C . . . . . put down all the
words ending in the letter R . . . . . put down the word or
words having a double OO together . . . . . etc.

BEHAVIOR #4

Pick up concept clusters which involve diet . . . . . (Learner
will pick up concepts or word cards which can be associated /
related to diet.   The learner must also justify / explain why
each particular concept was chosen.) . . . . . Pick up concept
clusters which involve pasting a stamp on an envelope . . . . .
(Explain and JUSTIFY) . . . . . Pick up concept clusters which
involve dialing a telephone number . . . . . EXPLAIN / JUSTIFY
. . . . . etc.

BEHAVIOR #5

(This activity involves using the concepts clustered around ANIM/
Pick up cat . . . . pick up horse . . . . put cat down . . . . pick
up cow . . . . pick up mouse . . . . put down mouse . . . . pick u
dog . . . . put cow down . . . . etc.

(This behavior involves using the concepts clustered around
APPLIANCE.)

Pick up stove . . . . pick up lamp . . . . pick up table . . . . put
lamp down . . . . pick up bookcase . . . . put down stove . . . .
put' down table . . . . etc.

ACTIVITY #5 CAN BE USED FOR EACH OF THE SUBSETS OF
CONCEPT CLUSTERS.

BEHAVIOR #6

Pick up kitten . . . . pick up milk . . . . pick up saddle . . . . pu
down mice killer . . . . pick up cheese eater . . . . etc.

(This behavior involves using the concepts clustered around ANIN

ACTIVITY #6 CAN BE USED FOR EACH OF THE SUBSETS OF
CONCEPT CLUSTERS.

BEHAVIOR #7

Compare (regroup) the following subsets into the appropriate con
cluster:

small, pink, round, blue, desk, butter, second, heavy, green,
tiny, chair, rectangle, light, black, banana, hexagon, ounce,
brown, bread, etc.

BEHAVIOR #8

Pick up defining. Give an example of defining . . . . Pick up
describing. Give an example of describing . . . . How does
defining differ from describing? . . . . Pick up comparing.
Give an example of comparing . . . . Pick up contrasting. Give
an example of contrasting. How does contrasting differ from
comparing ? . . . . etc.

These activities were designed to (A) articulate with meaning,
(B) increase letter recognition and a sight vocabulary, and (C)
relate ideas, the printed symbol, and experiences as a triple
association. Fourteen concept clusters will serve as an
introduction. These were chosen because of the nearness and
close relationship to everyday living. Other behaviors may be
developed to further increase recognition of printed symbols as
well as translating and associating these symbols.

Published by:

CISE Publications

Box 5060

Portland, Oregon 97213

	Monday	Tuesday	Wednesday
	Thursday	Friday	Saturday
	January	February	March
	April	May	June
	July	August	September
	October	November	December
	screwdriver	hammer	shovel
	rake	hoe	wrench
	file	saw	ounce
	pound	heavy	light
	scales	load	gram
	amount	gravity	ton

	bird	chicken	dog
	cat	pig	cow
	horse	mouse	dryer
	refrigerator	iron	vacuum cleaner
	toaster	stove	dress
	skirt	blouse	tie
	shirt	pants	jacket
	socks	shoe	blue
	yellow	orange	red
	white	green	brown
	black	eggs	bread
	hamburger	cake	milk
	potatoes	butter	beets

	soup	chair	sofa
	table	bookcase	lamp
	desk	dresser	bed
	rocking chair	penny	nickel
	dime	quarter	wallet
	receipt	check	half dollar
	dollar bill	zero	one
	two	three	four
	five	six	seven
	eight	nine	ten
	quantity	measurement	fraction
	decimal	percent	figure
	numeral	digit	integer
	fireman	policeman	men

	women	warehouse-man	typist
	sailor	truckman	custodian
	circle	square	rectangular
	octagon	oval	triangle
	trapezoid	small	smaller
	smallest	big	bigger
	biggest	dimensions	little
	miniature	huge	tiny
	giant	second	hour
	minute	day	week
	month	year	era
	age	season	night
	moment	instant	temporary
	duration	clock	Sunday

Appendix C

What you see here are tones of black
and white hues arranged to fulfill a
photo of an everyday familiar subject/
animal; at least to me it is.

Study the photo until you readily see what most people vision. Vision, then is arranging the various hues into a meaningful interpretation, for then once you see the subject, you have vision, before that you had only eye-sight. Vision is the ability to get meaning from the eyesight. My point is that the slow reader has difficulty interpreting his eye-sight into visual meaning. His eyes will cross the pages, reading words that do not/can not give him visual interpretations.[227]

---

227   Published in the interest of better vision by Optometric Extension Program Foundation,
      Inc., (Nonprofit), Duncan, Oklahoma. And if you need assistance of what you are
      suppose to see, glance on page 153 for an answer.

370

372

Although John Sheldon was born in Waukegan, Illinois, he was much on his own by working as a soda jerk at the Holiday Drug Store on 7th and Broadway, NE Portland and he graduated from Jefferson High School. He is a Korean veteran who served in the U.S. Navy. Afterwards and while working periodically at the Veterans' Hospital, Downey, Illinois, he eventually earned his BA in English from nearby Lake Forest University. He began his thirty-year teaching career in an isolated Aleutian community in Chenega, Alaska, and then served supervising the teaching of English by Micronesian teachers with his headquarters on Ponape, Caroline Islands, US Trust Territory (now titled the Federation of Micronesia). In the interim of the school years, he took advanced studies of which some were at the University of Alaska, University of Paris, University of London and Hellenic University at Athens, Greece. He took advanced studies in Browning at Northern Illinois University. He earned a MA degree at San Francisco, University. He was English chairman of North Division High School, Milwaukee, Wisconsin, with an accomplishment of introducing more Black literature into English studies. He was a curriculum chairman in the Mt. Diablo Unified School District, at the junior high level, endorsing multiple uses of texts by teachers' choices and the literacy testing of all students at the 6th and 8th grades through the exercise of writing both a personal and business letter for a satisfactory or unsatisfactory evaluation. Since retirement he traveled extensively and was first co-editor and then editor of the monthly periodical published by the South Salem Senior, Salem, Oregon, and is presently actively involved in that organization.